ONEIDA UTOPIA

ONEIDA UTOPIA

A COMMUNITY SEARCHING FOR HUMAN
HAPPINESS AND PROSPERITY

ANTHONY WONDERLEY

CORNELL UNIVERSITY PRESS
Ithaca and London

First published 2017 by Cornell University Press

Printed in the United States of America

Library of Congress Cataloging-in-Publication Data

Names: Wonderley, Anthony Wayne, 1949– author.
Title: Oneida utopia : a community searching for human happiness and prosperity / Anthony Wonderley.
Description: Ithaca : Cornell University Press, 2017. | Includes bibliographical references and index.
Identifiers: LCCN 2017025823 (print) | LCCN 2017027517 (ebook) | ISBN 9781501709807 (pdf) | ISBN 9781501712449 (epub/mobi) | ISBN 9781501702709 (cloth : alk. paper)
Subjects: LCSH: Oneida Community—History. | Noyes, John Humphrey, 1811–1886. | Collective settlements—New York (State)—History—19th century. | Utopian socialism—New York (State)—History—19th century.
Classification: LCC HX656.O5 (ebook) | LCC HX656.O5 W59 2017 (print) | DDC 307.7709747/64—dc23
LC record available at https://lccn.loc.gov/2017025823

Figure 1 is from the author's collection. All other images are from the Oneida Community Mansion House, used by permission.

To Patricia A. Hoffman

Contents

ILLUSTRATIONS

ACKNOWLEDGMENTS

If history is storytelling, it is a privilege and a joy for a teller of tales to have one worth telling. That is why my biggest debt of gratitude is owed to the person who has best presided over a complicated not-for-profit organization, a history museum called the Oneida Community Mansion House. Executive Director Patricia A. Hoffman hired me to work there and fostered my love and appreciation for a place where giants once walked.

While mindful of being helped by many, I must specifically acknowledge with gratitude those who have been generous—invariably so—with knowledge, information, and materials, including Lang and Nini Hatcher, Pody Vanderwall, Jessie Mayer, Nancy Gluck, Ed Knobloch, Paul Gebhardt, Walt Lang, Robert Fogarty, Kelly Rose, and Christian Goodwillie. Thank you.

I'm grateful to Randy Ericson for the opportunity to publish in the Richard W. Couper Press (Hamilton College Library) and thereby think through many of the ideas advanced here; and, at Couper Press, warm thanks to copy editor May Anne Ericson. I appreciate the helpful input from anonymous readers. Above all, this book was immeasurably improved by Michael J. McGandy, senior editor at Cornell University Press. *Mil gracias.*

The reader who arrives at the end of this book will learn that the failed Oneida Ltd. ended up as the property of distant hedge-fund financiers. With the passage of time, Oneida Ltd. became part of EveryWare Global Inc., an outfit with heritage consciousness and preservation vision. I thank EveryWare Global for its gift to the Oneida Community Mansion House of a substantial portion of the Oneida company's material legacy.

Thanks to Ellen Wayland-Smith for making available an advance copy of her book, *Oneida: From Free Love Utopia to the Well-Set Table,* and to Kathy Garner, who slogged through the manuscript, giving encouragement and help. Thanks to Pat Hoffman and Pody Vanderwall for arranging a subvention for this work out of Mansion House bookstore funds, and to Mr. Kevin Coffee (executive director in 2016) for acknowledging and seeing through the agreement. Thanks go especially to my mate, Pauline Caputi, who kept me going through this project in so many ways.

ONEIDA UTOPIA

Introduction

A Good Story Told Truly

The Oneida Community was, in author Chris Jennings's view, the most remarkable utopian experiment in American history.[1] The upstate New York commune comprised about 250 people dedicated to living selflessly as one family and to the sharing of all property, work, and love. It existed a little over thirty years (1848–1880). Founded by John Humphrey Noyes, a young man who believed himself appointed by God for the purpose, the commune espoused a nondenominational brand of Protestantism called Perfectionism—the idea that belief in Christ, if strong enough, could render one free of sin ("perfect") in this lifetime, once and forever. These Perfectionists were determined to bring heaven to earth by counteracting sin with selfless acts and by duplicating heavenly life. Heaven, they imagined, was a place in which all property is commonly owned and all relations—social and sexual—are equally apportioned. This was the doctrine of "Bible communism."

Oneida, then, was a religious cult but one that always had the feel of a secular utopia, a program to realize harmonious group living. It came out of a wave of communitarian enthusiasm that swept over the country during the 1840s. As many as one hundred thousand people may have participated in the movement. Although many communes were founded at this time, however, few lasted even a year. The Oneida Community, easily the longest lasting of

1

them all, has come to be the textbook example of American utopias from that tsunami of utopian excitement.[2]

The central principle of the Oneida Community as a utopia was that men and women should mingle in all activities. The intrinsic pleasantness of male-female company, it was thought, would make life enjoyable and work fun. As utopian reformists, the Oneida Perfectionists also claimed they could correct one of the greatest sources of human misery: unwanted, unchosen pregnancies. That was accomplished by practicing a form of birth control prohibiting males from ejaculating during sexual intercourse. The men did that to free the women from "propagative drudgery." The Perfectionists built what was probably the first communal home in America in which men and women lived in free association under one roof. In that building, the Mansion House, they practiced group or "complex marriage"—free love—which, it was said, liberated women from marital bondage. They developed innovative child-rearing practices. They achieved practical gender equality and freedom from household drudgery. They started up humankind's first eugenics program.

In addition to all that, Oneida was one of the most economically successful utopias of all time,[3] its prosperity based not on agriculture but on factory manufacture. The most lucrative product proved to be a metal animal trap introduced by a local blacksmith named Sewell Newhouse. The Community's innovation was to design and build machines to mechanize trap production. By the early 1860s, Oneida made over two hundred thousand traps a year and dominated the national market. Production on that scale led them to construct a factory dedicated to trap making and to hire outsiders—nonmembers of the commune—to work in it making traps in assembly-line fashion. That doubled trap production and brought in more money, which in turn paid for a second major industry—making silk thread for sewing machines, which were just coming into widespread household use.

Factory production of traps and thread placed the Oneida Community in the mainstream of American industrial development after the Civil War. Factory production brought prosperity and allowed the Bible communists to live as they wished. It also nudged them in the direction of greater materialism. Nevertheless, the Perfectionists were exceptionally good employers who formulated generous personnel policies, paid well, and instituted an eight-hour day.

Faced with dissension within and hostility without, the Oneida Community voluntarily brought the practices of complex marriage and communism to a close. The commune transformed itself, by vote, into a joint stock-holding company, the Oneida Community Ltd., in 1881. Former members of the Oneida Community became stockholders in a company chartered to continue the successful industries of the Oneida Community, to provide its shareholders with an income, and to take care of the Mansion House. As it happened, however, the company barely survived its first fifteen years and was saved by the return of the Oneida Community's now-grown children. The younger people, led by Pierrepont Noyes, John Noyes's eugenically conceived son, reorganized the firm to meet a new age of unprecedented industrial mass production and cutthroat marketing competition. They did so by focusing the company on the manufacture of silverware.

The making of cutlery or flatware had begun in Oneida Community times, but its quality was indifferent. To upgrade the product, the Oneida company began electroplating about three times as much silver to the base as was commonly done. The result was a new, high-end category of silver-plated ware called Community Plate. Next, the young executives invested heavily—and innovatively—in advertising and marketing. Oneida claimed to be the first to hire the best graphic artists around to design full-page color ads of Community Plate to run in such national weekly magazines as the *Saturday Evening Post, Good Housekeeping,* and *Better Homes and Gardens.* Committing to silverware was a big gamble, but it paid off. By the second decade of the twentieth century, the Oneida Community Ltd. had become renowned for its quality silverware and quality advertising

As the younger people restructured the company around silverware, they also embarked on an ambitious program of welfare capitalism—the employer's assumption of responsibility for the well-being of employees. The new directors first mandated that executive salaries would be kept low. Further, in hard times, everyone's pay would be reduced. The cuts, however, would start at the top and be proportionately greater there. Shortly after, company officials began providing their employees with generous pensions and health and welfare benefits, then a share of company profit, and subsequently a share of company ownership.

Central to Oneida's effort to improve workers' lives was the creation of an independent workers' community. To ensure that a high standard of living obtained there, the company quietly donated money and services to the City of Sherrill, just north of the Mansion House. To encourage private home ownership, the company sold lots to its employees below market value, then gave them cash bonuses to build houses. To encourage quality education, the Oneida Community Ltd. donated lots for schools, then paid more than half the cost of building the schools. The company assumed half the salary paid to each teacher from city tax money, then, for one dollar, made every teacher eligible to receive full company benefits. Teachers could live, with free room and board, in the company's central building. Finally, the firm funded Sherrill's electrical, water, and sewage systems, fire protection and garbage collection, and facilities for public health and recreation.

Since little government legislation in the interests of workers then existed, all this was done voluntarily by company officials. What the younger executives had chosen to do was to revamp the old Oneida Community concept of family so that it now applied to a corporate entity of nearly a thousand people. That company, carrying on the Community's industrial production, openly embraced the essence of the Oneida Community's outlook: selfless concern for others. Further, the company's core philosophy was that everyone involved in production deserved to share in the benefits of production.

The Oneida Community Ltd. never publicized these accomplishments and in fact denied being guilty of philanthropy. It was just good business, company officials maintained. Nevertheless, Sherrill—as a corporate creation dedicated to the health and prosperity of employees and neighbors— was one of America's greatest business successes. It seemed to many living in the shadow of the Mansion House that a second utopia had sprung directly from the people and values of the first.

During the twentieth century, the company shortened its name to Oneida Ltd. and went on to become, briefly, the biggest maker of silverware in the world. In the opening years of the twenty-first century, Oneida Ltd. went out of business.

This book, however, focuses on happier and more idealistic circumstances. My concern is to follow the Community and successor company for about a century, very roughly to 1950. To focus on that span of time is to emphasize that the Oneida Community developed into a major industrial maker of traps and thread. Then, the utopia turned itself into a company that became a major manufacturer of silverware. Commune and corporation are the same story of economic success, innovative thinking, and abiding concern for the welfare of others.

I attempt, in this book, to make an interesting chapter of the human experience better known and more widely appreciated. Others, it is true, have written about the same topic, or at least covered substantial portions of it. The books most readily available at this writing include a history of commune and company by Ellen Wayland-Smith and what has long been the best-selling account of the Oneida Community by Spencer Klaw.[4] The present work, however, is different from those two and is distinct, moreover, from every other major treatment of the Oneida story, popular or scholarly.[5]

The first innovation of this book is to focus on the group rather than on an individual. Especially is this so in the Oneida Community segment of the story in which John Humphrey Noyes is downplayed in relation to the commune. To emphasize the collectivity, one has to ask questions that are essentially sociological and economic rather than biographical. To do that, one must draw on a much wider range of evidence than is normally consulted, including artifacts and material culture generally.

A second innovation is the close attention paid, at every level, to what I regard as basic housekeeping chores of historical inquiry: context and, especially, chronology. All human organizations, ways of acting, and patterns of thinking are of their time, while being subject to change over time. Charting those changes is necessary, informative, and—often—illuminating. Everything—from the development of Noyes's theology, to the evolution of gender relations, to the transformation of economic structures—is approached here with a stronger sense of temporal methodology than I have seen in other works.

A third innovation is what this book is *not* about—the Oneida Community as a sensational sex cult. Gentle reader, I shall not withhold details of sex. But neither will I claim, as do others, that the essence of Community government resided in Noyes's ability to dole out the sexual favors of his nubile seraglio.

Each of these claims will now be explained more fully.

A Collective Story

Histories of the Oneida Community stress the importance of the commune's charismatic founder, John Humphrey Noyes. Since Noyes's leadership and teachings were crucial to the commune, it makes sense to visualize the group as—to use Lawrence Foster's paraphrase of Emerson—the lengthened shadow of Noyes.[6] And, if one does regard the Oneida Community as indistinguishable from Noyes, it is a short step further to assume that Noyes ruled the Community absolutely.

In contrast to that view, the present work accords higher billing to the collectivity than to Noyes. Noyes is not by any means ignored, and he remains on this stage, particularly in the opening scenes, which place him and his evolving doctrines in historical context. But the point throughout is to gaze beyond Noyes in order to paint on a bigger canvas that includes more people, more issues, and more trends. Such a view brings into focus the substantial achievements of the group. It was, after all, the Community that built Oneida and established its communal practices, largely in Noyes's absence. The commune developed group marriage arrangements that actually worked, conquered household drudgery, and achieved (as I argue) practical gender equality. Not Noyes alone but the group together carried out humankind's first eugenics program. The Oneida Community collectively fashioned a lucrative industrial enterprise capable of lasting into the future. There was one Noyes; there were two hundred others. It is common sense to take cognizance of more than one person.

If there is merit to seeking a larger perspective, why does no one try to do it? Perhaps the greatest obstacle to holistic perspective is Noyes himself. Excessive emphasis on Noyes is due, at least partly, to the degree Noyes dominates the written record. His writings were and remain today influential in the historiography of the Oneida Community. Noyes authored a substantial portion of the Community's published output.[7] He wrote voluminously, usually about himself, and in doing so was a conscious creator of his own image and legacy. He always presented the commune as an extension of himself, with the implication that he was its unquestioned ruler. Then and now, Noyes makes for interesting reading because of his explicit engagement with sex. In addition, he conveyed an unusually rich inner landscape of the mind, which remains appealing source material for psychologically inclined researchers. Finally, Noyes did historians an immense service by providing them with the history of his own circumstances—accounts that are readily available and apparently authoritative. Noyes, in sum, was effective. It is difficult to move beyond him.

Can one overcome this towering great man to achieve a collective history? The way I have gone about it is to seek out a range of voices to supplement Noyes's. To get at a Community point of view, one must look at what the Perfectionists wrote to explain themselves to the outside. This can be gleaned from many of their publications and from their magazine-newspaper, usually issued weekly, called, successively, the *Spiritual Magazine* (1848–1850), *Free Church Circular* (1850–1851), the *Circular* (1851–1870), the *Oneida Circular* (1871–1876), and the *American Socialist* (1876–1879). Especially valuable for understanding the Community's perspective is what they wrote about themselves for their own edification. Their communal diary, the "accurate transcript of the events and spirit of our daily life," was printed from 1866 into early 1868 as the *Daily Journal*.[8] An earlier edition, covering 1863 and much of 1864, exists as a typescript called the "Community Journal."

Voices from the outside world usefully supplement those from within. A good example of a visitor's view of Oneida is that furnished by William Hepworth Dixon, a prominent English literary figure who observed the Oneida Community running itself through peer-group pressure. Another is that of Charles Nordhoff, a scholar of American utopias, who was impressed by the bureaucratic governance of Oneida resulting from twenty-eight committees and forty-eight departments.[9]

In addition to voices inside and outside the community, I pay attention to what was *not* committed to writing. Often one can pick up on this by noting what happened when Noyes told the Bible communists what he thought should be done. Many of his projects were not carried out. Yet what one sees in the documentary record is that Noyes's opinions were recorded with care; audience reaction was not. This evidence needs to be sought elsewhere than in the traditional archive.

On one occasion, for example, Noyes proposed that the marking of individual graves be discontinued and that, instead, one large collective memorial be installed. This did not occur. On another, Noyes urged that the cemetery should have a summerhouse in which the living could sit contemplating the deceased piled together in a crypt beneath them. Nothing was done along these lines. As the Mansion House of 1862 neared completion, Noyes insisted that the decorative scheme of the central meeting area should depict the Lord's Supper. It never did. In 1863, Noyes advocated a scheme to make money by investing $10,000 of Community funds in the Commercial Bank of Indiana, an institution that, he assured his listeners, was highly profitable. The Perfectionists did nothing of the sort.[10]

The lesson suggested by these examples is that the disciples disregarded the master's word with some frequency. Further, ignoring Noyes was not an act demanding explanation in print. It may have seemed, in fact, more polite to let the matter pass in silence. The historian attends to what is said, written, or done, of course, but the historian of the Oneida Community must also consider what was not said, written, or done.

In addition to seeking out views supplementing those of Noyes and paying attention to silences, I am alert to the physicality of Perfectionist life. Archaeologists and other specialists in material culture understand that objects express the personal and social lives of their makers and users. Non-textual evidence from the Oneida Community includes maps and photographs, naturally, but also comprises artifacts of the communards: quilts and furniture, for example, domestic objects and industrial products. All may testify to aspects of daily life and thought. In a larger sense, settlement pattern and built environment—how the group settled into the world around them—furnish other clues about how the Perfectionists planned, lived, and worked together. The biggest artifact of all, their communal home, was the product of group decision making and a repository of communal values.

Time and Change

This book, then, is distinguished from other Oneida histories by its supposition that the Oneida Community is a more significant topic than its leader. A second distinction is that I pay greater attention to the temporal dimension of the story. Chronicling what happened as time passed may seem a pedestrian thing to do in a history, but I believe it to be innovative in this context. Other studies tackle the story of the Oneida Community by concentrating on it at a single point in time. Or they flatten out time by constructing an idealized picture of one moment's duration to show how the Community functioned for thirty years. Or again, they present the Community as static and timeless by leaving out historical change altogether.

An instructive example of overlooking change is afforded by an account of Oneida's early days written in 1913 by Community member George E. Cragin. As a young boy, Cragin had been present at the founding of the Oneida Association. As a young man, he was one of the first Oneidans to be sent into the outside world to acquire professional training (as a physician). John Noyes once declared him fit for the "School of the Prophets," meaning, apparently, that Cragin was regarded as suitable for Community leadership.[11] As Cragin neared the end of his days (he died in 1915), he wrote a number of reminiscences about long-ago Community life. One explained the origin of trap making.

> At that time, and for several years, the idea of making steel traps for a living was far, very far from our ideals as to means of support. "Horticulture a leading means of subsistence" was our published watchword, and the despised and lowly trap making was consigned to apparent oblivion. . . .
>
> In those days we had visions of a second garden of Eden so far as fruit raising was concerned, and devoted all of our means available to this end. We invited Henry Thacker, a noted fruit grower at Owasco Lake, N.Y., to join us as our horticultural chief. He entered heartily into our plans for fruit growing but warned us that we had selected a bad locality. In fact he said it was the worst place so far as concerned climatic conditions for fruit raising that he had ever seen, and that our efforts in that direction would end in failure. Undismayed by this opinion we launched out into an extensive scheme of fruit raising and spent a good deal of money and labor in covering our home domain with the finest variety of peach, plum and cherry trees together with many smaller fruits and vineyards.

A few years showed us, without any manner of doubt, that Mr. Thacker was a true prophet and our frost bitten and blighted orchards were turned into brush heaps for the fire.

Cragin went on to indicate that it was Thacker who grasped the economic potential of metal animal traps that were made by another Community member, Sewell Newhouse. "Why you have a perfect gold mine in that Newhouse trap," Thacker is supposed to have told John Noyes. "You can drive every other trap clean out of the market." Cragin concluded the anecdote by emphasizing: "Our horticultural flag had been nailed to the mast and, sink or swim, we were going to do our best to make a success of fruit growing."[12]

The burden of Cragin's song is that disappointment with fruit trees led to the beginning of the trap industry. This is often repeated, most recently in Wayland-Smith's book.[13] It is not true. Or so I believe, partly because I cannot find such an occurrence documented. More important, Cragin's view rings false because Community writings state the opposite.

By the early 1850s, the Community's love of working in "bees"—volunteer task groups—had become intertwined with the commune's interest in "horticulture." Horticulture meant fruit trees, as Cragin recalled, but it also included the tending of berry bushes, vineyards, and vegetable gardens. It contrasted with "farming" or "agriculture," which denoted the keeping of domesticated livestock and the raising of grain in large mono-crop fields. Horticulture was to be the Community's chief source of food. But more than that, horticulture provided spiritual enrichment to men and women working together out of doors. The horticultural ideal, I argue in chapter 5, paved the way for practical advances in female standing and, in the terms of their day, gender relations that were essentially egalitarian. Horticulture did not disappear with a dramatic burning of trees in the 1850s, as Cragin suggested. On the contrary, it remained one of the Community's major concerns for about a decade. The masthead slogan Cragin mentioned (actually it was "Horticulture is the leading business for subsistence") was featured in the Community's newspaper from 1853 to 1864.

Although horticulture never went up in flames, it was pushed into the background by the successful manufacture, in Community factories, of animal traps and sewing machine thread. With industrialization came dependence on hired labor, which divided men and women during the workday. Increasing industrialization also encouraged interest in financial profit, which weakened the earlier focus on horticulture and spirituality. Even then, however, horticulture remained deeply etched in Perfectionist memory. As late as 1878, a Community member affirmed that they still thought of their domain as a horticultural garden of Eden. They had never been tempted into farming, Harriet Skinner affirmed, and had always devoted the greater part of their land to "the gardeners, the vine-dressers and fruit raisers."[14] During the Community's later factory years, the Bible communists nostalgically recalled horticulture as the happiest period of communal life.

To state, therefore, as Cragin did, that failed fruit-tending caused successful trap-making is to miss an important chapter in the Community's economy, outlook, and social life. Worse, to repeat Cragin in this matter is to forfeit not only recognition of change but also the ability to inquire into its significance. This particular assertion, for example, prevents one from seeing that relations between men and women were not inscribed in stone and were not in 1875 what they had been in 1853. Sensitivity to the temporal dimension is always sound policy in historical studies. In stressing chronology, this book emphasizes changes in Community life that took place in the course of three decades.

And as change occurred over time within the Community, so also did change occur with John H. Noyes. Since members of the Community believed in Noyes's teachings, any treatment of Community life must supply some description of them. Noyes's theology comprised several wide-ranging propositions, the most fundamental of which was the doctrine of Perfectionism. Noyes did not invent that belief, but he did develop it to an unprecedented extreme. He formulated a scheme of history in which God makes sequent covenants with groups of people and Christ puts in an extra appearance. Noyes envisioned heaven as a communist household of sexual bliss. He propounded an afterlife in which sleepy souls await activation to rise out of the sod.

Most Oneida Community histories convey the impression that Noyes's theology was a seamless whole in which constituent beliefs fit logically together in timeless fashion. My reservation with such summary analysis arises from the suspicion that the individual concepts did not spring de novo and simultaneously from Noyes's brow. In fact, the thoughts were reactions to interests and passions of the day, including revivalism, millennialism, utopianism, and spiritualism. Not only were Noyes's ideas the products of different circumstances; they occurred at different times and accumulated over time. That means that, like deposits laid down at an archaeological site, his notions should be peeled off in layers so they can be examined, individually, in context. Such an approach has the virtue of clarifying Noyes's intellect and, often, shining a new light on it.

When one considers events chronologically and contextually, as is done here, it becomes clear that Noyes's views were a pastiche never glued together tightly. Further, paying attention to the order and setting of Noyesian thought helps to explain why the Oneida Community, as a religious cult, also had the feel of a nonreligious utopia. Oneida had a foot in that camp because Noyes was influenced by secular communitarian theory. The specific example of the Fourierist Brook Farm commune near Boston inspired him to venture beyond his brand of Christianity into a wave of utopianism then sweeping the country. When Noyes planned out the coming Oneida Community, he envisioned it as a Fourierist phalanx or association in which amorous attraction replaced Fourier's "passional attraction" as the motivating power.

And, as mentioned above, tracing change over time also helps one to proceed beyond what Noyes said about himself. A specific illustration of this can be found in Noyes's 1849 autobiography, *Confessions of John H. Noyes*, subtitled *Confession of Religious Experience, including a History of Modern Perfectionism*. The pamphlet provides a wealth of personal detail still repeated in studies of the Oneida Community. It does not, however, furnish a history of Perfectionism as a movement apart from and preceding Noyes. That view, also, is perpetuated in works on Oneida that fail to distinguish the doctrine of Perfectionism from Noyes's belief in, say, the return of Christ or the two-age theory of divine judgment. Supplying those lacunae is the job of the opening chapters of this book, which explains, chronologically, the development of Noyes's religion and thinking.

Curiosity about change over time underlies this book and has done much to shape its interpretations. For example, a researcher interested in the nature of Noyes's leadership and influence on the Community might wonder, among other things, how much time Noyes actually spent at Oneida. The answer is that he was absent roughly half the time, including a period from early 1849 through late 1854.[15] In and of itself, this information does not speak directly to the importance of Noyes or the character of the Community. Yet realizing that Noyes was not physically present during six formative years, the most important time in Community development—knowing that, as I say, is likely to affect one's feeling for what the Oneida Community was all about.

Uncle Johnny's Woman Farm

This book differs from other Oneida treatments in its interpretive preference for collectivity and in its attention to changes wrought by time. Here is a third. This book is distinctive for not telling the story of John Noyes as priapic prince of the primal horde called the Oneida Community.

It is true that, in the public mind, the Oneida Community probably always connoted scandalous sexual practices. From the outset, Putney clergyman Hubbard Eastman raged that Oneida Perfectionism was nothing more than "perfection in sin" and nothing less than "the worst of spiritual maladies with which man's moral nature was ever infected." The Oneidans, thundered the *New York Observer* in 1852, are a foul body living, at best, in concubinage. Under the guise of seeking spiritual enjoyment and professing to be perfectly holy, the *Observer* continued, the Perfectionists practice "the freest licentiousness as the highest holiness." A quarter of a century later, Professor John Mears, of the clergymen's crusade against the Community, lambasted Oneida as an outgrowth of vile passion, a hotbed of harlotry, and a pernicious institution based on "a system of organized fanaticism and lust." This kind of sensationalistic coverage lasted well into the twentieth century in the form of such lurid men's magazine articles as "Uncle Johnny's Woman Farm" (see figure 1).[16]

The group and its leader were pegged with the reputation of being notorious throughout the existence of the commune and far beyond it.

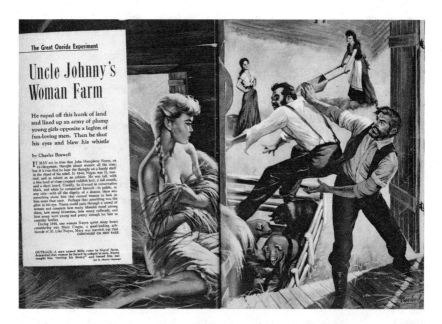

FIGURE 1. "Uncle Johnny's Woman Farm," 1959. This men's magazine article by Charles Boswell continued a long tabloid tradition of spotlighting Oneida Community sex.

Serious students of the subject, however, long eschewed the titillating tone of tabloid coverage. The first academics to study Oneida distanced themselves from any hint of sensationalism by adhering to research agendas not greatly dissimilar to those advocated in this book. Sociologist Maren Lockwood Carden, whose research was conducted in the early 1960s, concluded that the Oneida Community was a religious despotism under Noyes in which people were motivated by faith to give up their selfhood. The most obvious coercion, however, was in the form of peer-group pressure applied by Perfectionists to one another. She thought it wrong, in any event, to judge the whole from Noyes, because no individual can be held accountable for a group's organization or for its success or failure.[17]

In an article summarizing doctoral research in history (also conducted during the 1960s), Robert Fogarty asked why the Oneida Community was so successful as a utopia. His answer was that the Perfectionists who got Oneida off the ground were youthful, in possession of practical skills, and highly motivated in their convictions. Their leaders ensured collective survival by stressing manufacture over agriculture. The blend of business and spirituality they promoted was effective enough to help Oneida retain its religious enthusiasm over many years. Together, followers and leaders endorsed the same familial model of social life and shared the same inclination for flexibility and practicality. Oneida was closely linked with secular communitarian developments, but to get at that larger perspective, Fogarty cautioned, one would have to move beyond Noyes and sex.[18]

Although Carden and Fogarty recommended research into the sociology of group behavior and into socioeconomic trends, those directions were not followed. Instead, subsequent studies tended, not unlike the tabloids, to concentrate on sex. Klaw's best-selling work on the Oneida Community, for example, depicts communal life as revolving largely around sex, with Noyes in authoritarian control. Wayland-Smith's more recent book says much the same.[19]

An important factor contributing to this atmospheric change in interpretive stance is a letter written by John Noyes's eldest son, Dr. Theodore Noyes, to anthropological researcher Anita Newcomb McGee in 1892—almost a dozen years after the Oneida Community ended and six years after John Noyes died. Community attention, according to Dr. Noyes, focused on its young females as a pool of desirable sexual partners. Exercising the right of "first husband," John Noyes deflowered the girls in order to usher them into the Community's marital system of complex marriage. The young women so initiated felt strongly bonded to Noyes. This provided him with leverage to influence their actions. Armed with a cooperative bevy of compliant young females, Noyes controlled men by determining their access to sex and to particular sexual partners. Noyes's supervision of sexual intercourse was the basis and main business of Oneida Community government.[20]

The first to document the existence of the letter was Carden, who evidently treated it with circumspection. Others subsequently seemed to be affected by it. I would say most writers on the subject (including Klaw and Wayland-Smith) advocate some version of Dr. Noyes's views as an accurate characterization of the Oneida Community.[21]

As is true of any piece of evidence, however, Dr. Noyes's letter should be considered with respect to its consistency with other evidence. It should be examined critically in context, especially as regards its possible bias. I will return to this topic in due course. Here I note that, for me, Dr. Noyes's letter does not outweigh the preponderance of evidence and is better viewed as a cautionary tale. Know your primary sources, of course, but also know your secondary sources well enough to detect derivative claims with long careers. In any event, repeating an assertion does not make it so.

This book, in sum, is unique in its attempt to provide a broad account of the Oneida story, one based on historically sound methodology. It stands apart from other works also by *not* focusing on Noyes as a sexual despot. What I aim to show is that the Oneida Community and what it became is a bigger, more interesting topic than Noyes's personal sex cult.

The primary theme in what follows is that the Oneida Community collectively fashioned a lucrative enterprise based on factory manufacture. For the Bible communists, the welfare of everyone, including workers, was regarded as paramount. When the commune turned itself into a company, the new organization, the Oneida Community Ltd., built on its industrial heritage to become a successful producer of silverware. At the same time, the successor organization kept faith with the earlier one by ensuring that all who worked at Oneida could prosper. As a century-long story of economically successful social idealism, the narrative that follows is an unusually upbeat American saga. I wrote it to remind others of our better angels, what is large-spirited in ourselves.

CHAPTER 1

Perfectionism

John Humphrey Noyes (see figure 2) provided posterity with accounts of his time, which while seeming historical, never looked beyond the circumstances of Noyes. Among his retrospective efforts was an autobiographical tract subtitled "A History of Modern Perfectionism," a work notable for its silence on the subject of Perfectionism as a movement separate from Noyes. That is the job of this chapter. Noyes, and Noyes with reference to the coming Oneida Community, will be introduced in historical perspective. The work of understanding his ideas in historical context begins.[1]

This story properly starts nearly two decades before the founding of the Oneida Community in the person of the greatest revival preacher in nineteenth-century America. On November 28, 1830, Charles Finney addressed a gathering at the Third Presbyterian Church in Rochester, New York. A few years previously, the people of this congregation "had declared themselves impotent before a God who 'foreordained whatsoever comes to pass.'" Human beings, they also said, were incapable of altering their individual spiritual states. Finney rejected the fatalistic notions of what he called hyper-Calvinism and old-schoolism. Christ's atonement did away with human helplessness and passivity by making salvation available to anyone choosing to accept it. A truly penitent individual, sincerely suffused with faith, was thereby saved. In the epiphany Finney had experienced a

FIGURE 2. Oil-on-canvas portrait of John Humphrey Noyes, 1862, by William Tinsley. This is the only known likeness of Noyes painted from life.

decade before, he found not only that his sins were gone, but that he could no longer sin against God.[2]

The concepts Finney preached that day were those he said he always advanced, including "repentance, faith, justification by faith, sanctification by faith; persistence in holiness as a condition of salvation." But on this occasion, Finney also emphasized that God has made man a moral free agent. Humans are inclined to sin, and sinners will suffer endless punishment in the afterlife—if they do not choose otherwise. The capability of choosing good over evil means sin and disorder can be overcome in this world. Finney, in the words of historian Paul Johnson, "stared down from the pulpit and said flatly that if Christians united and dedicated their lives to the task, they could convert the world and bring on the millennium."[3] In saving themselves, those experiencing saving grace could save the world.

Perfect Revivals

Rochester, in 1830, was the front line of American development. New York had just become the most populous state in the Union and was accounted the most dynamic following completion of the Erie Canal in 1825. With population tripling in five years and flour mills springing up overnight, Rochester was the quintessential canal boomtown and center of transformation in upstate New York.

But Finney's Rochester also happened to be at the geographic epicenter of revival enthusiasm. The surrounding region experienced at least 1,343 religious revivals between 1825 and 1835, the majority of them packed densely between 1829 and 1832. This broad swath of upstate paralleling the Erie Canal was so scorched by white-hot fires of religious zealotry that it was known then as the "Burned-Over District" or, more simply, the "Burnt District." Finney rated the exuberant upturn in Christian faith as the greatest advance of religion ever seen in America. Another prominent minister of the time called it the greatest revival the world had ever seen. Historically, Finney's own Rochester revival was the biggest event of them all, probably the most important revival in American history.[4]

The Rochester success owed much to Finney's careful orchestration of events. He ensured, as much as he could, a judicious blend in his audiences of the pious and the potentially converted. Among Rochester's prominent citizens were a number of individuals previously identified as susceptible to conversion. These Finney placed in his front row "anxious bench," to receive repeated exhortations to find God. Frequently they did, an outcome that brought the meeting to a spectacular close. To supplement the revival events, Finney organized a network of zealous workers who conducted prayer meetings and house-to-house visitations.

But however well planned the operation was, revival success hinged on effective public speaking, and Finney's ability to connect with an audience was legendary. Seemingly, he packed every hall; every individual within hung on his every word and gesture. Finney's preaching, however, was neither histrionic nor given to what he regarded as cheap theatrical tricks. On the contrary, his delivery was measured and composed in the manner of a courtroom advocate drawing his interlocutors to an ineluctable conclusion. However logical Finney's reasoning might seem, what most impressed was his persuasive expression in language that was clear and accessible.[5]

Finney's eloquence in Rochester swept aside the last vestiges of Calvinist predetermination and replaced them with a viewpoint common to revivals of the Burnt District "awakening": the importance of human-centered religion and individual decision-making. Sin was not a permanent condition but a problem to solve. Finney's notion of free agency, furthermore, was not an abstraction of political science. In religious context, it related to the individual choosing to be open to the deeply felt emotion of saving grace coursing through the body. It spoke to an intense longing for higher spirituality at a time when Christ's return (the millennium) was expected daily.

Heightened concern with spirituality led naturally in the direction of Perfectionism as formulated some decades earlier by British theologian John Wesley. Perfection, in Wesley's view, was wrought in the human heart by divine grace through faith. Faith is not a substance God automatically deposits in a passively receptive soul. It is a condition the individual apprehends, pursues, and seeks to practice. If, therefore, faith is practicable in this life through individual effort, and if salvation from sin comes from faith in the resurrection of Christ, then perfect holiness—or, at least, moving in that direction—becomes a theoretical possibility in this, the mortal world. It is not necessary to die to be saved.[6]

Finney's notion about the penitent being cleansed of sin on acceptance of Christ was broadly consistent with Wesley's. In 1830, however, Finney was a Presbyterian offering innovative ideas drawn not from Wesley but, as he thought, from his own revelatory experience. At the time, Perfectionism seems to have been viewed as coalescing around Finney but independently of him. The movement began in New York City about 1828, then rapidly diffused outward to Albany, south central Massachusetts, and then into upstate New York. As preached by a fiery orator named Hiram Sheldon, Perfectionism gained a significant number of converts near Syracuse in 1833–1834.[7]

The key tenet of the Perfectionists was that freedom from sin resulted from faith in resurrection. Perfectionists also maintained, however, that they were sanctified and of Christ, whereas those lacking sufficient faith were sinners and of Satan. A contemporaneous definition emphasized that Perfectionists "believe that every individual is either wholly sinful, or wholly righteous and that every being in the universe, at any given time, is either entirely holy or entirely wicked. Consequently they unblushingly maintain that they themselves are free from sin."[8] Biblical support for this view was drawn from 1 John 3:5–10: "If we walk in the light . . . the blood of Jesus Christ his Son cleanseth us from all sin. . . . Whosoever abideth in him sinneth not; whosoever sinneth hath not seen him, neither known him. He that committeth sin is of the devil. Whosoever is born of God doth not commit sin; for his seed remaineth in him; and he cannot sin, because he is born of God."[9]

Perfectionism was a faith-based doctrine with little obvious reference to good deeds or public morality. This gave pause to many who worried that the essential core of the new "salvation from sin" teaching was arrogant self-righteousness, a path likely to lead to dangerous excess. Some Perfectionists did, in fact, proclaim freedom from law and custom because the regenerate, as historian Whitney Cross put it, "were guided by the Holy Spirit through the prayer of faith and must follow their impulses to the exclusion of external authority." Particularly outspoken in such antiauthoritarian sentiments were Perfectionists of the Burnt District who declared they would be governed in their conduct solely by immediate inspiration, and not by any civil authority or false ecclesiastical writ.[10]

Noyes the Perfectionist

One of those converted in the great religious outburst was twenty-year-old Dartmouth graduate John Humphrey Noyes, who experienced saving grace in his hometown of Putney, Vermont. Noyes's conversion occurred in 1831 at a revival conducted in the Finney manner by a follower of Finney who remains unnamed in the historical record. What we do have is an account describing how the revival transformed the little New England town.

During the 1820s, Putney was home to a brilliant society given over to "music and dancing, jewels and plumes, fine horses and martial parade," according to Harriet Noyes, the younger sister of John. That happy lifestyle was shattered "suddenly and totally" by financial disaster. One by one, the leading men went bankrupt, their failures setting off a "reign of estrangements and separations. Pleasant windows were darkened and every courtesy chilled." These conditions of humiliation and distress, Harriet discerned, were what prepared Putney for the great transformation effected by the Finney revival. "A more powerful control cannot be imagined," she recalled wonderingly. "It made a new society wherever it went. It abolished caste; it raised up the low and humbled the proud; it changed the customs. Vain show of dress and beauty was all forgotten in the solemnity of its presence. The dance gave way to the prayer-meeting, and for a time religion was supreme over business. It was the talk in barrooms and stores as well as in the churches."[11]

The reaction of John Noyes to the revival experience was to abandon immediately an incipient law career and to begin a new one. Looking to become a Congregationalist clergyman, he launched into study at Andover Theological Seminary—the major training ground for the country's Protestant clergymen. Subsequently he transferred to the seminary of Yale College in New Haven—the place one went for cutting-edge religious theory. In the latter place, Noyes's intention to become a minister and missionary went by the wayside as he imbibed the radical fumes of Perfectionism in the air around him.

Won over to the new faith by late 1833, Noyes initiated his own scholarly study of Perfectionist doctrine (this occurred with every new interest) but quickly sensed that something was missing. There must be, he suspected, more to redemption than faith alone. His answer was that a public declaration was needed, one committing the speaker to the Perfectionist faith in the eyes of God as well as of mortals. In future years, stating this sentiment would become a distinctive practice of the Oneida Community. In 1834, "Confessing Christ" was Noyes's first theological innovation, one he explained in this fashion.

> Faith, as a grain of mustard seed, was in my heart; but its expansion into full consciousness of spiritual life and peace, required yet another step, viz. confession. The next morning I recurred to the passage which had been my guide in my first conversion, viz. Rom. 10: 7–10, and saw in it—what I had not seen distinctly before—the power of Christ's resurrection as the centre-point of faith, and the necessity of confession as the complement of inward belief. As I reflected on this last point, it flashed across my mind that the work was done, that Christ was in me with the power of his resurrection, and that it only remained for me to confess it before the world in order to enjoy the consciousness of it. I determined at once to confess Christ in me a Savior from sin at all hazards.[12]

Noyes's profession of faith took the form of preaching a sermon titled "He That Commiteth Sin Is of the Devil." That took place in a New Haven church on February 20, 1834, a day later commemorated as "High Tide of the Spirit," the Oneida Community's spiritual new year's day.

Noyes's announcement of Perfectionist leanings electrified the New Haven community. Do you seriously claim, he was asked incredulously, that you do not commit sin? Noyes replied that he did not regard himself "as perfect in any such sense as excludes the expectation of discipline and improvement." He did not pretend to perfection in externals, he elaborated ambiguously, but "only claim purity of heart and the answer of a good conscience toward God." The reaction of church and school officials was to rescind Noyes's warrant to preach, to which Noyes retorted, "I have taken away their license to sin, and they keep on sinning. So, though they have taken away my license to preach, I shall keep on preaching."[13]

He did. For three years, Noyes became an itinerant preacher who always had the safe haven of his parents' Putney home whenever needed. He could count on some physical presence, being five-foot-eleven and broad-shouldered. On the other hand, he suffered from a throat ailment that often kept his volume low and sometimes prevented speech altogether. On the whole, he seems to have been a reasonably effective speaker who impressed by his diffidence, sincerity, and evident intelligence. One who witnessed his early sermonizing said he stood, polyglot Bible in hand, doing little more than reading and collating "the testimony on the subjects of the Second Coming of Christ and Salvation from Sin. It sufficed for these classes that the truth he brought out confounded the Orthodox sects." Another person thinking back on Noyes's early days remembered the blue eyes, the red hair, and a face that "shone like an angel's."[14]

Noyes believed God had appointed him to bring the true word to humankind in advance of the coming of Christ and the heavenly kingdom. From the first moment of that commission, he felt ready to assume the mantle of Perfectionist leadership. "God gave plenty of evidence in 1834, that he had appointed me foreman of his church," Noyes recalled. "Finney was the leading man before, but he had gone out of the country, and his dispensation had worn itself out. His men had become independent of him. Boyle, his right hand man, came out publicly and put himself under me."[15] Certainty that he was the earthly representative of the highest power always remained the central pillar of Noyes's consciousness. The conviction surely afforded him considerable self-confidence and would, in years to come, underwrite his claim to being final authority in all matters.

Noyes was recognized from the outset as an important spokesperson of Perfectionism. He was known for his biblical scholarship and respected for having the best theological training obtainable. He immediately put his mark on Perfectionism in the form of an influential periodical he published with James Boyle out of New Haven from August 1834 to about March 1835. "It was astonishing," Noyes later recalled, how many of the original members of the Oneida Community "had been brought into the faith either directly or indirectly by the paper published at New Haven."[16] Called the *Perfectionist,* it served as the chief written communication among the widely scattered Perfectionist groups. It linked Noyes to numerous Perfectionists in central New York.[17]

Spiritual Marriage

The Perfectionist movement was centered not in New Haven but in the Burnt District and especially in the vicinity of Syracuse, New York. There, at Manlius, the first large convocation of the new faith took place in the fall of the same year Noyes publicly confessed Christ. When British writer William Hepworth Dixon inquired into the origins of Perfectionism some thirty years later, he was able to obtain accounts from two of the first participants, both of whom would later be members of the Oneida Community. One was the wonderfully named Marquis de Lafayette Worden. The other was Jonathan Burt, on whose property the Oneida Community would start up. What the two men related, through Dixon, constitutes our primary source of information about how the early Perfectionists acquired a lurid reputation.

Present at Manlius in 1834 were all then accounted the leading lights of the movement: Erasmus Stone, Jarvis Rider, Hiram Sheldon, and Lucina Umphreville. It was on this occasion, Worden indicated, that the Perfectionists proclaimed themselves separate from the world. And more than that, they "rejoiced in deliverance from what they called Babylonish captivity, or the legality of the churches, and no doubt this sentiment finally affected their feelings and practice in various ways, and especially was applied to domestic and social relations."[18]

At Manlius, the Perfectionists went on to debate whether matrimonial vows would still be considered binding "in the new heaven and the new earth." Their answer was no. The new heavenly day dawning would put an end to all legalities. All such bonds were already loosening, "including those of prince and liege, of cleric and layman, of parent and child, of husband and wife." The kingdom of heaven was at hand, they thought, and in that new state of being every man should be happy in his choice of a mate. "And it was not only right, but prudent, to prepare betimes for that higher state of conjugal bliss."[19]

That seems to have been the general opinion to which Lucina Umphreville, the most renowned female Perfectionist of the Burnt District, offered a somewhat different view.[20] Umphreville claimed, on the authority of visionary insight, that men and women were not only chaste and pure in heaven, but also entirely innocent of licentious thoughts and sexual acts. To emulate heavenly behavior and to prepare for the coming rule of Christ on earth, Umphreville urged that mortal people, likewise, should be celibate and avoid marriage.[21]

Umphreville's concept of sexless gender relations gained credence from a dream experienced by Erasmus Stone. In his mind's eye, Stone reported, he had seen a sky filled with a mighty host of men and women. "A sudden spirit seemed to quicken them," Dixon was told. "They began to move, to cross each other, and to fly hither and thither. A great pain, an eager want, were written on their faces. Each man appeared to be yearning for some woman, each woman appeared to be moaning for some man. Every one in that mighty host had seemingly lost the thing most precious to his heart."[22] The meaning of this dream, Stone helpfully explained, was that "in the present stage of being, men and women are nearly always wrongly paired in marriage; that his vision was the day of judgment; that the mighty hosts were the risen dead, who had started from the grave as they had been laid down, side by side; that the trouble which had come upon them was the quick discerning of the spirit that they had not been truly paired on earth; that the violent pain and want upon their faces were the desires of every soul to find its natural mate."[23] Reports of Stone's dream electrified the convocation, apparently putting the stamp on the idea of a spiritual affinity between a man and a woman as being a mystical bond that, ordained in heaven, was purer than any sexual or legal relationship forged in this world. Did Stone originate the concept?

The notion of spiritual marriage as a sexless and therefore pure union of man and woman had long been a tradition of the Christian church. Perhaps Stone learned of it from such a source, or perhaps he was familiar with Emanuel Swedenborg (1688–1772), a Swedish mystic whose doctrines would influence the spiritualist movement in coming years. According to Swedenborg, God causes "conjugal pairs"—true lovers—to be born and search for each other in the course of human life. "The Lord provides similitudes for those who desire love truly conjugal, and if they are not given in the earths, He provides them in the heavens." The doctrines of Swedenborg were, in fact, known in the region, according to Joscelyn Godwin.[24] Then, too, the term "spiritual wifery" may have been used in upstate New York as a euphemism for extramarital affairs.[25] In any event, Dixon's impression at the time was that Manlius was the birthplace of spiritual wifery in America.[26]

Seemingly bolstered by Stone's dream, Umphreville now held that "this sort of friendship between male and female saints in these latter days and in the Perfect Church, was not only allowable in itself, but honourable alike for the woman and the man," Worden related. This "lady champion of no-marriage and no-intercourse" began to preach that, like Saint Paul, "the man was not without the woman in the Lord," and "'they that are accounted worthy to obtain that world do not marry, but are as the angels of God.'" What obtained between a man and a woman was purely spiritual.[27]

Umphreville accepted the Reverend Jarvis Rider as her spiritual partner, and the pair became the first couple of mystic union. Dixon described the two of them publicly declaiming that their companionship was a relationship "of high attainment and lasting peace," a bond of perfect and holy chastity.[28] Stone's vision, and the example set by Rider and Umphreville, spawned a spate of spiritual marriages in central New York during 1835. Hiram Sheldon discovered his celestial partner to be an attractive lady who was single. Erasmus Stone bonded with a woman described as beautiful, intelligent, and married to someone else.

Spreading quickly through the Perfectionist world, tidings of these doings reached a circle of believers in the south central Massachusetts towns of Brimfield and Southampton. This group happened to include a number of forceful young women, among whom the recognized leader was one Mary Lincoln. "Reports of what Lucina Umphreville was doing in the burnt district of New York had begun to excite the imaginations of these young and clever girls," according to Dixon. "Was Lucina the only prophetess of God? Could they do nothing to emulate her zeal?"[29]

When a trio of well-known Perfectionist speakers (Simon Lovett, Chauncey Dutton, John Noyes) gathered at Brimfield in March, Lincoln and another young woman, Maria Brown, entered Lovett's room and shared his bed—without having sex. The point was to demonstrate their superiority over the way of flesh. In a thrilling sequel, Lincoln and another woman claimed they diverted divine retribution for the act by scaling a mountain, nude, in a violent storm.[30] Even though no sexual union had transpired, Noyes reckoned the affair a great scandal for Perfectionism and disassociated himself from it.

A run on spiritual wifery followed the "Brimfield bundling." The epidemic of celestial affinity swept Southampton to such an extent that a prominent male Perfectionist boasted "he could carry a virgin in each hand without the least stir of unholy passion." What was euphemistically styled the "gospel liberty" spread to New Haven, where Simon Lovett paired spiritually with one Abby Fowler. Mary Lincoln of Brimfield fame marked out Chauncey Dutton as her special affinity.[31]

Sexual Communism

John Noyes thought it presumptuous and dangerous to flout the spirit over the flesh in this fashion. He himself, however, formulated a similar conceit to describe an unrequited love. The woman was Abigail Merwin, thirty years old (Noyes was twenty-two), attractive, and intelligent. Merwin's influence gained entrance for Noyes and his doctrine into the New Haven Free Church, where he had confessed Christ. Although he was smitten with her, Noyes outwardly displayed only "calm brotherly love." Even that form of companionship was short-lived—begun in March, over by mid-July—and Noyes scarcely ever saw her again. However, when he heard Merwin was engaged to be married in late 1835, he wrote her a letter indicating that, even though she might be with another man corporally, God had joined her to Noyes in immortal and, presumably, spiritual marriage.[32]

Noyes also thought the Perfectionists' advocacy of spiritual wifery brought them very close to Shaker doctrine. The Shakers, a religious sect founded about 1779 near Albany, called themselves the United Society of Believers in Christ's Second Coming in the conviction that their founder, Englishwoman Ann Lee, was an incarnation of Christ. In following her teachings, they initiated the kingdom of Christ on earth, the millennium. Based on the belief that lust was the cause of evil, Shakers were celibate and practiced a nearly complete segregation of men and women.[33] "Every element of Shakerism was present," Noyes mused. "The Shaker doctrine of the Leadership of Women was there. Lucina Umphreville was the incipient Mother Ann at the West, and Mary Lincoln at the East. The Shaker doctrine of chastity was there." Indeed, if the Shakers had been alert to the situation in 1835, "they might have established new societies in Central New York and in Central Massachusetts."[34]

The enthusiastic pairing up of the Perfectionists was regarded as entirely chaste. However, such claims were revealed to be hollow when platonic affection suddenly flowered into sexual love at Bridgeport, just north of Syracuse. There, living in a house together in the summer of 1836, were Lucina Umphreville and Jarvis Rider, but now no longer a spiritual couple. Umphreville's new partner was a man named Charles Lovett. Rider's was the woman of the household, said to be "much appreciated and loved for her beauty of character and goodness of heart." Becoming suspicious of the goings-on, the woman's husband attacked Rider but, just as quickly, backed off with abject apologies. "But," Worden concluded the tale, "in the sequel there was some reason to believe that the relation became so far carnal as to lay just foundation for scandal."[35]

Jonathan Burt's version of the story was that he and the owner of the house, Thomas Chapman, were engaged in canal work some distance away. It was in Chapman's absence that Umphreville and Lovett and also Chapman's wife and Rider became spiritually united, "and, as it afterward appeared by their own confession, entered into sexual intimacy as well." Burt continued, "The result was that Chapman on his return beat Rider with a horse-whip and kicked him out of his house. In the midst of this operation Chapman was taken blind. In consequence he desisted from his blows, and called Rider back into the house. I was present at this catastrophe. The termination of the affair was an entire alienation of Chapman from his wife and from Rider; and she, being of a delicate constitution, sank under the troubles that came upon her, and died soon after."[36]

Chapman being struck blind was a nice detail impressing many as an act of God, one that put the stamp of approval on celebrating special affinity with coitus. Soon after, Hiram Sheldon and Sophia Cook, Erasmus Stone and Eliza Porter, and probably other couples cemented their formerly platonic affiliations with what Whitney Cross called "the new physical sacrament."[37] This was the form of spiritual wifery that would become familiar to Americans during the spiritualist craze of the 1850s. True love was a divinely preordained state. When two people recognized a spiritual spouse in each other, their discovery sanctified sexual intercourse and superseded any legal bonds.[38]

The progression from the spiritual to physical plane did not surprise Noyes. "Religious love is very near neighbor to sexual love, and they always get mixed in the intimacies and social excitements of Revivals. The next thing a man wants, after he has found the salvation of his soul, is to find his Eve and his Paradise. Hence, these wild experiments and terrible disasters." More than natural, the culmination of desire in the carnal act might be inevitable. Noyes took to heart the demonstration that the sexual drive is a mighty power—"a stream ever running. If it is dammed up, it will break out irregularly and destructively."[39]

"A multitude of stories were afloat about the fantastic sayings and doings of western Perfectionists," Noyes recalled sadly. "Many of those stories, I knew, were true."[40] The newly revealed carnal dimension of spiritual wifery compromised Perfectionism, he thought. After Bridgeport, Noyes gave up the attempt to bring the far-flung and obstreperous movement into the fold by traveling about and engaging in firsthand disputation. Noyes retreated to Putney with the intention of starting over by assembling his own group of followers.[41]

The first result of Noyes's new tack was to formulate an original perspective on human sexuality. Written at the start of 1837, the announcement of "the theory of absolute communism in love" was referred to as the "Battle Axe Letter," after the name of the publication in which it later appeared.

When the will of God is done on earth, as it is in heaven [Noyes affirmed], *there will be no marriage.* The marriage supper of the Lamb, is a feast at which *every dish is free to every guest.* Exclusiveness, jealousy, quarreling, have no place there, for the same reason as that which forbids the guests of a thanksgiving dinner to claim each his separate dish, and quarrel with the rest for his rights. In a pure community, there is no more reason why sexual intercourse should be restrained by law, than why eating and drinking should be—and there is as little occasion for shame in the one case as in the other. . . . The guests of the marriage supper may have each his favorite dish, each a dish of his own procuring, and that without the jealousy of exclusiveness. I call a certain woman my wife—she is yours, she is Christ's, and in him she is the bride of all saints.[42]

It is possible that Noyes's heaven of sexual activity owed something to Swedenborg's afterlife in which the nuptial union of conjugal pairs "is not momentary, but incessant and total." If so, Noyes never acknowledged the debt and, on the contrary, distanced himself from the Swedish seer by accusing the latter of encouraging sexual promiscuity for men.[43] In any event, Noyes's sexual communism contradicted Swedenborg's notion of heavenly monogamy.

Although Noyes wrote this letter on learning that Abigail Merwin had married, the thesis was more than a sour-grapes reaction to being spurned. It did much more than merely elaborate on either spiritual wifery or monogamous marriage.[44] Noyes's vision of sexual communism redefined assumptions about morality and purpose. If sexual desire is God-given, it cannot be bad or shameful. If sexual desire is irresistible, it should be directed to serve holy purposes. And, logically, if all things in heaven are shared, sex should be brought into line with communism in other matters.

Noyes's "great idea of a universal marriage" was issued with stern warnings that the policy was not to be undertaken in anything less than a state of complete holiness. It was a program that would not be attempted for another decade. As for himself, he said he "never knew woman sexually till I was married, and that I never knew any woman but my wife until we entered into our present complex marriage in 1846."[45]

At the height of revival enthusiasm about 1830, the popular exhorter Charles Finney advanced a brand of Protestantism stressing free agency and the Wesleyan belief that perfect holiness might be attainable. In this milieu, the new religion of Perfectionism insisted on the literal truth of all that—now.

Personal sanctification and salvation from sin could be achieved in this life-time. Rejecting preordained outcomes, Perfectionists regarded salvation as, simply, a matter of individual choice and faith.

Regenerate Perfectionists were in theory free from external authority, a belief encouraging them to suppose they were free of all legalistic bonds. The bonds they frequently insisted they were free of were marriage rela-tions, a line of thought that led them away from valuing physical contact between husband and wife. Perfectionists near Syracuse in 1834 took up the notion of spiritual affinity, a mystical bond of true love between a man and a women forged in heaven. Accordingly, some of the leading evangelists paired themselves up, platonically, to demonstrate mastery over the flesh. Such rela-tionships tended to become sexual and brought to Perfectionism a reputation for sexual scandal long preceding that of the Oneida Community.

One convert to the new faith was John Humphrey Noyes, a young Ver-monter who came to believe that faith-based Perfectionism needed one more precept to work—in effect, an on-switch. The individual, Noyes proposed, activated his or her state of inner redemption by publicly announcing alle-giance to Perfectionism. What prompted this suggestion or how it related to outside circumstances is not clear. But, for John Noyes, the confession of Christ was equally an acknowledgment of being divinely appointed to advance God's work. That, one would suppose, brought a great inner strength of certainty. Thereafter, Noyes became an important figure in the Perfectionist movement. He wielded influence mainly by publishing a peri-odical that enjoyed wide currency. The lesson learned here about the power of the press would be taken to heart in coming years.

Noyes had some impact on early Perfectionism. But the movement, in turn, made its mark on him as Perfectionism focused increasingly on gender relations and, increasingly, became infamous for its sexual behavior. These were the circumstances in which Noyes formulated a theory of sexual com-munism. If all things in heaven are held in common and if people there truly love one another, then the way of heaven is that all men and women should love each unselfishly in all ways. Noyes did not, at the time, elabo-rate the concept. Nor did he and his followers practice what he preached. In due course, however, sexual communism would become the keystone of communistic living in the Oneida Community. Further, and as the Oneida Community was to discover, sexual communism implicitly accorded men and women the same right to engage in sex. It was a concept charged with potential to push earthly relationships in the same direction of equality.

CHAPTER 2

Putney

This chapter continues to focus on Noyes and on those aspects of his philosophy useful to understanding the future Oneida Community. At the same time, his thinking is related to a larger context of beliefs and trends in the outside world to which Noyes was responding. Noyes's first disciples are introduced; the roles they played in the coming commune are outlined. And finally, a review of the Putney years is aimed to clarify why the Oneida Community assumed both a religious and a secular character.

For more than a decade, Noyes enjoyed the security of Putney, Vermont, a place that offered the sanctuary of family money and standing. He assembled a small band of disciples with whom he printed religious tracts and studied doctrinal matters. Over time, the group assumed collective ownership of the money and property originally owned by individual members. In addition, the Putneyites developed several distinctive habits foreshadowing later developments in the Oneida Community.

Noyes, newly married, developed an unusual form of birth control that would prove crucial to instituting free love. He elaborated his Perfectionist theology and began to grapple with some of the difficulties a faith-based religion posed to the creation of an actual organization run from the top down.

Conducting comparative research on the utopian endeavors of their time, the Putney group came especially to admire the Brook Farm Association.

When that commune collapsed, the Putneyites declared themselves to be complete communitarians and, a year later, proclaimed that heaven had come to earth among them. This and other actions outraged the neighbors and forced Noyes and his band to flee town. They found refuge with a small Perfectionist group in upstate New York.

Recruiting Disciples

Noyes retreated to his hometown to repair, as he said, "the disasters of Perfectionism." Disavowing earlier efforts "to reorganize and discipline broken and corrupted regiments," Noyes intended to reestablish the faith by devoting himself to "the patient instruction of a few, simple-minded, unpretending believers, chiefly belonging to my father's family. . . . The Bible school which I commenced among them in the winter of 1836, proved to be to me and to the cause of holiness, the beginning of better days."[1] The storm of opprobrium descending on him after his views on sexual communism were published in a Philadelphia periodical, *The Battle Axe and Weapons of War*, in August 1837 strengthened his resolve to withdraw from the public arena. Ensconced in Putney, the twenty-five-year-old Noyes set about building up a cadre of Perfectionists uncontaminated by the views of others.

How does one recruit disciples? What can a callow young man offer to inspire loyalty and love? What people most vividly recalled of Noyes was his attractive personality. "When you were in his presence, you knew you were with someone who was not an ordinary man," was the way one woman put it. "Old members of the Community have said to me," Noyes's son Pierrepont testified, "that those who got within the effective area of Father Noyes's personality were reluctant to lose him; that life seemed brighter and more worthwhile when he was about." He was a source of light and power for all about him, said another. "His was a golden dream and always we were bent on sharing it with him." An atmosphere of good feeling seemed to surround Noyes, a third remembered. "It was a pleasure to sit near whether he was talking or silent. A river of living water seemed to issue from him. His life was so harmonious that the effect of contact was musical. One forgot one's trouble in his presence."[2] Noyes offered the pleasure of his company, which many experienced as irresistible.

At least partly because of Noyes's charismatic drawing power, people found it easy to believe he was divinely appointed. From there, it was a short step to agree God had equipped Noyes with the means to interpret gospel truths hidden from others. And more—Noyes was in active communication with heaven. Via spiritualistic linkage he called inspiration, Noyes could relay advice and information directly from the apostles in the earliest Christian church. Corinna Ackley, who grew up in the Oneida Community during the 1870s, remembered Noyes as a man "always sitting in his big arm-chair with his eyes shut and when I asked why, I was told he was communing with St. Paul."[3] With all that, Noyes could reward a disciple's faith with the great gift of certitude about the meaning of life.

The dimension of Noyes uppermost at Putney must have been the offering of divine truth, because by 1838, Noyes rigorously asserted his divinely appointed status. He found it necessary, his mother said, "to come out with the declaration that all who expected to attach themselves to him must take a subordinate place and have confidence in him as qualified by the special grace of God to take control both temporal and spiritual." The mother was an authority on this because Noyes had bullied her unmercifully into admitting that he—Noyes—was no longer her son but rather her father by virtue of his commission from God. In Putney, Noyes brooked no opposition and recognized no equals.[4]

Noyes initially recruited three of his siblings: Harriet, nineteen years old; Charlotte, sixteen; and George, fourteen. This very young group was impressionable but not "simple-minded," as we use the term today. All three would prove to be important collaborators in Noyes's publishing efforts over the years.

George, the most cerebral of the trio, would found the Community's museum and explain the intricacies of diverse philosophical viewpoints in the pages of Oneida's periodicals. For a time and in the absence of his elder brother, he conducted the Oneida Community's evening meetings. In the far future and close to the time of his death (1870), he would help—with apparent enthusiasm—to initiate the Community's eugenics program by fathering two offspring. George, however, comes across as rather colorless in Community memory in contrast to his sisters, who evoked real fondness.

"They could criticize without personal animus," Jessie Kinsley, a child who grew up in the Community, recalled. "They could reconcile a sore heart to see its fault; they could stimulate ambition to rise out of littleness of Spirit, both for itself and others. They were great hearted and made you feel great hearted." Harriet gave up marriage prospects and a teaching job when she accepted her brother's teachings. Thereafter, she staunchly supported John and, just as staunchly, waged war against sin and worldliness. Her nephew, Pierrepont Noyes, remembered her as beautifully homely, "with many freckles, sandy hair and almost masculine features." The quality of being "masculine" often was applied to her, possibly because she looked like her older brother. And like him, she was a systematic thinker with an eye for practicalities. After studying Oneida Community diet, for example, she turned the knowledge to account in the form of a cookbook tourists could buy. The most organized of the siblings, Harriet was effectively the Community manager.

Artistically inclined Charlotte would be looked up to as adviser to the girls and youthful women of the later Oneida Community. She inspired the most lasting memories of warmth. It was "Aunt Charlotte Maria—beautiful Aunt Charlotte who, on one of my first homesick days [away from Oneida], took me in her arms and comforted me," Pierrepont Noyes recorded years later. Jessie Kinsley's memory of her was "of a gentle teacher who made English History delightful—a loving friend who always made criticism seem like love, and a gentlewoman who wanted me to keep my hands clean and to stand straight, sit erect and 'breathe deep.' There was unspeakable reverence for the beauty of her character in my heart. I wanted to be like her."[5]

After the siblings, Noyes recruited disciple Harriet Holton to be his wife. Holton, thirty years old, lived with her grandparents in nearby Westminster, Vermont. She had seen Noyes preach and had corresponded with him. Holton became an enthusiastic fan of Noyes's teachings and a substantial donor to his cause. Noyes proposed marriage to her with the explanation that it would help him to settle down. "I am conscious of possessing by the grace of God a spirit of firmness, perseverance, and faithfulness in every good work, which has made the vagabond, incoherent service, to which I have thus far been called, almost intolerable to me." He would welcome a comfortable domestic situation, Noyes said, then added bluntly that, while he respected many of Harriet's qualities, he felt no particular affection for her. Finally, Holton was invited to join Noyes in this life with the understanding that she faced the prospect of sexual communism, a primary and universal union "more radical and of course more important than any partial and external partnership." Harriet accepted the bizarre offer entirely on Noyes's terms: "I feel that the Lord had directed you to me, and that I was formed in part to contribute to your happiness and usefulness in this act of your drama."[6] With unstinting devotion, Holton upheld her end of the bargain for the remaining forty-eight years of Noyes's life. She would be revered in the Oneida Community as "Mother Noyes," the epitome of selflessness and good cheer.

The core group of Noyes siblings and wife expanded with the addition of George and Mary Cragin. George had been a figure of some prominence in efforts to improve the lot of New York City's fallen women. Mary, a teacher and Sunday school instructor, was brought into the Perfectionist fold from her study of Noyes's writings. When George, in turn, was converted, he was fired from his job editing a periodical called the *Advocate of Moral Reform*. The unemployed couple took shelter in the home of Abram Smith, Perfectionist preacher of Rondout (Kingston), on the middle reaches of the Hudson River. Noyes repeatedly reproved Smith for asserting independence during these years. Smith, however, always worked his way back into Noyes's good graces. In this instance, Smith carried on a torrid love affair with Mary while George did the house chores and farmwork. Noyes rescued the Cragins from this situation and brought them to Putney in late 1840.[7]

Other important figures at Putney and later at Oneida included John Skinner, formerly a Quaker school teacher and one of Noyes's earliest converts; William Woolworth, a farmer and wagon maker; and John Miller, a Putney storekeeper who for the next fifteen years ably served the Perfectionists as accountant and financier. All these Putney people would be among those looked up to at Oneida as the "central committee," an informal board of advisers close to Noyes.[8]

By the early 1840s about two dozen adults had gathered around Noyes. They lived in various Putney locations, including three residences: the Noyes family home, a house built by John Noyes in 1839, and another belonging to a family named Campbell. For the better part of a decade, the Perfectionists of Putney served as the printing crew for publishing religious tracts. Noyes had always been drawn to the printed word with the idea that the penny press of his day represented a technological revolution in communication. Harnessed to the gospel cause, the press would spread the good word and constitute the central, regulating office of Noyes's church. His experience with the short-lived *Perfectionist* magazine strengthened this view. Now, with Harriet Holton's dowry, Noyes bought his press.[9]

They thought of themselves as a Bible study group and, after 1841 when they built a chapel, a society of inquiry devoted to strengthening their religious faith. Filled with earnest conviction, the young zealots—mostly in their late teens and early twenties—threw themselves into Bible study daily at 5 a.m. The remainder of the morning was devoted to printing, farming on land obtained from the Noyes family estate, and managing a general store in downtown Putney. In the afternoon they cultivated the mind by engaging in an hour of individual study of a selected religious topic. The next hour was spent in common discussion of the subject; the hour after that was given over to arriving at a unanimous conclusion in the matter.[10] These activities foreshadowed the Oneida Community's emphasis on intellectual development and on the group meeting as forum for decision making. Other possible precedents for later Oneida practices included a dietary preference for fruits and vegetables and a tendency toward cooperative child care.[11]

The Oneida Community's later move toward gender equality was not, however, prefigured in Putney practice. The Perfectionists, to be sure, were aware of women's rights issues being raised in the outside world.[12] Actual gender equality, however, was not a salient issue to them. Noyes and his disciples insisted that although the two sexes complemented and completed each other, men were the better half. "The husband is the head of the wife" (Ephesians 5:23); "I permit no woman to teach or to have authority over men" (1 Timothy 2:12). Such was the biblical justification quoted at Putney and, again, at Oneida to describe the standing of women. "To man is assigned the place of head of the woman," Charlotte Noyes Miller affirmed, "but woman is the glory of man, and neither is without the other 'in the Lord.'"[13] Noyes, as Corinna Ackley indicated, was strongly drawn to Saint Paul. Because of that preference, the Perfectionists of Putney, and later of Oneida, referred almost exclusively to that misogynist apostle when expressing their belief that, in the divine nature of things, women were inferior to men.

Noyes's little group was not self-sufficient. The only enterprise producing an income was the store. Its profits, however, fell far short of the group's considerable expenses. "But," Harriet Skinner remembered, "we were like a boy in his minority going to school. We knew our father was rich and would set us up in business when we were old enough; and meanwhile we were not afraid to spend the pocket-money which he freely gave us."[14] In fact, Noyes and his followers were able to concentrate on religion because they were financially supported by about $16,000 contributed by Harriet Holton Noyes and nearly $20,000 from the estate of Noyes's father.[15]

Noyes's authority was unquestioned throughout the Putney years, even to the extent of determining marriage partners for his followers, including his siblings. Harriet, for example, was wed to John Skinner. Charlotte was paired with John Miller. George was joined to a local girl of the Campbell family. When it came to the subject of matrimony—what marriage is, who marries whom—Noyes's ideas about heavenly relations surely received earnest consideration in their study sessions. Theory aside, however, Noyes and his followers "continued to walk in all the commandments and ordinances of common morality *blameless*," according to Harriet Skinner. "There was probably, never a people where the law of chastity was more inviolate or its spirit more respected."[16] The Putneyites were not indulging in extramarital sex.

Nevertheless, the townspeople of Putney knew the licentious reputation of Perfectionism and knew also that Noyes advocated sexual communism. Further, the Protestant majority of Putney regarded the Perfectionist doctrine of salvation from sin as heretical. Here were grounds for local distrust and suspicion liable to flame into active expression at any time, as they did with Joseph Smith's contemporaneous Church of Latter Day Saints. However, unlike the Mormons, who were repeatedly driven out of town by outraged locals, the Perfectionists of Putney were long shielded from public antagonism by the high regard in which the Noyes family was held. "The responsibility and general popularity of the Noyes family was one of the prepared conditions for the safety of the Community germ. Though it was the wealthiest family in town, it was one which always attracted the good-will rather than the envy of the less fortunate" was the opinion of Noyes family member Harriet Skinner. The Noyes family, she said, was unostentatious, approachable, hospitable.[17]

The Perfectionists of Putney were left in peace to follow their own inclinations for more than ten years.

Perfecting Perfectionism

During his years in Putney, Noyes's thinking developed in several ways that would affect beliefs and practices of the future Oneida Community. One was his startling invention of safe—relatively safe—sex. Although Noyes's marriage proposal had been a cold one, it resulted in a union that generated a certain amount of heat. We know this because, years later, Noyes reminisced about the intimacy of this period. What he mainly recalled was developing a technique for birth control requiring the man to forgo ejaculation in sexual intercourse.

> I studied the subject of sexual intercourse in connection with my matrimonial experience, and discovered the principle of Male Continence. And the discovery was occasioned and even forced upon me by very sorrowful experience. In the course of six years my wife went through the agonies of five births. Four of them were premature. Only one child [Theodore] lived. This experience was what directed my studies and kept me studying. After our last disappointment, I pledged my word to my wife that I would never again expose her to such fruitless suffering. . . .
>
> [In the summer of 1844] I conceived the idea that the sexual organs have a social function which is distinct from the propagative function; and that these functions may be separated practically. I experimented on this idea, and found that the self-control which it requires is not difficult; also that my enjoyment was increased; also that my wife's experience was very satisfactory, as it had never been before; also that we had escaped the horrors and the fear of involuntary propagation. This was a great deliverance. It made a happy household.[18]

Noyes's technique of *coitus reservatus* would have tremendous implications for the practice of sexual communism. Later, Noyes described the practice of sexual intercourse without male ejaculation as "the very soul of Oneida, the principle to which the Community in some sense owes its existence."[19] In the absence of male continence, it is difficult to imagine how a commune committed to sexual relations with multiple partners could end up as anything other than a support group for pregnant women and an ever-increasing pool of juvenile dependents. At the same time, the recognition that women were freed from the necessity of pregnancy and that their experience of sex could be "very satisfactory" were ideas with radical potential for developing gender relations of greater equality.

Turning from sexual to political relations, Noyes also pondered an essential organizational dilemma of his religion. How could one reconcile having one leader directing group action with a group ethos of essentially independent and individualistic character? To Burnt District Perfectionists, perfect holiness meant exemption from man-made, formal codes of behavior and from all customary strictures constraining action. Noyes agreed in theory. He also knew that, in practice, freedom from legalistic restraint made for undependable disciples. So Noyes hedged. "Those who are led by the spirit of God, though they can not come under law, may yet come under rules," he argued, "and may act acceptably under the conjoint influence of internal impulses and external regulations."[20] Like the disciples of old, the regenerate could maintain a system of mutual instruction and profit from being taught. God works through human means and human leaders auxiliary to God's leadership. This clearly meant Noyes, who, in person during the Putney years, insisted on his dominance. In print, however, the point usually was conveyed with circumspection.

The Putney sojourn also afforded Noyes the opportunity to polish his theology, which was published in a new periodical called the *Spiritual Magazine*. The more important articles were pulled together into a volume issued in 1847. That book, *The Berean: A Manual for the Help of Those Who Seek the Faith of the Primitive Church*, was regarded as something of a Bible to members of the later Oneida Community.

What Noyes laid out in these writings was that salvation from sin "was the great object of the mission and sacrifice of Christ." How, he asked the reader to ponder, "is this union, by which Christ dwells in the soul and saves it from sin, to be attained? The witnesses of the New Testament answer with one voice—by faith." The true believer became one with Christ, dying and rising from death with Christ into a resurrected, sanctified state.[21] This was familiar Perfectionist ground. Noyes, however, went beyond John Wesley in asserting that the true believer is not merely forgiven the consequences of specific sinful acts, but completely purified of sin. Remission of sin is once and forever. Redemption being permanent, it is impossible to backslide from the condition, to fall from grace. "Periodical repentance, which implies continuance in the sins repented of, is of most horrible hypocrisy."[22] Once attained, salvation from sin is absolute.

A logic so extreme raises a problem in understanding what takes place in the condition or quality of faith that results in salvation. Earlier Noyes had proposed that public confession activated redemptive status. But what came before? What led up to perfection? Did faith of a high magnitude suddenly blossom into being? In response, Noyes embarked on what would prove to be a long journey of theological equivocation. Even as he insisted sanctification was absolute and forever, at Putney he argued it was also conditional and progressive.

When Noyes had confessed his perfection, it will be recalled, he also thought there might be room for improvement. Being perfect but not perfect seems difficult to grasp, and Noyes's subsequent elaboration of the concept was not entirely illuminating. Most Perfectionists, he mused, would not be able to achieve sanctification instantaneously. "The process by which full salvation is effected, is one that requires time," Noyes explained, "because it is not merely a spiritual operation, but an exhibition and application of *truth*."[23] "Every believer in Christ may, in a valuable sense, claim to be *perfect*," he elaborated. "He is perfect in the sense of having in him the germ of all righteousness; but he may at the same time be very *imperfect* with reference to the expansion of that germ into actual experience."[24] Noyes believed that the primitive church recognized two grades of believers: the fully regenerate and those of lesser faith. He presumed, as the latter statement implies, that the same would be true in his church as well.

To envision righteousness as something that could improve took religious Perfectionism (based on the doctrine of salvation from sin) into the realm of social perfectionism—belief in the perfectibility of society through human effort.[25] There was potential for confusion here if the two kinds of perfection were not clearly distinguished. They were not. On the one hand, Noyes did not specify how one might achieve sanctification as the result of following some specific course of action. On the other, he apparently encouraged the ambiguity by insisting, at Putney, that the righteous would have "an unquenchable desire of progress."[26] One can also imagine practical benefits to blurring the distinction between perfectionisms. If a group wished to move beyond faith toward action, for example, a healthy dollop of social perfectionism might go far to encourage socially constructive purpose.

Competing Millennia

In addition to developing a technique of birth control and to exploring the limits of Perfectionism, Noyes at Putney also revised his views on the millennium. The Burnt District Perfectionists who spoke of the kingdom of heaven being at hand were expressing a widely held conviction that Christ's return was imminent. With it, as foretold in the last section of the New Testament, the Book of Revelation, would come the millennium, a thousand-year reign of Christ with the righteous over a united heaven and earth. That period would conclude, it was generally supposed, with resurrection of the dead and delivery of final judgment. Noyes agreed with this and also thought that the return of Jesus would be heralded by "an unexampled succession of wars, pestilences, earthquakes, eclipses and famines."[27] Indeed, most agreed that Christ's advent would signal the apocalyptic end of days. Noyes was in tune with all this, but he expanded on it. For him, advent and final days were incorporated into a much broader vision of human destiny.

His reading of the Bible, as far back as divinity school, led him to assert that Jesus had made a return appearance to the mortal world a short time after his resurrection and ascent into heaven. To accommodate this additional advent event, Noyes formulated a scenario of the past in which human history was the outcome of compacts made by God with two groups of people. Noyes called them covenants, imagining that each was a set of behavioral expectations for humans, which God judged when the term of the contract expired.

God's first covenant was with the Jews. The task of this, his chosen people, was to follow an explicit body of law spelled out in the Ten Commandments of Moses. For approximately two thousand years, as it seemed to Noyes, God had poured "the sunshine and rain of religious discipline" upon them. But when Christ came, "he said that the fields were 'white to the harvest.'" Due to the preaching of Jesus and his apostles, the preparation for judgment was completed. The resulting verdict was negative. The divine sentence was to allow the Romans to conquer Jerusalem in AD 70 and to end the national existence of the Jews.[28]

Prior to that, however, and after the resurrected Christ departed the first time, the disciples gradually became fully regenerate. This early apostolic church, called the "primitive church" in Noyes's writings, demonstrated, for the first time in human history, that complete redemption from sin was attainable in this life. Christ, at that point, returned to the primitive church on earth and rendered the judgment bringing the age of the Jews to a close.

The second age, the time of the Gentiles, began with the departure of Christ and the primitive church from the physical world to the spiritual plane soon after. Their withdrawal to heaven meant that no earthly body of religion was in the direct line of apostolic succession. Claims by any of the formal churches to ecclesiastical authority since that time, therefore, were false.[29]

God's compact with the Gentiles was that, freed from Mosaic and earthly laws, they could aspire to the new dispensation of salvation from sin. The age will conclude with the reemergence of Christ and the primitive church into this world and judgment passed, in turn, on the Gentiles. That event, Noyes learned in an apocalyptic vision, was close at hand.[30] "For nearly two thousand years the Gentile crop has been maturing," he explained, "and we may reasonably look for the Gentile harvest as near."[31] Portentously, he thundered on: "Between this present time and the establishment of God's kingdom over the earth lies a chaos of confusion, tribulation and war such as must attend the destruction of the fashion of this world and the introduction of the will of God as it is done in heaven. God has set me to cast up a highway across this chaos, and I am gathering out the stones and grading the track as fast as possible."[32] Time was running out, and Noyes, at least early on, felt a great urgency to convert and thereby save as many as possible.

It was only at the conclusion of this scheme—that is, at the third coming of Christ and the second epoch-ending destruction—that Noyes fell into step with the popular view of the matter. Concern with the doomsday connotations of the millennium increased steadily during the 1830s, strengthened by the apparent rise of calamity in the world, including freakish weather and the financial crash of 1837.[33] Finally, what had built up to a frenzy of end-time excitement culminated in a millennial movement started by William Miller, a Baptist minister of Hampton, New York.

Millerist doctrine was loosely organized around the prediction that the world would end in 1843 or 1844 with the return of Christ and the rendering of judgment on humankind. The arguments Miller advanced in favor of his reading were clear. The Bible was literally true, he averred, and, almost literally, provided the world's termination time. Armed with a few simple rules of interpretation provided by Miller, any person could consult the source, decode the primary text, and reach the same conclusion.

The ideas were conveyed in millions of copies of books, pamphlets, periodicals, and tracts, including six hundred thousand copies of the Millerite publication *The Midnight Cry* in the year 1842 alone.[34] Partly as a result of this outpouring of print, Millerism became a substantial movement numbering roughly fifty thousand adherents in New England and upstate New York, with perhaps another million or so inclined to take it seriously. Millerism, however, lost credence when the final prediction for the end of the world (October 22, 1844, the "Great Disappointment") proved to be a day like any other.[35]

Noyes's views of the end were broadly similar to Miller's in imagining that the advent of Christ meant the end of the world. And, as with Miller, the Bible was true also for Noyes. However, since that source did not clearly state many of the doctrines Noyes imputed to it, he—unlike Miller—had to explain why such things were hidden and why only he could see them. "The Bible furnishes radical principles on which a spiritual mind can stand and reason firmly concerning things within the veil," he explained. "The Bible must not be asked to lead us step by step into the holy of holies, but only to point the way, consigning us to the specific guidance of 'the spirit of wisdom and revelation' Eph. 1:17."[36] In contrast to Miller, therefore, Noyes advanced a theology that must have seemed murky and filled with special pleading.

Considering the Millerites to be his main competition in biblical exegesis, Noyes set about refuting them in a blizzard of articles from 1840 on. It is difficult to imagine, however, that his anti-Miller prose swayed many Millerites. Millerism, on the other hand, attracted many Perfectionists.[37] Noyes must have gritted his teeth as he sat in Putney watching waves of the rival brand of millennialism lapping around him.

His reaction to Millerism is discernible in two changes of doctrine at this time. First, he conceded violent apocalypse to Millerites, claiming instead that the coming of Christ and all it entailed was likely to be a peaceful event. The Book of Revelation was, after all, such highly figurative material that we should "allow prophecy a wider field of fulfillment than this world." When one took a more expansive view of things, the coming change now looked more like, say, a gorgeous temple of everlasting peace and developing faith.[38] The judgment of the world, he concluded in contradistinction to Miller, "will be a gradual spiritual operation, effected by truth and invisible power, without any of the physical machinery which alarms the imaginations of most expectants of the great day."[39]

Second, Noyes sharpened the contrast of his interpretation to Miller's by emphasizing the importance of the human contribution to the preordained outcome. In Millerism, people were passive recipients of divine action. One sought redemption, of course, but Christ was coming whatever one thought or did. Noyes, in contrast, began to describe people as God's colleagues who helped God to effect an outcome. "As the Bible is the great manual of Spiritual Philosophy," Noyes now explained, "our main business as co-workers with him, is to serve as door-keepers to the Bible—to do what we can to make all men 'meditate therein day and night;' and especially to bring forth into due prominence the *spiritual* doctrines of the Bible."[40] Noyes, then, began to emphasize human participation as meaningful.

A gentler and more gradual millennium and a Christ people could work with—these were doctrinal changes with implications for Perfectionist behavior. The first freed Noyes's disciples from keeping a vigil for the end. The second encouraged individual engagement with God's plan as actively as did any of the communal programs of the day.

Communal Antecedents

The Perfectionists defined themselves in increasingly formal terms during the Putney years. In 1842, they declared it was consistent with republicanism "to have a foreman." Theirs was John Noyes, now explicitly named as president of their little theocratic government by virtue of authority vested in him from heaven.[41]

Next, they began to visualize themselves as owners in common of their goods and money. Two years after naming Noyes as their leader, they drew up a document of incorporation stating: "All property of every kind which we are now severally possessed of or which shall hereafter come into our possession so long as we remain in the Corporation, shall be held as the property of the Corporation."[42] Although this sounded like communism, the condition set forth was limited to four owners, all men (John and George Noyes, John Miller, and John Skinner). A constitution issued in 1845 greatly augmented the participatory membership by taking into account individuals contributing time and work to the commonweal.[43]

As they became a community of pooled property, they took an interest in similarly inclined groups around them. Among the examples of religiously based communities to consider were several German sects that had fled Lutheran oppression in the Old World. These included the Zoarite and Rappite sects of Ohio and Pennsylvania. However, the one closest to the Putneyites was the Ebenezer Community of True Inspirations established near Buffalo, New York, in 1843.

About eight hundred Ebenezers resided in several agricultural villages in which land and buildings were owned in common. Domestic life centered on communal kitchens with common dining areas. The Putney Perfectionists, very likely, were attentive to a notion of divinely sanctioned leadership among the Ebenezers broadly similar to their own. The German system of governance was a council of elderly men receiving guidance from a medium through whom, they believed, God spoke.[44] The Putneyites probably also learned that the piety of each individual Ebenezer was evaluated annually by a committee of those deemed highest in spiritual standing. This internal hierarchy bore an intriguing resemblance to a kind of ranking later instituted in the Oneida Community called the principle of ascending fellowship (see chapters 4 and 5).

However, the brand of sectarian communitarianism best known to the Perfectionists of Putney was not the Ebenezers but the previously mentioned Shakers, a religious sect committed to celibacy and notable for completely separating men from women in daily life. By 1830, Shakers may have numbered about five thousand members residing in some nineteen societies located in several states. Each society was an essentially autonomous and self-sufficient farming settlement that also produced such salable products as garden seeds, medicinal herbs, preserved fruits and vegetables, finely wrought furniture, and other goods. A society, typically, was divided into four families, each comprising a cluster of buildings with about a hundred people. In each family, men and women worked separately at tasks that they, in common with the world around them, regarded as gender appropriate. Each of the families had parallel organizations for men and women, each with its own leaders. Children, brought into the family with their parents or adopted by the order from orphanages, were kept physically apart from the adult world.[45]

Noyes, as we have seen, was familiar with the Shakers and had been studying their doctrines since about 1834. Shaker theology may have influenced his thinking (as we shall see) on the subjects of God's duality and Pentecostal communism. Noyes, of course, profoundly disagreed with the Shaker idea that sex was bad and that such a view could be justified from scripture. "An unauthorized and evil use is made of the text, 'In the resurrection they neither marry, nor are given in marriage,'" he insisted, "when it is taken for proof that the distinction between the sexes—the very image of God—is to be obliterated in heaven, and all the glorious offices and affections growing out of that distinction are to have an end."[46] He did, however, regard Shaker abstinence as an ethically justifiable form of birth control.

At the time the Putneyites were studying them, the Shakers were increasingly recognized for successful communal living. Noyes himself—much later in time—credited that sect with having demonstrated the practicality of communal life.[47] And because the Shakers recognized no personal ownership, they also demonstrated the possibilities of communism.

Oddly, in view of the fact that Ebenezers and Shakers were being studied for their communal characteristics, neither was essentially communitarian. Nothing, that is to say, in theological doctrine required their members to live together or to own property in common. Neither Ebenezers nor Shakers nor any of the other religious groups practiced communitarianism at the outset. All had taken it up to maintain themselves separately from society and to keep the allurements and hostility of the outside world at arm's length. For Ebenezers and Shakers, communism and co-residence were defensive measures tacked on to a theocratic credo.[48]

In addition to these sectarian precedents, there were also various kinds of nonreligious communards who looked hopefully on the world around them with a view to changing it for the better. Idealists of this stripe imagined they could fashion a utopian state of harmony in which social life could be satisfying for all. They offered a model for better living that they assumed others would admire and want to imitate. Society, thereby, would be improved voluntarily and peacefully. Nonreligious communitarianism or utopianism was thus a reform movement similar to abolitionism and women's rights in its intent to better the world.

Secular utopianism of this sort began in America in 1825 with the creation of a community in Indiana called New Harmony. Its founder, a wealthy Welsh reformer named Robert Owen, was a staunch believer in environmental determinism. Human character, he was convinced, is formed by the individual's background and upbringing. Give a person a good environment, and that individual will do the right thing. Owen tried to provide the community with basic necessities of life and with the opportunity to enjoy cultural activities. In exchange, each resident was to contribute labor. Having no entrance requirements, however, Owen ended up with a crowd of argumentative freeloaders. New Harmony collapsed within two years.[49]

In 1841, the utopian community of Brook Farm was founded near Boston by a group of transcendentalists including the writer Nathaniel Hawthorne. In the transcendental philosophy of Ralph Waldo Emerson—the central figure of the movement—every human being contained a portion of the godhead, the deity pervading all nature. Humans, of course, are part of nature, but because people are endowed with mind, they have the responsibility to improve themselves. Humans should develop that divine essence into complete self-reliance, spiritually and intellectually, in part through constructive engagement with life.

Brook Farm was an attempt to provide that constructive engagement. By pooling their labor, individuals would have more time to enjoy artistic, intellectual, and recreational pursuits. It was a joint-stock arrangement requiring each participant to buy shares in the enterprise and thus assume responsibility as a co-owner. Further, each was supposed to work three hundred days a year, about nine hours a day. Most of the Brook Farmers knew nothing about farming or making things, however, and there was nothing to compel or organize work. In consequence, Brook Farm was always in financial arrears.[50]

The brand of nonreligious communitarianism that the Putneyites studied most closely, however, was neither Owenism nor transcendentalism but Fourierism—a popular movement that swept across America in the early 1840s. The originator of the movement, Frenchman Charles Fourier (1772–1837), believed humans acted according to instincts and talents he called "passions." There were supposed to be twelve passions distributed among 810 personality types. If the precise mix of personality types were assembled in the correct number of people living together in a common residence (a phalanstery or phalanx), the result would be social harmony— utopia. Work would become enjoyable—"attractive"—because people were following out their innate self-interests and doing what they were meant to do. The key assertion of Fourierism was that "passional attraction"—meaning personal inclination and occupational leaning—rendered labor attractive. Further, phalanstery life would improve the lot of women. Working closely together with men, women would be liberated from the isolated households that had doomed them to the economic servitude of domestic work (see figure 3).[51]

The American Fourierist movement, called Associationism, may have numbered as many as one hundred thousand adherents. As with Millerism, the dissemination of Associationism resulted, in large measure, from the printed word, especially in the form of Albert Brisbane's columns on the subject that ran in the *New York Tribune* in 1842–1843.[52]

Associationism, like Millerism, influenced Noyes's thinking. It taught him that work could become fun if men and women engaged in it together. Fourieristic writing equipped him with the vocabulary to express the benefits of communal labor and of communal residence in a unitary home. More generally, Brisbane and Fourier probably reinforced the love Putneyite Perfectionists were developing for fruit trees. Brisbane and Fourier also may have ignited the interest in gender equality soon to flower at Oneida.[53]

Noyes and his Putney disciples, then, were well aware of communitarian developments in the world around them as they became, self-consciously, a community owning property together. Yet the Putney Perfectionists vociferously denied that they themselves were moving in any similar direction.

FIGURE 3. *Vue générale d'un phalanstère*, lithograph by Jules Arnout, early 1840s. In late 1844, Albert Brisbane "returned from France with a huge engraved aerial view of an ideal phalanx, which helped to spread the doctrine to impressionistic American audiences" (Guarneri, *Utopian Alternative*, 28). This copy of the same print, still on view in the Mansion House, was presented to the Oneida Community by French Fourierist Victor Considerant in 1875.

"Our object in coming together," Noyes declared in 1843, "was not to form a Community after the fashion of the Shakers and Fourierites, but simply to publish the gospel and help one another in spiritual things." When they constituted themselves as a corporation in 1844, they reiterated that, since their object was publishing the gospel, "neither the attention nor the expense required by a primarily communistic enterprise" could possibly be spared.[54]

The idea that they might take up a communitarian lifestyle was rejected well into 1846. "I am every day more persuaded, that to build here slowly and silently a little Community in which the true gospel shall be thoroughly embodied will tell more effectually on the interests of God and man than to push forward extensive organizations at first," Noyes wrote in February. "Formal community of property is not regarded by us as obligatory on principle but as an expedient," he stressed the following month. "We are attempting no scientific experiments in political economy, or in social science, and beg to be excused from association in the public mind with those who are making such experiments." In the middle of March, Noyes wrote that a union of social interests had "always been a secondary matter to us.

Our primary object has been to publish the gospel of salvation from sin, and to form a Spiritual Phalanx."[55]

A Confessed Community

Suddenly, however, the Putneyites became communitarians. "The frost and ice of selfishness and exclusiveness melted and disappeared under the warm rays of unselfish brotherhood," one of them recalled of 1846. "The spirit of Communism, which left this world with the Primitive Church, reappeared and came down on this little body of believers who were together in one place, and no man said that aught of the things he possessed was his own, for they had all things common. They had held their external property in common for years, and so had enjoyed partial Communism, but the spirit that now controlled them would eliminate all selfishness; it would have Communism of life and of the affections; in short, vital, organic society."[56]

Group marriage among the leading couples began in the spring of 1846. The custom of mutually criticizing one another to achieve individual improvement and greater piety was instituted (see chapter 4). At about the same time, they announced their commitment to commonality of residence. Having consolidated themselves in the three Noyes-Campbell houses, they began to dream of building a unitary home, a grand phalanstery. Entering into a new social order, one of them said, "we stood forth a confessed Community." "In 1846," Noyes affirmed, "we commenced Community life at Putney."[57] Now they thought of themselves as the "Putney Community."

What had happened? According to Noyes, the transformation began with the initiation of free love. It came about when he was overcome by desire for Mary Cragin, who by all accounts radiated a powerful sensual allure. "Her only ambition was to be the servant of love," it was said, "and she was beautifully and wonderfully made for this office."[58] Noyes emphasized that both parties longed for each other. They resisted consummating their love, however, until discussing the matter with their respective spouses, Harriet Noyes and George Cragin. The latter two then acknowledged wanting each other, and so on. The result was the commencement of complex marriage.[59]

But a communitarian way of life involving more than sex was occasioned by more than lust. Back in 1844, the communards of Brook Farm had cast aside their transcendentalism to embrace Fourierism. Almost immediately, the Brook Farmers began building an enormous unitary residence intended to be the country's first phalanstery.[60] The Putneyites monitored these developments closely. When the *Harbinger*, a prestigious Fourierist publication, was located there, Brook Farm, in Noyes's estimation, became "the foremost and brightest of the Associations," "the chief representative and propagative organ of Fourierism." Years later, Noyes recalled how the Putney Perfectionists admired the *Harbinger* "and undoubtedly took an impulse from its teachings." He and his congregation "drank copiously of the spirit of the *Harbinger* and of the Socialists; and have always acknowledged that they received a great impulse from Brook Farm."[61] Finally, Noyes took notice of the way Brook Farm became the religious center of Associationism by claiming that the teachings of Fourier were essentially Christian in nature.[62]

The proximate cause of communitarian living at Putney was the death of Brook Farm. In March of 1846, the well-publicized phalanstery, still incomplete, burned down. It was perceived as a calamity that extinguished the hopes of the commune. This was the moment Noyes and his followers embraced complete communitarianism and launched into the social experiment soon to become the Oneida Community. "In 1846, after the fire at Brook Farm, and when Fourierism was manifestly passing away," Noyes wrote, "the little church at Putney began cautiously to experiment in Communism."[63] The Putney Community, it was implied, was a continuation of the Boston commune. The timing suggests Noyes aspired to fill Brook Farm's niche, and perhaps to assert leadership over what he saw as a movement of Christian socialism—as well as to enjoy sex with Mary Cragin.

After a year of their new communitarian lifestyle, Noyes and his Putney followers issued this summary of their beliefs: "We believe that the kingdom now coming is the same that was established in heaven at the second coming of Christ. God then commenced a kingdom in human nature independent of the laws of this world. That kingdom, withdrawn to heaven, has been strengthening and enlarging itself ever since. We look for its reestablishment here."[64]

The document goes on to say that God had gathered them together "to be the medium of establishing on earth the institutions of heaven." Accordingly, the Putney Association had trampled underfoot "the domestic and pecuniary fashions of the world. Separate households, property exclusiveness have come to an end with us." The efforts of the Perfectionists apparently had been crowned with complete success. Their manner of heavenly living had brought the resurrection state into being around them. "There is a power among us that can conquer death." Therefore, on June 1, 1847, the Putney Association proclaimed: "The Kingdom of God Has Come."[65] Noyes, characteristically, was the first to assert that living in the heavenly fashion had brought its just rewards. As soon as he said so, the story was told, "there was a tremendous clap of thunder, although the day was clear and there were not thunder clouds visible." This seemed clearly to be "a supernatural signal" that God approved the proceedings.[66]

Earlier, Noyes had described people as God's coworkers capable of aiding the divine scheme. Now that logic was followed out in claiming that the efforts of the Putneyites had been instrumental in bringing heaven to earth—without apocalypse. The Kingdom of God, it turned out, was established "not in a formal, dramatic way, but by a process like that which brings the seasonal spring."[67]

This struck many as blasphemous. Local sensibilities were further jarred by Perfectionist claims that death was overcome and Noyes could perform miraculous cures. Public outrage was stoked higher by the Perfectionists' apparently licentious behavior. Adultery, at least, was an indictable offense, and in late October of 1847, Noyes was arrested on that charge. Warrants for the arrest of other Perfectionists were also issued, with the result that several fled Vermont. By the end of 1847, the Putney Association, then numbering about thirty adults, was broken up.[68]

Burt's Pledge

Meanwhile, Perfectionists in the Burnt District of New York were following events in Vermont with considerable interest. They called two conventions in September 1847 to consider the kingdom of heaven newly arrived in Putney. At the first, in Lairdsville, the New Yorkers approved the Putney press and agreed to cooperate with Noyes's group. The elected moderator of this meeting was Jonathan Burt, the man who had watched Chapman beating Rider a decade earlier. At the second, in Genoa, New Yorkers resolved to establish the kingdom of God for themselves by forming, in emulation of Putney, a "heavenly association" somewhere in central New York. One of those pledging his life, fortune, and sacred honor to the enterprise was Burt, and one of the places considered was his property near Oneida between Syracuse and Utica.[69]

Burt was set on redeeming his pledge. In late November 1847, he was joined on the south bank of Oneida Creek by several families of Perfectionists from nearby East Hamilton: the Hatches, the Nashes, and the Ackleys—Joseph and Julia. This union was the beginning of what for years would be called the Oneida Association and, subsequently, the Oneida Community.

The most prominent feature of Burt's property was a lumber-sawing facility known as the Indian Sawmill, formerly owned by Native American Oneidas of the once powerful Iroquois (Haudenosaunee) Confederacy. Oneidas had long been pressured to emigrate to the west, away from encroaching whites. At the time Burt acquired the facility, only about 150 of them remained in the vicinity.[70] In addition to the mill, the little Perfectionist settlement comprised a motley assortment of structures clustered around the Burt residence.

Noyes, who had posted bond, left Vermont and ended up at Burt's home at the beginning of 1848. When invited to join the New York association, Noyes—fugitive from justice, shepherd of a dispersed flock—naturally accepted. Immediately he wrote to his Putney disciples, urging them to come.

Among the constructions on Burt's property was a log cabin built by the Oneidas. This appealed to Noyes, who wrote: "There is some romance in beginning our Community in the log huts of the Indians."[71] The idea was also attractive to the other Perfectionists, who maintained they inherited Native American land never cursed by private ownership.[72] "We virtually took the land," was the way Harriet Skinner explained it, "from the hands of the Indians themselves, for the white settlers had not paid their debt to the State when they passed their titles to us. And so this soil scarce knows the touch of private ownership, for the Oneidas held their lands in common."[73] That the Oneida Community was meaningfully connected with the Oneida Indians because both valued common ownership was a conceit the Perfectionists long enjoyed.

In a January letter to Putney, Noyes, ensconced in Burt's home, began to express himself in the language of social reform. "Our warfare is an assertion of human rights: first, the right of man to be governed by God and to live in the social state of heaven; second, the right of woman to dispose of her sexual nature by attraction instead of by law and routine and to bear children only when she chooses; third, the right of all to diminish the labors and increase the advantages of life by association."[74]

Noyes, at the time, was composing a theoretical tract proposing that the coming commune would be both a religious community and a secular utopia.

Noyes, in summary, withdrew from the Perfectionist movement to recruit his own cadres untainted by the excesses of other Perfectionists. Noyes offered potential disciples a mesmerizing personality to go along with religious certainty. His first recruits included his siblings, their future spouses, the Cragin couple, and Noyes's new wife, Harriet Holton. All these early disciples acknowledged their fealty to Noyes as emissary of God and the primitive church. In future years, several of them would constitute the core of the "central committee," an informal group of advisers close to Noyes.

Holton supplied the money to purchase a printing press with which Noyes established a newspaper-like journal for disseminating his views to the world. Noyes and his adherents would continue to publish a periodical, more or less biweekly, for upward of forty years. The group numbered about two dozen adults who, when not printing, devoted themselves to group study of religious topics. There was no pretense of equality in gender relations: men were superior to women. Nevertheless, a few precursors to later Oneida Community practice are discernible in Putney precedents, including a high value placed on intellectual discourse and a taste for forging group consensus in collective discussion.

Noyes, in the meantime, was improving the conjugal occasion by developing a form of birth control that would prove crucial to practicing sexual communism at Oneida. Also during the Putney years, Noyes developed the doctrine of salvation from sin to the radical position that salvation, once attained, was absolute and forever. Having gone so far with the purely faith-based religion, he began adding qualifications to make it governable and functional. When he considered the essentially individualistic and egalitarian nature of Perfectionism, Noyes decided that a hierarchical organization would be acceptable, providing a divinely appointed leader could impart beneficial instruction. To that he added the caveat that becoming perfect was likely to be a gradual process. Perfectionism, he implied, was not only progressive; it was something that might reasonably be mistaken for or combined with social improvement.

Many Americans during the 1830s expected the return of Christ and the end of the world momentarily. Noyes had incorporated these events into a complicated interpretation of history involving two world ages and three advent occurrences. In contrast, the contemporaneous Millerite movement offered a much simpler reading based on information anyone could check in the Bible. Noyes reacted to the challenge of Millerism by dropping the requirement for violent apocalypse and emphasizing the importance of human contribution to God's plan. These revisions to the millennial agenda may well have encouraged Perfectionists to assume a more active engagement—more than passive faith dictated—in the enterprise of building a Zion on earth.

Having adopted common ownership of property, the Putneyites studied various communal programs being pursued all around them. There were religious communitarians including the Ebenezers and the Shakers. There were also nonreligious efforts to build a better world, which included the Fourierist or Associationist movement. Although the Putney Perfectionists particularly admired the literary Associationists of Brook Farm near Boston, they denied any desire to organize themselves in a similar fashion.

Nevertheless, at the moment Brook Farm died, the Putney group became suddenly and completely communitarian. The timing suggests that Noyes, visualizing the Putney group as Brook Farm's replacement, aspired to leadership in the utopian movement.

After a year of living communally, communistically, and duplicating the lifestyle of heaven, the Perfectionists thought they had succeeded in imitating that realm and thereby drawing it to earth. Their announcement that heaven had come, in conjunction with their newly established group marriage, provoked hostility from those around them. Fleeing Putney, Noyes's group joined their fortunes to those of a small Perfectionist band coalescing on the property of Jonathan Burt in upstate New York.

CHAPTER 3

Oneida Birthed and Left Behind

Noyes had a head for phrenology, a craze that swept America during the 1830s and '40s. Phrenology was the belief that the skull revealed the individual's personality. A phrenologist analyzed a subject's character by examining the cranium at thirty-seven locations, called "organs" or "faculties," each regarded as the seat of an emotional or intellectual quality. Accounting for a quarter of the total brain size, the most important faculty, by far, was "amativeness," or sexual desire. The physical prominence of amativeness led to an emphasis on sex as the foremost human concern. "Poetical maidens," one of America's leading phrenologists announced to the young women of Victorian America, "you think your love is as pure as that of angels, and as far from desire for sexual commerce as earth from Heaven." But love, he insisted, is a function of amativeness, which leads to "sexual action; which creates desire for coition." Phrenology's assertion that the sexual drive is socially dominant must have seemed, to Noyes, like scientific confirmation of his own views.[1]

By way of introducing himself to readers in 1837, Noyes shared a phrenological analysis of his personality performed by a New York practitioner named Brevoort. "You have need of crying, O Lord, increase our faith, for you have no marvellousness at all," Brevoort reported to Noyes. "But what if I should tell you," Noyes rejoined, "that I am accounted by those who know me, the veriest visionary in the land?" Brevoort would not believe it, because, to him, phrenology was science that never lied.[2]

Although Noyes scored well in the amativeness department, his highest phrenological marks were in a faculty called "causality," said to indicate intelligence and the inclination to reason causally. Noyes, according to phrenologist Lorenzo Fowler, "came to be a member of this [Oneida] Community from principle. He first thought it out—investigated the whole subject. He did not come here because he loved so many, or wished to surround himself with so many friends,—but because he has satisfied himself that this is the best way to arrange society." Fowler concluded that Noyes was driven to find a reason for everything. "Intellectually, Mr. Noyes should be known for a disposition to investigate principles, to go back to the origin of things, to study cause and effect, or the why and the wherefore," phrenologist Samuel Wells affirmed similarly.[3]

The phrenologists were correct about Noyes thinking things through on one important occasion. It occurred in 1848—after fleeing Vermont, finding asylum in central New York, and awaiting the arrival of adherents from Putney. The Oneida Community is introduced in this chapter through Noyes's imagination: what he planned, how he envisioned its life and purpose. Then we turn to the amazingly successful commencement of the commune and its abandonment immediately after by Noyes. The chapter concludes with a look at Noyes, now in Brooklyn, adding the final theological touches to what would become religious doctrine in the Oneida Community.

Bible Argument

Sheltering in the home of Jonathan Burt in February 1848, Noyes systematically contemplated the nature of the association about to coalesce on the banks of Oneida Creek. The resulting document, *Bible Argument: Defining the Relations of the Sexes in the Kingdom of Heaven*, was a blueprint for the coming association. In it were reasoned out most of the important principles that would become reality in the Oneida Community.

In addition to looking forward, *Bible Argument* looked back. Retrospectively, this tract was a partial synthesis of Noyesian theology, the elements of which had been accumulating in piecemeal fashion over the years. Noyes professed freedom from sin (1834), asserted heaven was a place of free love (1837), developed a two-part scheme of world history (1830s), invented male continence (1844), and advocated a communal lifestyle (1846). These thoughts had never been drawn together into a unitary framework. Now Noyes set forth his first public defense of group marriage initiated a short time before in Putney. He also provided his first substantive explanation of the free-love doctrine advocated in the Battle Axe Letter a decade earlier.

As synthesis, however, the work was far from comprehensive, because it was focused on sexual association. *Bible Argument* is, in fact, Noyes's magnum opus on sex, celebrating free love and sexual intercourse with startling candor. Though it must have shocked many at the time, there was nothing surreptitious in Noyes's actions. The treatise was published in the Oneida Community's *First Annual Report* of early 1849, a pamphlet mailed out to prominent public figures in New York State to inform them what was occurring at Oneida.[4]

More than anything else, *Bible Argument* was meant to justify a communitarian venture duplicating life in heaven—a place of group matrimony—in order to bring that kingdom to earth. Noyes's plan was twofold. On the one hand, complex marriage would hasten Christ's return, bringing it to earthly fruition through the practice of righteous, unrestrictive love. On the other, collective marriage would transform society and correct its ills. Noyes's essay, as it pertained to the latter point, was a prospectus for social reform through associative action, a plan recasting Fourierism around the practice of free love. Accordingly, two lines of argument were advanced in support of complex marriage. The first, concerned with the advent of Christ and the coming of heaven, was religious.

This exposition began with the assertion that group or "complex" marriage is both the way of heaven and the earthly means for bringing heaven about. The Bible tells us there is no marriage in heaven, Noyes conceded, but that does not mean, as Shakers suppose, that there is no sex. The true meaning is that there is no monogamous or exclusive marriage. In the kingdom of God, there is a state of unrestrictive love for several reasons.

First, sex is a natural act because God created human maleness and femaleness as fitted to each other to achieve perfect union physically and spiritually. Heterosexual bonding is a holy act because God is a bisexual duality in whose image men and women were created, "and of whose nature the whole creation is a reflection."[5] In coitus, the conjoined partners selflessly recreate and draw nearer to the godhead as the spirit of God passes between them.

Second, it is illogical to suppose God excluded from heaven a sacrament so important and good. "It was manifestly the design of God, in creating the sexes, to give love more intense expression than is possible between persons of the same sex; and it is foolish to imagine that he will ever abandon that design by unsexing his children, or impede it by legal restrictions on sexual intercourse, in the heavenly state."[6] Noyes found it inconceivable that God would not feature sex in heaven.

Third, any restrictions or exclusiveness in marriage are incompatible with the biblical emphasis on common ownership and, inferentially, complete communism. In the heavenly state, all property is communally owned, as was the case in the primitive Christian church at the time of Pentecost. This would be called "Bible communism" in the future, although that term is not used here. That sexual exclusiveness is incommensurate with communism is demonstrated by "the love-relation required between all believers by the express injunction of Christ and the apostles, and by the whole tenor of the New Testament. 'The new commandment is, that we love one another,' and that not by pairs, as in the world, but *en masse*." In heaven, Noyes insisted, "the intimate union of life and interests, which in the world is limited to pairs, extends through the whole body of believers."[7] Logic tells us, then, that complex marriage exists in heaven.

The relevance of complex marriage to earthly existence is that the heavenly kingdom is coming and Christ is returning. Christ must have control over the marriage system "and arrange sexual conditions according to the genius of his own kingdom, before he can push his conquests to victory over death." Establishing the heavenly conditions of marriage is "the very means by which the resurrection power is to be let in upon the world."[8] This theological purpose is stated more clearly in a summary of Noyes's religion appearing in a preface to the text of *Bible Argument*.

> [We believe] that the second advent of Christ took place at the period of the destruction of Jerusalem; that at that time there was a primary resurrection and judgment in the spiritual world; that the final kingdom of God then began in the heavens; that the manifestation of that kingdom in the visible world is now approaching; that its approach is ushering in the second and final resurrection and judgment; that a church on earth is now rising to meet the approaching kingdom in the heavens, and to become its duplicate and representative; that inspiration, or open communication with God and the heavens, involving perfect holiness, is the element of connection between the church on earth and the church in the heavens, and the power by which the kingdom of God is to be established and reign in the world.[9]

This was similar to the affirmation of June 1847, and like that statement, it meant that Noyes and his disciples regarded themselves as the earthly duplicate and representative of the kingdom of heaven. It is they, through the practice of perfect holiness, who will serve as the medium for establishing God's kingdom here.

There are, however, two differences between this and the earlier statement. One is that heaven, which arrived in Putney in 1847, had not yet come to Oneida. Without explanation, the event has now been moved to the future. The second is that perfect holiness, the means by which resurrec-tion power is to be let into the world, is here defined chiefly as complex mar-riage. What the Oneida Community intended to do to expedite the earthly appearance of heaven was to duplicate the heavenly state by engaging in heavenly sex.

That, of course, was Noyes's religious justification for complex marriage. A second argument in favor of free love was that it had value as a secular program that would correct social evils, relieve human misery, and reorga-nize society. "It is the special function of the present or body-church, (avail-ing itself first of the work of the primitive church, by union with it, and a re-development of its theology,) to break up the *social* system of the world, and establish true external order by the reconciliation of the sexes."[10] Noyes, as social reformer, defined and criticized problems to be remedied. These difficulties, however, were not so much social issues as they were categories of human misery. Noyes's subject was how much unhappiness there was in the world due to the demands of, first, monogamous marriage and, second, reproduction.

Monogamous marriage, Noyes observed, is an artificial and unsatisfy-ing institution because sexual love is not naturally restricted to pairs. "Men and women find universally, (however the fact may be concealed,) that their susceptibility to love is not burnt out by one honey-moon, or satisfied by one lover. On the contrary, the secret history of the human heart will bear out the assertion that it is capable of loving any number of times and any number of persons, and that the more it loves the more it can love." Monogamous marriage is a source of misery and dysfunction because "it gives to sexual appetite only a scanty and monotonous allowance, and so produces the natural vices of poverty, contraction of taste, and stinginess or jealousy."[11] The solution is to love without restrictions. "A system of complex marriage, which shall match the demands of nature, both as to time and variety, will open the prison doors to the victims both of mar-riage and celibacy; to those in married life who are starved, and those who are oppressed by lust; to those who are tied to uncongenial natures, and to those who are separated from their natural mates;—to those in the unmar-ried state who are withered by neglect, diseased by unnatural abstinence, or plunged into prostitution and self-pollution, by desires which find no lawful channel."[12]

Reproducing our species, the second source of hardship, increases the mis-ery of both parents in a monogamous marriage. For the husband, it greatly augments the labor he must perform to support his family. For the wife, "the infirmities and vital expenses" of pregnancy waste her constitution;

"the awful agonies of child-birth" threaten her life; and, if she survives, "the cares of the nursing period" reduce her further.[13] For women, reproduction is a fearful curse with baneful effects.

The solution to these problems is to control reproduction, to refrain from having children unless the parents want and are ready to take care of them. The proximate answer, of course, is male continence, the distinctive form of birth control Noyes developed in Putney but described in *Bible Argument* for the first time. The justification for it is laid out not in the language of religion but of logic—a line of reasoning based on a distinction mentioned in the previous chapter. Sex, Noyes reasoned, comprises two aspects: the amative function consisting of sexual attraction, amorous desire, and the sex act itself; and the propagative function, meaning ejaculation, conception, and reproduction. The amative and propagative functions can be separated by prohibiting male climax.[14]

The primary purpose of sex without male ejaculation is to prevent conception. There are, however, other benefits. "Our method," Noyes explained, "simply proposes the subordination of the flesh to the spirit, teaching men to seek principally the elevated spiritual pleasures of sexual intercourse."[15] Further, this technique of birth control will open the door to "scientific propagation," or eugenics. Here Noyes predicted "stirpiculture," a program of selective breeding that the Oneida Community would undertake twenty years later. "We believe the time will come when involuntary and random propagation will cease, and when scientific combination will be applied to human generation as freely and successfully as it is to that of other animals," Noyes indicated.[16]

"The foregoing principles concerning the sexual relation," he abruptly concluded, "open the way for Association." Amativeness and complex marriage draw men and women to one another so that "the same attractions as draw and bind together pairs in the worldly partnership of marriage" are magnified in the larger social body.[17] Free love was to be the engine and ligature of communal existence. The other side of the coin was that unrestrictive love with birth control frees men from the tyranny of excessive labor and emancipates women from "propagative drudgery"—the burden of bearing unwanted children. Complex marriage also is the antidote to division, jealousy, and strife that plague every organization in which men and women are forced, by custom and law, to be monogamous.

Circling back to the communitarianism most familiar to his readers, Noyes asserted that free love corrects a fundamental error of Fourierism. Massing a large number of people together, Fourierists hope for harmony from compression but find only inert density—a lifeless organization. For an association to live, every member must enjoy vital relations with other members. Complex marriage kindles "vital society," and, in the association Noyes imagined, "strength will be increased, and the necessity of labor diminished, till all work will become sport." In vital society, Noyes added, each individual surrenders selfish conjugal and property interests to the use of the whole.[18]

Appropriating Fourier's concept of work as pleasurable and fulfilling, Noyes now peeled the idea away from "passional attraction" and affixed it to a different and simpler thought: men and women should work together. "Loving companionship in labor, and especially the mingling of the sexes, makes labor attractive."[19] Noyes's vision of what is to come closes, accordingly, with the proposal that men and women should mingle in every aspect of daily existence. This will become the keystone of associative life at Oneida. By 1854, the concept was described as an established fact:

> The Social Theory of Bible Communists contemplates delivering man from the curse of hard work, and woman from the curse of excessive propagation, and bringing about an entire amalgamation of the sexes in all useful industry. The two first propositions prepare the way for the third. Woman could scarcely be the help-meet of man in his work, while he tills a cursed ground, and she is exhausted with excessive child-bearing; but let the expense of maternity be properly reduced, and labor lightened by Association, and the way is prepared for the marriage of man and woman in their daily employments. These principles are in practical operation. . . . Hard work and excessive propagation are abolished, and men and women mingle in their occupations to a considerable extent.[20]

Mingling, in the mind of Noyes writing *Bible Argument*, did not mean, as we have noted, that men and women were equal. The presumption in complex marriage at Putney and Oneida was that males would behave as chivalrous gentlemen to their lovers because, in the divine nature of things, females were the inferior sex. Such opinions were unremarkable and perhaps even typical of American society. At Oneida, mingling was not designed to contradict established attitudes toward gender, nor to advocate equal rights for women. Mingling, nevertheless, as a real-life rubbing of elbows, would pave the way for practical advances in female standing in the Oneida Community.

A final point to note of the utopian plan advanced in *Bible Argument* is that the new society would have, as Fourier stipulated, a unitary residence, a phalanstery. "A community home in which each is married to all, and where love is honored and cultivated, will be as much more attractive than an ordinary home, even in the honey-moon, as the community out-numbers a pair."[21]

Utopian Success

One of the last points of Noyes's prospectus, a communal home, was the first to receive the full attention of the Perfectionists gathering at Oneida Creek in early 1848. There was not enough housing for the forty-seven immigrants from Putney, adults and children. As other small bands of Perfectionists came in from New England and New York, the group expanded to about ninety people in need of shelter with winter approaching.

Noyes selected the location for a new shelter at the base of a knoll across the creek. After purchasing that eighty-acre property, Perfectionists began building on it in early March.[22] All pitched in. "Attraction and zeal have made artisans of nearly the whole Association," they said at the time. This was the first enterprise that enlisted the Vermonters from Putney with the other joiners as a whole Community, Perfectionist Harriet Worden recalled, and all—"the women no less than the men"—worked together. Impressed with their accomplishment, they duly noted that many valuable lessons "in regard to gregarious and attractive industry were learned in this operation."[23] By late December, their new home was habitable.

When they stood back to look at it, they saw a big rectangular box three stories high. The design was attributed to a newly arrived member from Syracuse, an architect named Erastus Hamilton. Hamilton, at least, softened the stark look of the building by adding such decorative embellishments as a crenellated cupola above and, below, an arcaded walkway the Perfectionists called a piazza (see figure 4).[24]

"Mansion House" was the name they bestowed on the new building. To them, it meant large dwelling or stately residence.[25]

That designation may have followed an Associationist tendency to call a large community structure a "mansion."[26] But inherent in the Mansion House itself was a more significant concept and a more interesting precedent. Noyes, in *Bible Argument*, had drawn on Fourieristic writing when he called for a unitary residence to overcome the problem of isolated households, each one a nest of egotism and exclusiveness.[27] So did the other Perfectionists whose dream of a phalanstery in Putney was now realized in Oneida.[28] The Mansion House, in other words, was a Fourieristic unitary dwelling in the minds of its builders. The architectural antecedent familiar to them was the phalanstery begun at Brook Farm—a rectangular three-story, wood-frame building with a plain, vernacular look. The Oneida structure was merely a

FIGURE 4. Early Mansion House complex, about 1851. A drawing by Charlotte Miller depicts the original Mansion House of 1848, a three-story structure (*center*) that grew quickly with the addition of two wings and a woodshed. The Children's House of 1849 is visible behind the Mansion House, and to the right is the Francis farmhouse.

smaller version of the Massachusetts prototype (60 as opposed to 175 feet in length).[29] Of course, in contrast to the phalanstery at Brook Farm, the one at Oneida was actually completed. In fact, the Oneida Community's Mansion House probably was the first phalanstery to be realized in America—that is, the earliest communal dwelling designed to house men and women living freely together under the same roof.[30]

As soon as spring came, a second house was built on the summit of the knoll overlooking the Mansion House, this one for the Community's children. Child raising, carried on as a cooperative activity separate from the adult world, was one of the most distinctive features of Oneida Community life. It meant youngsters would be raised and educated together by a few care providers. Children would be apart from parents most of the time, and parents would have to accept the arrangement. Oneidans, of course, loved their children as much as parents everywhere. However, parental love was institutionally discouraged if it became "sticky"—that is, exclusionary in its focus. When that happened, it became a sin called "philoprogenitiveness." Originally a phrenological term, the word was used by the Perfectionists to mean loving one's own progeny more than those of another. There are several vivid accounts from later in time illustrating how this actually worked, the pain it could cause, and the discipline required to conceal that pain.[31]

The Oneida children's department apparently came into existence as a matter of convenience. The adults simply concluded that it was "altogether a more comfortable task to take care of six in the new way, than it had been to wait on one in ordinary circumstances." To be sure, one had to overcome the natural apprehensions of mothers giving up their children into the care of others. "But the wounds of philoprogenitiveness were soon healed," according to the Community's *First Annual Report*, "and the mothers soon learned to value their own freedom and opportunity of education, and the improved condition of their children, more than the luxury of a sickly maternal tenderness." Further, mothers recovered all the more quickly from the pain of separation as they realized that occasional visits with their offspring brought more pleasure than ever came from "constant personal attendance."[32] However casually this system came about, one might assume the next step—building a separate building for the children—was worthy of notice. In fact, it received only scant mention in the next annual report.[33]

Unlike the concept of the unitary home, the Oneida method of child raising did not originate in a body of theory. Although Fourier wrote extensively on the subject, Albert Brisbane passed on virtually nothing of that to American readers of his column in the *New York Tribune*.[34] Likewise, Noyes said nothing about raising children collectively in *Bible Argument*. The Oneidans were, to be sure, familiar with the Shaker practice of keeping youngsters together and apart from adults. If that provided a precedent, however, it was a very limited one, offering little guidance for separating real parents from real offspring. What seems likely is that the Perfectionists drew on their own experience in the matter. In Putney, women in the three main houses had pooled their labor in food preparation and child care in order to free each other up for more Bible study.[35] Such a background comports with the Perfectionists' report that those who superintended the establishment of the children's department were Putneyites Mary Cragin and Harriet Noyes.[36]

Whatever the source of their inspiration, the Bible communists of Oneida had created a new compact living arrangement with a new system of collectivized child care. The Mansion House and the Children's House spatially concentrated household work and child care, which, performed cooperatively, lightened the drudgery of what was regarded as feminine work. Though not remarked at the time, this arrangement revolutionized the social and spatial aspects of the domestic sphere.

The new arrangement also achieved an important goal of Associationism: liberating women from the isolated household with its attendant drudgery. One of the benefits Charles Fourier claimed for phalansterian life was that it would correct the evil of "parcelled" homes, which consigned women to a state of degradation and dependence.[37] American Fourierist Albert Brisbane described women living in separate households as absorbed in the "ceaseless round of petty domestic cares" and overcome by anxiety and monotony. In the present mode of isolated households, he moaned, men "see their wives obliged to drudge continually in miserable little kitchens and at a round of menial labor."[38] By socializing domestic work in a compact living space and collectivizing child care, the Oneida Community instituted a significant measure of social reform at the beginning of the commune's career.

Out of the experience of building the Mansion House came two more traits characteristic of Oneida Community life. The first was a distinctive women's costume permitting feminine mobility—short dress and pantalettes. Noyes, in *Bible Argument*, had inveighed against the prevailing women's fashion, which exaggerated the physical characteristics of femaleness. This was immodest, he judged; and worse, such clothing shackled that sex "which has the most talent in the legs." Do away with dishonest and confining apparel, he urged. Instead, model feminine dress on the clothing of children, which was thought to be both functional and comfortable. Then, he enthused, "when the partition between the sexes is taken away, and man ceases to make woman a propagative drudge, when love takes the place of shame, and fashion follows nature in dress and business, men and women will mingle in all their employments, as boys and girls mingle in their sports, and then labor will be attractive."[39]

Oneida Community women were reminded of this sentiment when they tried to help in the construction of the Mansion House. In frustration and defiance of fashion, Mary Cragin and Harriet Noyes altered their clothing so they could move around more freely. "This was in June, 1848," Harriet Skinner reported. "In the present mellow state of public sentiment, it is impossible to appreciate the heroism that was then required, to appear in the semi-masculine attire, now so much applauded. There seemed to be but one opinion in the world, that it was unfeminine and immodest; and the whole atmosphere was charged with this accusation." The Oneida clothing may well have inspired the famous "bloomer costume," an innovation normally credited to Elizabeth Smith Miller in nearby Peterboro in 1851.[40] Shortly after transforming their clothing, Oneida Community women also began wearing their hair short to save the hour of vanity time required to brush and put up long tresses.

A second result of the first works project was the development of a labor pattern that translated Fourieristic work teams ("series") into an American idiom of informal cooperation. "This practice of doing work 'by storm,' or in what is more commonly called a 'bee,' in which the men, women and children engage, has been found very popular and effective," the Community reported in early 1850. "It may be employed in a great variety of occupations, especially of out-door business, and always contributes to enliven and animate the most uninteresting details of work."[41] In this fashion, the Oneida Community hit on "bees"—volunteer task groups that promoted happy mingling—as their preferred method of getting things done.

Proving indispensable to the working together of men and women in real life, the short dress and the bee operationalized mingling. And it was mingling—not passional attraction—that made Associationism work. Of perhaps thirty communities founded on Fourier's principle, hardly any lasted more than two years. "Fourier had a glorious scheme of 'Attractive Industry,'" Harriet Skinner observed more than a quarter century later, "but it was intricate and artificial. In practice the Community have found that the gregarious element, and especially the combination of the sexes, is the main secret." In conceiving mingling as a motive power for communitarian success, Noyes, as historian Carl Guarneri put it, "out-Fourierized the Fourierists."[42]

Almost immediately, then, the Bible communists completed the first phalanstery, transformed the domestic environment, invented new fashion, then re-created the workplace and gender relations within it. The Oneida Community, starting up, surely would have been hailed as the poster child of world communitarianism and socialism—had anyone noticed. They themselves were not much given to boasting and had other things on their minds. One was that Noyes walked out on Oneida in February of 1849.

Hades in Brooklyn

Like a man suffering a midlife crisis, Noyes seemed eager to be free of the new commune. He informed his disciples, as he left, that "he was bound to obey God in all cases, and he felt at liberty to do so without first consulting this Association. Man's judgment was a small matter with him; the one that judged him was the Lord. And he had reached a position where he walked surely; he knew he was right before he went ahead. God would defend whatever course he took, and whoever undertook to judge him would find in the end that he was their judge."[43] What he first felt at liberty to do was to travel. Noyes went off to Niagara Falls with Mary Cragin. He went to England in order, he said, to converse on the ship with publisher Horace Greeley, who, like Noyes at this time, lived in New York City. He visited the Shaker center at Mount Lebanon, New York, to inform them that he had just laid the foundation for a society destined to subvert the Shaker faith.[44]

In early 1849, Noyes had directed his old friend, Abram Smith, to purchase, with Oneida funds, a house in Brooklyn. Noyes promptly relocated there, and there he remained for nearly six years. The only explanation offered was that Noyes needed "a more quiet place for reflection, and a better opportunity to act upon the Association than a residence directly in it."[45] Perhaps a dozen members joined Noyes to make up what they called the Brooklyn branch of the Oneida Community.

Noyes earlier had begun to consider the problems of converting Perfectionism—a faith-based and absolute credo essentially individualistic and antiauthoritarian in spirit—into a more tractable and governable religion. In Putney, he had asserted that Perfectionists could follow a leader, that attainment of righteousness might be a gradual process, and that the attainment process might involve improvement of a behavioral sort. Among the questions still unresolved was this: If one accepted Noyes's views and felt unity with Christ, when did one become perfect? How, more specifically, would one know when sanctification was achieved? Who was to say? Who decided?

Now, newly arrived In Brooklyn, Noyes returned to the problem of formulating criteria for advancing to perfection. In 1849, he introduced a general scheme of spiritual hierarchy within the Oneida Community, which placed himself at the top. According to the doctrine called "ascending fellowship," all should "seek for association with those that are better than ourselves. Select out the best that we know of."[46] The option of spiritual grading in this system rested solely with the spiritually superior party. Specific criteria for evaluating a person's standing, however, were not forthcoming. The closest Noyes himself came to issuing grades was when he announced that brother George and Erastus Hamilton were people of "the spiritual department," men possessing the same inspiration as himself. But he immediately took that back in a subsequent talk, which pointedly addressed the internal hierarchy of the apostles. The Bible, Noyes emphasized, "intentionally failed to specify relative importance about rank."[47] In the end, Noyes withheld rules for advancing to sanctification. Nevertheless, he did indicate that it was he who would pass judgment on another's state of righteousness.

The Perfectionists who joined Noyes in Brooklyn—many of them former Putneyites—seemed to imbibe Noyes's fierce spirit of self-righteousness. It was they who committed an act of fanaticism uncharacteristic of the later Oneida Community. In early 1851, several Brooklynites, including Mary Cragin, formed themselves into a committee to study the effects of dolls on their children. They concluded that playing with the toys was an improper activity because it encouraged little girls to yearn for motherhood. Dolls distracted the young folk from growing in knowledge of God, acquiring an education, and learning to help the greater family. Comparing the doll spirit to "worship of images," Noyes approved the findings. The children, for their part, were said to be well satisfied that the doll spirit had seduced them into "pleasure-seeking, frivolity, and lying, and voted that they be burned up. Accordingly, the dolls were stripped without delay and laid on the coals, all hands rejoicing in their condemnation." More than a century later, Noyes's granddaughter still found the incident heartbreaking.[48]

At about the same time he confronted the crisis of the doll spirit, Noyes acknowledged that the Perfectionists were running out of money. "The great question is whether we are spiritually ready, whether we have fulfilled our obedience to God so that he can allow us to support ourselves." Noyes advised the people in Oneida to take up peddling, "providing things to sell and training men as salesmen."[49] Those in Brooklyn were supposed to make gold chains and operate a shipping business with a river sloop named the *Rebecca Ford*.

The craft was purchased in 1850 with the idea that transporting lime-stone from Kingston down the Hudson River to New York City would be profitable. Noyes loved the boat and lay awake thinking about it. The more he thought about it, the more he "wished it might be manned by Commu-nity men," a Brooklyn Perfectionist reported. "Then our folks could take a pleasure trip up the river any time they chose. We are all much elated at the prospects which open up to us in connection with this business. It was agreed that it should be a Community school of navigation."[50] The sloop, operated by a hired crew, made about sixty passages and brought in some $1,250 that first year. But it imparted little sailing knowledge to its owners, who, in July 1851, were happily sailing the craft downriver when it was struck by an unex-pected gust of wind. The cargo of stone shifted, and the vessel went down almost instantly. Two passengers trapped below were drowned. One was Mary Cragin, who earlier that day had visited the house in which she carried on the affair with Abram Smith a decade before. The day of her death, Smith was captain of the *Rebecca Ford*.[51]

Noyes mourned her passing. In the depths of his depression, he began to think a great deal about death. And death was a subject that spurred him into a fresh round of religious interpretation. What happens to people when they die, Noyes explained that fall, is that they go to an afterlife called Hades. "Hades" was a Greek word employed in the King James Version of the Bible to mean the abode of the dead, usually without implying that it was a place of rewards or of anguish and punishment. Noyes, who knew his Bible well, used the word in the same sense. Hades, the land of the dead, is where all people go, good or bad. There, they await resurrection. Most await salvation from sin.

Hades is a dark, sleepy place of rest and inactivity. Dead people there are incorporeal shades largely excluded from perception of matter in our world. They do not know much because, being virtually asleep, their level of consciousness is low. The prospect did not appeal to Noyes, and he was pretty sure Mary Cragin felt the same.[52] In the larger scheme of things, Hades is one of three realms or worlds around us, the other two being heaven and the physical reality experienced by the living. The Bible says (here Noyes was unusually close to literal meaning) that "the Lord himself will descend from heaven . . . and the dead in Christ shall rise first" (1 Thessalonians 4:16). "Those that are in Hades will first have to rise up to a level with us," Noyes emphasized, "before we shall together meet Christ and the New Jerusalem." He began to refer to the expected coming of Christ as a collision or conjunction of the three worlds that would begin with the appearance of the dead among us. "It seems to me that this is to be the place of the meeting," Noyes wrote in November 1851.[53] As resurrection time approaches, believers in Hades "will begin to lead that department up into communication with us."[54] At the head of the host would be Mary Cragin, because God appointed her to be the leading woman of the Perfectionist church—in Hades. Noyes expected to see her soon.

After modifying the doctrine of the advent of Christ in this fashion, Noyes improved the occasion by bringing his theology up to date with the big news of the day: spiritualism. This was a religious movement touched off by reports of rappings—spirits knocking on wood—near Rochester in 1848. Spiritualism asserted not only that the soul lives on after death, but that it retains earthly ties and is directly accessible to the living. Requiring no church or body of dogma, spiritualism was an immensely appealing and wonderfully democratic faith. It swept the country with galvanic force. By the early 1850s, there were an estimated 1.5 to 4 million believers in spiritualism, compared to about 2.8 million Protestants (Baptists, Congregationalists, Methodists, Presbyterians), in a population of some 23 million. America was becoming a land of spiritualists.[55]

Noyes had no quarrel with the theory of spiritualism. He was, as we have seen, a practicing medium who claimed direct psychic communication with the primitive church. His line to Saint Paul, however, was only one of many possible channels. Noyes believed there was an invisible realm of spirits all around him, one in which numerous presences clamored for his attention. "Every person," he mused, "has strange flitting fancies from time to time; but a person in the ordinary state does not feel bound to believe them, because he attributes them to nothing higher than his own imagination. But let one enter the *aura* of the world of spirits, and become conscious that his thoughts originate not in his own imagination, but in the unseen intelligences above him, and, until he has become familiar enough with the strange company he has entered, to examine and discriminate its characters, he will feel bound to believe all impressions, and so for the time will be more or less at the mercy of devils."[56] Noyes, then, questioned the plausibility of other mediums who lacked his discernment in the matter. He was also dubious about the substance of most messages from the spirit world because few spirits had anything of value to convey to the living.

Noyes interpreted the increasing popularity of spiritualism as evidence for the correctness of his own views. Rappings and other noise from the spirit world indicated the dead in Hades were beginning to wake up in anticipation of resurrection. The reported spiritualistic phenomena began in the Burnt District of New York at precisely the time the Oneida Community commenced operations in that region.[57] Rappings, therefore, attested to the truth of Oneida doctrine and, presumably, to the effectiveness of Oneida practice in hastening the return of Christ.

In early 1852, the *Circular*, moved from Oneida to Brooklyn the year before, announced plans for a "Concentric Convention" to take place on February 20, the day commemorated for Noyes's first confession of Christ. The convention would be a spiritual one bringing mortal believers together with delegates from the primitive church above and from Hades below. Details were scant: "We believe that there will be an actual and interesting meeting of three worlds at that time; and we believe that whoever has a heart big enough to attend that meeting has a heart big enough to comprehend the enterprise we are engaged in, and to cooperate with us and heaven in its fulfillment."[58] The only report issued of the convention stated that the event resulted in "a somewhat interesting change of position."[59] The Oneida Community announced it would give up complex marriage.

This was a response to hostility in the outside world, bubbling up again, to Perfectionist sexual doctrine. At Oneida, as we shall see, they were under serious legal attack from the Oneida County district attorney. In Brooklyn, Noyes was feeling the heat from criticism appearing in the *New York Observer* in 1851 and early 1852. The newspaper described Noyes's followers as a "disgusting order of united adulterers" who practiced "unrestrained indulgence of the human passions." Noyes was marked out for special calumny as the head of the order who proclaimed "promiscuous intercourse of the sexes as compatible with the highest state of holiness on earth." Noyes taught that "unbridled licentiousness is the law of heaven," according to the *Observer*.[60]

The Concentric Convention evidently provided Noyes with the means to inform his followers that abandoning a practice supposed to be key to bringing heaven to earth was sanctioned by the highest authorities. He acknowledged, however, that ending complex marriage was a matter of expediency to placate critics. Since that audience reacted with scorn, the conciliatory gesture seemed futile, and complex marriage was reinstituted several months later.[61] And, since there seemed little to be got from public séances, Concentric Conventions ceased to be emphasized in Community writings. However, the concept of three worlds, sometimes approaching each other closely, would remain a feature of Oneida Community thinking for years to come.[62]

Noyes's ideas about the resurrected dead coming among the living in the near future implied that any barrier between life and death was insubstantial. Death, therefore, was not properly a pretext for intense mourning. In time, the Community came to cultivate an upbeat attitude toward mortality. "If we preserve our cheerfulness on the death of a brother or a sister," a Perfectionist explained, "it is because we do not think of our friends as lost to us, but still reckon them one with us in faith and purpose—only separated by a thin partition that may soon be removed."[63] The Community strongly discouraged displays of maudlin sentimentality. "If it were God's will that a brother or sister be called to another field of activity, those left behind should accept the decree not only willingly but gladly," Pierrepont Noyes recollected. "Although for a time there might be tears, no spirit of mourning was encouraged or tolerated." The proper attitude was one of smiling godspeed.[64]

Mary Cragin was eulogized in subsequent Oneidan writings as a saint credited with, among other things, initiating complex marriage and the Oneida system of child rearing.[65] Her memory was burnished and kept fresh. When a new Community graveyard was established in 1868, Cragin's remains were transported from Esopus for inclusion in the new cemetery. Prior to her reburial, Community members assembled in their meeting hall to examine Cragin's bones, and especially her skull. "All who knew her, recognized the contour—so beautifully feminine. The interest was intense—no nervousness—no repugnance—no sorrow. It was impossible to keep the eye off from it. What relic could be such a reminder as that? . . . . Mr. Cragin expressed a wish that the skull might be retained. The wish was unanimous. It is to be varnished and preserved."[66] One historian remarked of this incident that, given the Oneidans' conviction in the rightness of their beliefs, "it is surprising that they were not more out of touch with the world around them and more inclined to celebrate and develop their peculiarities."[67]

A material result of Noyes's spiritualist interlude and his fascination with Cragin's place in the afterworld can still be seen in the Oneida Community cemetery. The deceased were interred in neat rows, each grave marked by a low and modestly plain headstone. Cragin's tombstone, brought with her remains from Esopus, is different, much bigger than anything else in that part of the cemetery. Situated next to Noyes's (later) grave in the front row of the original layout, it seems to look over the other interments in a proprietary fashion—an appropriate vantage for a soul regarded as the queen of Hades.

What happened in Putney inspired central New York Perfectionists to start up their own heavenly association on Oneida Creek in late 1847. Noyes, fleeing legal difficulties, was given refuge there, as well as the opportunity to compose *Bible Argument*. In this, his first substantive rationale for free love, Noyes also advocated common ownership of property (Bible communism) and a social environment in which men and women would reside in a unitary home, love one another, and work together.

The new Oneida Association was an amalgam of Noyes's Vermont contingent with an approximately equal number of non-Putney New Englanders and New Yorkers. The nascent Oneida Community forged itself in the collective act of building a common residence in 1848. A social innovation emerging from that project was the collectivization of child care. Further, the raising of children was removed from the adult world with the construction, in early 1849, of a separate home for the youngsters. The Mansion House and the Children's House spatially concentrated household work and child care, which, performed cooperatively, lightened the drudgery of what was regarded as feminine work. Two other traits typical of Oneida life date from the commune's inception: the invention of a new women's costume and the realization that Community members liked working together in "bees"—volunteer task groups that promoted the happy mingling of men and women.

As soon as the Mansion House was completed, Noyes left. Later, from the vantage of his Brooklyn residence, Noyes wrote that, although he seldom visited Oneida, those in Oneida should know that "he [referring to himself in the third person] has done and will do what he can, consistently with other duties, for the good management and success of that Community . . . but he assumes no such care over it or responsibility for it, as would exclude the sovereignty of God or the responsibility of its members."[68] Ensconced in New York City for about six years, Noyes would continue to affirm his authority over Oneida while simultaneously trumpeting his independence from it.

Noyes asserted dominance when he proposed a system of spiritual hierarchy and ascending fellowship, with himself at the pinnacle. Soon after, the death of Noyes's favorite lover plunged him into a phase of eschatological speculation. When people die, Noyes reasoned, they go to Hades to await resurrection. When Christ returns, the millennium will begin in Hades with the dead rising up out of the ground. Spiritualism, at the time, was extremely popular. Noyes related his thoughts of afterlife to that movement by identifying the souls in Hades as the entities being contacted by spiritualists. In early 1852, Noyes announced plans for a "Concentric Convention"—a Brooklyn-centered séance that would link our world to souls in Hades and in heaven. Under attack from a New York newspaper at the time, Noyes apparently used the event to sanction temporary retreat from complex marriage. All these theological innovations related, as they always had, to Noyes's circumstances. They resulted from Noyes reacting to the world around him. We should note also that, with the exception of *Bible Argument* linking complex marriage and male continence to Christ's coming and a Fourieristic New Eden, Noyes did not pull his doctrines together into a larger synthesis.

Bible Argument, ascending fellowship, Hades, and, perhaps, Concentric Conventions were Noyes's last doctrinal innovations. This is not to say Noyes ceased to theorize. But the major conceptual forays of the future tended to be more secular than religious—suggestions for practicing complex marriage, a book placing the Oneida Community in the context of the utopian movement, and a tract explaining the scientific basis of eugenics. These topics, furthermore, elaborated on ideas expressed earlier. The gospel according to Noyes, then, was essentially complete by the early 1850s. Accordingly, succeeding chapters turn from examining Noyes's thinking to showing how the Oneida Community brought his ideas to life.

CHAPTER 4

Creating a Community

The book Noyes would write placing the Oneida Community in the context of the utopian movement offered no synthesis of his religious doctrines. Stranger still, Noyes's chapter on the Oneida Community in that book was essentially a history of John Humphrey Noyes and the Putney Community, with a few pages of Oneida financial summaries tacked on at the end.[1] Noyes was not alone in doing this sort of thing during the 1870s. Other nostalgic accounts of the communal past penned by the old guard of Putneyites told the story of Putney, how Putney moved to Oneida, and how, apparently, Oneida was nothing but Putney up to the time of writing. For those authors, it was as though a quarter century of Oneida Community existence was nonexistent and, by implication, meaningless.[2] The legacy they left presents something of a historiographic problem in that their narrative tends to pass, in the absence of a history of the Oneida Community, as Oneida Community history.

This book now shifts toward presenting the history the Oneidans never wrote about themselves. To this point, we have examined Noyes and his ideas in historical context while noting the brilliant beginning made by the association on Oneida Creek. This section focuses on how the Bible communists of Oneida took up Noyes's ideas and adapted Putney antecedents to create a new community with its own communal character during the early 1850s—while Noyes was in Brooklyn.

The Hubbard Affair

As Noyes smarted from the insults of the *New York Observer* and grieved for Mary Cragin in Brooklyn, the Bible communists of Oneida were staving off a legal assault from the court system that threatened their very existence. The case originated with a neighbor of the Perfectionists, Noahdiah Hubbard, and with the circumstances of his daughter, Tryphena, the Oneida Community's first local convert. The twenty-one-year-old woman had been in the residence of Jonathan Burt when Noyes lodged there at the beginning of 1848. Stealing a glance at the manuscript he was working on—*Bible Argument*, she was astonished to learn his sentiments on marriage and sex. Nevertheless, Tryphena Hubbard was won over to Perfectionist doctrine by the end of the summer.[3] She was welcomed into the Community in a way that would not give offense to local canons of morality. The Perfectionists had her married to one of their number, a young man named Henry Seymour.

Early the following year, Tryphena's father became "somewhat excited" when he learned the details of the Community's marriage arrangements. Hubbard probably threatened Noyes, who admitted his departure from Oneida was caused by Hubbard's enmity. "Mr. Noyes's absence had the effect of quelling the excitement against the Association," it was noted at the time. Noahdiah Hubbard chuckled to hear "the old he-one of the flock is scared off" and demanded Tryphena's return. Tryphena refused, and loudly denounced her father. For two years thereafter, Hubbard made a skulking nuisance of himself around the Mansion House—visiting, prying, stealing, radiating hostility, and manifesting a "sneering and contemptuous spirit."[4]

Community life proved to be difficult for Tryphena. She was criticized for being despondent and unthankful. She came under judgment, the Perfectionists reported in late 1850, "for insubordination to the church and excessive egotism amounting to a kind of insanity. Yesterday the family had a meeting, and it was unanimous judgment that Tryphena be placed under the special charge of Henry Seymour, and required to submit herself to him as her head and the representative of the church."[5] Seymour's supervisory program included criticism and, in keeping with disciplinary norms of the day, physical punishment. At first, whipping seemed to produce good results. However, in September 1851, the intensely pressured Tryphena began crying at night, speaking incoherently, and wandering about. Seymour went to the

Hubbard house to report her apparent insanity. "At first Tryphena's father spit out his wrath, but her mother checked him, saying it was no time to talk so now; she would forget all the past, and see what is best to do. When Henry informed them of all the means he had had taken, her mother inadvertently exclaimed: 'You ought to have been whipped yourself.' He made no reply, but afterward said he had used his best judgment and done as well by her as he knew how."[6]

The whipping of Tryphena provided Mr. Hubbard with a basis for legal action. Seymour was indicted by the Oneida County Office of the District Attorney in Utica for assault and battery in October 1851. Other Community men were served warrants for arrest, apparently as accessories. Several Community members were summoned to Utica to give testimony. "Sensitive and high-minded women," according to Parker, "were asked obscene questions about the most private experiences." They answered honestly, that author added, but never forgot the ignominy of the ordeal.[7]

The Oneida Community believed they had reached an out-of-court settlement with Hubbard later that fall. They would pay Tryphena's expense at an asylum and, after release, pay her an annual sum ($125–200) determined by the state of her health. They also agreed to pay for a divorce if that was what Tryphena wanted.[8] District Attorney Samuel Garvin consented to the agreement and said he would drop the charges. Garvin, however, made no move to quash the proceedings. On the contrary, he seemed to grow increasingly angry with the Community and may have encouraged Hubbard to maintain the suit. Hubbard, at any rate, abrogated the agreement and began to make noises about prosecuting the Perfectionists for the seduction of Tryphena. Garvin considered the Oneida Community "worse than any whorehouse" and made it clear he hoped to prosecute an action against the Community as a house of ill repute.[9]

The Perfectionists were greatly distressed. Noyes, in Brooklyn, announced himself willing to have the Oneida Community disbanded to avoid further trouble. In April, John Miller dutifully conveyed the offer from Oneida to the district attorney in Utica.[10] Ending the Oneida Community was fine with Garvin, but he still did nothing to dismiss the case.

Just as the Oneidans conceded total defeat, a sympathetic neighbor encouraged them to strengthen their resolve. Timothy Jenkins, a lawyer of nearby Oneida Castle, had earlier been the county's prosecuting attorney and was, at the moment, the district representative to the United States Congress. He understood that Garvin's case really was being tried in a court of public opinion and was, at heart, a political affair. Jenkins and his brother Whipple, also an attorney, advised the Perfectionists not only to stand their ground but to fight back.[11]

That summer, the Oneida Community waged a public relations battle for the hearts and minds of their neighbors. In June, they held what they called a peace offering, a strawberry festival.[12] It turned out to be a big neighborhood party attended by hundreds who happily gorged themselves on berries served with sugar, cream, biscuits, and butter. While they were at it, the Community staged another strawberry get-together to show their appreciation to the Oneida Indians for *their* neighborliness. At both events, visitors feasted on strawberries notable for their flavor, lusciousness, and size.[13] These fruits, developed after only a year under the care of gardener Henry Seymour, were a timely demonstration of the Community's horticultural prowess.

In July, the Oneida Community collected the signatures of the leading citizens of their area on a petition to Garvin. The document invited the district attorney to imagine the time had come to back off.

> We, the undersigned, having understood that a prosecution in behalf of the people against several of the prominent members of the Oneida Community had been commenced and is now pending, beg leave to say, that in our judgment, if there has ever been any cause for such a prosecution, it has been wholly removed, and does not now exist, and in our opinion it is not demanded or deemed advisable, on the part of the people at large out of that Community best acquainted with their present management and conduct, that the prosecution should be further carried on against them, and we recommend that it be discontinued.[14]

This was political push-back Garvin understood. The court declared *nolle prosequi*—prosecution ended—in September 1852. The Oneida Community paid court costs of twenty dollars and proceeded to enjoy friendly relations with the outside world for over twenty years. As for Tryphena Hubbard, she lived out her life in the Oneida Community in a quiet and seemingly normal frame of mind. "In the excitement of the persecutions attending the founding of the Community," a medical doctor noted years later, "she was temporarily insane for a few months." As of 1870, she was described as completely recovered.[15]

Hubbard's case came close to destroying the Community. But the Bible communists of Oneida prevailed and did so without help from Brooklyn. The embattled upstaters were not aided by the Concentric Convention. They did not act on Noyes's suggestion to capitulate. Apparently they did not follow his recommendation to pay Hubbard off. The victory was Oneida's. It resulted from Jenkins's "kind offices and friendly advice" and the good relations forged locally by the Community.[16] The Oneida Perfectionists never called attention to this accomplishment. And never, during

Noyes's long sojourn in Brooklyn, did they assert independence of him. "I beg of Oneida," Noyes had advised his central New York followers in the course of their Hubbard difficulties, "to take comfort in the view that their tribulations are exactly what they need to reduce them to their proper magnitude as an auxiliary to Brooklyn."[17] That, apparently, is what they did. The Oneidans never claimed to be doing anything other than carrying out Noyes's wishes. Why? Who were the Bible communists of Oneida? What made them tick?

Community Members

Few of the people Noyes left behind in Oneida had any background in Fourier-ism or experience of communitarian living in other associations. On the other hand, they had assets Noyes never considered in *Bible Argument*, including a storehouse of practical knowledge. The professions or skills of men at the begin-ning of the association were listed as farmer (4), carpenter and machinist (2), blacksmith (2), cabinetmaker (2), shoemaker (2), miller (2), schoolteacher (2), printer (1), wagon maker (1), gunsmith (1), and lead pipe maker (1). Some were "conversant with several other professions, such as those of editors, architects, harness-makers, masons, &c." These people, as Fogarty observed, "were neither poets nor political anarchists, but farmers and mechanics who knew how to run a mill, plow a field, and lay a foundation."[18]

They were rural and small-town New Englanders and New Yorkers com-fortable with physical toil. Most, probably, were of the "middling" sort, although some came from truly disadvantaged backgrounds. Years later, when the Oneida Community was comfortably prosperous, a column in its weekly newspaper remembered such "Stories of Poverty." One of them was by Julia Ackley, who started life among eleven siblings on a hardscrabble farm. Julia was three when her mother died. Thereafter, the young girl lived in a succession of households, exchanging labor for room and board. At the age of twelve, she moved in with a married sister:

> Although I had all I wanted to eat of the plainest kind of food I had to work very hard all the time. During those six years my sister gave birth to four children, and after her third child was born her health failed to such a degree that the heaviest of the work came on me, which I had thought hard enough before. The barn was located at quite a distance from the house. It was one of my duties to milk every morning and night, and if my brother-in-law was from home I was also obliged to feed the cattle. In blustering, wintry weather it was pretty tough for a girl of thirteen,

thinly clad, to wade through the snow and drag the hay down from the loft while my fingers and toes were nipped with the frosty air. But the hardest of all was the carrying of the water. . . . For eight months in the year we had to bring water from a spring in the woods, thirty-five rods from the house. Besides being a long distance, every step of the way back was up-hill. . . . When fifteen it was my custom to take the family-washing down to this spring and do it alone. It would take me nearly all day after doing the housework in the morning. . . .

We lived in an old log-house, and it was a common thing in winter for the snow to sift through the roof, covering my bed and the floor so thickly that I could only get out of bed in the morning by stepping into a snow-drift. I was never well dressed, and had nothing pretty or becoming to wear as other girls had. . . . But the greatest trial of this kind which I had to endure was going barefooted.[19]

Ackley's account concludes with the statement that, in the Oneida Community, she found emancipation from household drudgery and social slavery. Community life seemed very good to Ackley, a hard worker disposed to work hard for the Community.

The first Oneida Perfectionists were serious, professing Christians, almost all of whom came out of conventional Protestant denominations. The greater number had been Congregationalists (about 28 of them), Methodists (ca. 15), Baptists (ca. 11), or Presbyterians (ca. 6). Nevertheless, they were "seekers"—folk dissatisfied with the customary preachments, distressed by religious uncertainty, and searching for answers.[20]

They were convinced they had found the answer in Noyes's Perfectionist teachings. As devout believers, they joined Noyes in his purpose and, in so doing, dedicated themselves to the highest possible cause. A good example of this sentiment was penned by Joseph Ackley (Julia's husband) when he cast his mind back to the founding of Oneida. Here is how he described joining Burt on Oneida Creek in a letter to his granddaughter born a quarter century later in the Oneida Community.

Well, 45 years ago this morning I started out in the mud and rain with your Grandmother and three little children, the youngest your mother, a baby about nine months old, for this place. . . . Rain and sleety snow accompanied us on our journey all day. Outwardly everything seemed very unpropitious, but inwardly there was hope and joy. Do I hear you asking what was our motive and why did you leave friends and a father's house and go among strangers? I will tell you briefly. The thought did not once pass through our minds of finding a better home or of accumulating money or worldly honor or fame in any way. We had our eyes fixed upon something that seemed far more lasting than anything this world can give. There was something within us that made us think and feel that we were called of God to unite with a people who we believed loved God with all their hearts and were not selfish but were laboring to build up a society where the love of God should be the prevailing spirit. In taking this step I lost my good name, my worldly fortune, was disinherited by parents, and for years had no other expectation than that I was forever disinherited.[21]

Members of the Community thought they were subordinating themselves to God with the recognition that Noyes was "the chosen representative of Jesus Christ, and the ordained one who is to set up the kingdom of heaven in this world." A Community member frequently "confessed" or publicly avowed Noyes "as my head, and the medium that shall modify me and organize me into Christ's body."[22] Such homage was rendered voluntarily. It seemed proper to acknowledge Noyes as paramount because he radiated an effulgent magnetism that made people happy in his presence. Then, too, the prevailing sentiment was that Noyes was divinely inspired, and peer pressure encouraged one to go along with all of this. Hence, Community members made much of Noyes and happily, even sycophantically, repeated his maxims. They tried hard to carry out his wishes and realize his dreams (see figure 5).

FIGURE 5. The Oneida Community, 1863. This portrait, titled *Group No. 1*, was sold to tourists in several formats and sizes. John Noyes stands proprietarily in the right foreground.

The communards bowed to God and to Noyes as an exercise of free will and ongoing voluntarism. They were not coerced to do so, although they knew of a different perception abroad in the land (and emphasized in recent scholarship) that they were vassals to a Rasputin-like tyrant. "Some of the papers say that if Mr. Noyes takes a pinch of snuff all the Community sneeze" was how the Perfectionists joked about the notion that Noyes determined all.[23]

Called of God to build an unselfish world, drawn to Noyes as a leader chosen by God—these are beliefs of a very general nature. What the Bible communists thought of more specific doctrine is surprisingly difficult to discover. As Perfectionists, they must have believed that feeling unity with Christ would result in sanctification. One of them announced precisely that "for some time past my mind has been directed to the doctrine of Salvation from Sin, with the purpose of making it practically my own. I have believed that entire Salvation was possible in this world, and that I should have it; but I can now say, it is mine. I believe that Christ is in me, and that his victory over sin and death is mine; his righteousness is mine. Not that I have done some great thing. I have only ceased 'going about to establish my own righteousness,' and have submitted myself to the righteousness of God."[24] This sentiment was rarely enunciated, presumably because the principle of ascending fellowship prevented the personal announcement of one's own perfection. This statement came from John Freeman, a recent joiner who may not have been fully cognizant of Community etiquette in the matter.

Nor did they say much about non-spiritual betterment as a means to attain salvation from sin. Noyes, it will be recalled, left the door open as to whether social perfectionism might be linked with religious Perfectionism. Consequently, it must have been easy to compound the two concepts. That occurred when a craze for educational self-improvement swept the Community in 1850: "This [education] is the passion which is at work in all classes, and which will be encouraged at any expense, until it has full possession of the body. It is, we believe, the beginning of the resurrection—the working of that mighty power which raised Christ from the dead, and which, as it is received by faith, is adapted to quicken all the elements of life and character. We expect to be saved, and raised to immortal fruitfulness, by the infusion of this very principle which we are even now conscious is having its own way in our central nature."[25] This, also, was very rarely expressed, presumably because equating a course of action with faith would have seemed heretical in the light of more sober reflection.

What Bible communists said most frequently was simply that religion was an ongoing project requiring attention and effort. "It seems to me," the old Putneyite William Woolworth remarked after working to perfect himself for nearly twenty years, "that salvation is a continual yielding of our life to the spirit of truth."[26] Internalizing Noyes's idea that sanctification was a progressive affair, the Perfectionists avowed repeatedly that they were improving spiritually. Spencer Klaw's observation that self-improvement was the central purpose of life at Oneida makes sense with reference to this generalized notion of religious advancement.[27]

Rites and Integrative Practices

Many traits typical of the Oneida Community emerged during the commune's early years, including the commune's fashion of worship, or, more accurately, the almost complete absence of formal ritual. With the possible exception of his strange "Concentric Convention," Noyes never insisted on much in the way of participatory religious exercise. His followers in Oneida, for their part, harbored a general mistrust of engaging in any behavior that might seem ostentatious or pretentious. They did not like public displays of emotion. They avoided anything smacking of "idolatry"—outward signs of formulaic belief, including such material symbols as crosses. A strain of ideological indifference to cant and formula may have resulted from a religious outlook in which every act was an expression of faith. In any event, the Oneidans disliked "legalism"—fussy rules and unvarying routines of any sort. The Oneida Community seemed "to have an almost fanatical horror of forms," Charles Nordhoff observed in the course of doing fieldwork on American communitarian societies.[28] There were, as a result, only two overtly religious exercises at Oneida, both of which acknowledged Noyes's theology and his spiritual preeminence.

One was "Confessing Christ"—that is, publicly professing one's faith. Noyes, it will be recalled, insisted that confession was essential to achieving the regenerated state: "A whole-hearted, and everlasting surrender to the faithfulness of God alone, can secure the fulfillment of his promises to faith." Confession was also a demonstration of commitment, which, as Noyes put it, "leaves no way for retreat."[29] Those starting out at Oneida in 1848 adopted the confession as Community liturgy. "We children said, 'fess Christ' or 'fess Christ a good spirit,'" Pierrepont Noyes recalled, "without clear understanding but with firm confidence that we were in some way acquiring merit." To adults, confession was not so much a claim of salvation as it was an affirmation that "Christ had the power to free their lives from sin," according to the same source.[30]

The other religious exercise was commemorating the date of Noyes's first confession of Christ on February 20, 1834: the High Tide of the Spirit. The most memorable High Tide was the Concentric Convention in Brooklyn.

At a High Tide in Oneida a few years later, a member reported that he quit work in the trap shop a little early "to be ready for the celebration appointed at four. The scene in the parlor—the three long tables lined on both sides with happy faces—the cake, the apples, the bread and wine, the music and the cheering—the toast and speeches—and especially the allusion to old times—to the gospel of 1834 and the progress toward the resurrection which we have made since—stirred my heart very pleasantly. After the banquet I attended milking service again at the barn."[31] Most High Tide celebrations were modest affairs of this sort.

During the 1850s, the Community was swept by enthusiasm for a ritual-like activity called the "Bible game." It was actually several games, all of which boiled down to identifying chapter and verse of a passage read aloud.[32] Later in time, there were attempts to introduce a new holiday—"High Tide of the Flesh," on August 20—and new rituals, including parenting songs for couples about to conceive children. None of these ever really caught on.

The Oneidans did, however, develop at least two distinctive institutions: mutual criticism and the evening meeting. Although both delivered participatory satisfaction akin to church services, neither was regarded as primarily a rite of worship. They were viewed as social events essential to harmonious group life throughout the tenure of the commune.

Noyes learned what he called "mutual criticism" as a divinity student at Andover and passed it on to the Putney and Oneida communities. The technique effectively combined peer pressure with self-examination. Sometimes it was practiced as part of the evening meeting. More commonly, responsibility to examine an individual's defects and weaknesses devolved on a committee. Each criticizer was supposed to specify "every thing objectionable" in the subject's character and conduct. The person being examined was expected to receive the criticism meekly, gratefully, in silence—and then to act on it. The experience required seeing oneself through the eyes of others, and that, in turn, fostered humility and encouraged selflessness.[33]

Mutual criticism could touch on anything ranging from boorishness ("His utterance is labored, tedious and awkward") to vanity ("He talks for effect and walks for effect; he flourishes his handkerchief for effect; takes out his letters and watch for effect"). One who belabored humor was urged to take his comic acting less seriously. Another who was humorless was advised to "cultivate the laughing spirit, and to read the jokes in Harper's Magazine."[34] Criticism aimed to correct unbelief, too much belief in spiritualism, moodiness, excessive legalism, and cruelty to animals. The technique could be applied as a health measure to reduce fever and stimulate the healing agencies of the body. "It was a common thing for the Committee to repair to a sickroom and criticize the patient," Pierrepont Noyes remembered. Many cures, it was claimed, resulted from mutual criticism sessions.[35] Most of all, mutual criticism was used to root out resentments, irritations, and other issues of attitude or behavior potentially disruptive to communal life: hardness of heart, complacency, egotism, jealousy, selfish love for one person. At Oneida in the early years, the power harmonizing and directing their commune "lay not in any code of laws, nor in the commanding influence of any man, or set of men, but in our *system of Free Criticism.* . . . Here is the whole mystery of government among us."[36] Mutual criticism, it seemed to them, was the foundation of regulation and order, "especially necessary as the counterpart of our Social Theory [complex marriage], which throws down all barriers, and sets us afloat under circumstances that expose us to a variety of dangers,—such dangers as the world suppose it is impossible for us to sail through without shipwreck."[37] Mutual criticism was how the Bible communists held one another to the same high standards and how, along with the practice of ascending fellowship (see below), they governed themselves.

Pleasanter than mutual criticism was another institution crucial to communal stability: the evening meeting. The idea, very likely, was suggested by group get-togethers at Putney. At Oneida, every day ended with a gathering of the adult Perfectionists. Initially the convocation occurred in the parlor on the ground floor of the Mansion House. The second Mansion House, built in 1862, was actually designed around a theater space for daily meetings. These communal gatherings were strongly stamped with the democratic character of a New England town meeting in which anyone—or, at least, any man— had the right to speak his mind. At Oneida, "all important questions are brought before the Community for decision," they said, "and in the general assembly every person, male and female, has a voice and a vote." Visitor Charles Nordhoff observed that nothing at Oneida was attempted without first obtaining general consent in the evening meeting.[38]

The earliest meetings were devoted to discussion of business matters and reading of correspondence. Then the proceedings were opened to general conversation and confessions of religious faith. Later gatherings included singing of hymns and reading of news items. Then, "the last half hour of the Meeting was, as a rule, a time for religious expression," according to Jessie Kinsley. "Mr. Noyes frequently had something to say in the form of a 'Talk,' and his thought was commented on by others. Meeting ended, not with a *set* prayer but with our own peculiar form called '*Confessing Christ,*' when we would express our desires and emotions in confessing Christ in us a guide and leader." Combining worship with business, the evening meeting assured individual involvement in community affairs and bound all the Perfectionists together in common purpose.[39]

Though not a publicly enacted event, ascending fellowship was in principle similar to mutual criticism and the evening meeting in its socially integrative effects. This system of spiritual ranking (see the previous chapter) functioned "to uplift character and draw all toward the plane of goodness attained by the most Christlike and therefore most central members," according to religious scholar Richard DeMaria. The pursuit of ascending fellowship discouraged the formation of cliques and interest groups that might cause internal discord. Conversely, adherence to the principle was said to produce peace, happiness, improvement, and collective success. Hence, ascending fellowship probably contributed to the smooth operation of Community life.[40]

Community members, for their part, internalized the implications of ascending fellowship, then administered its logic to one another. It was easy to understand, Pierrepont Noyes thought, "and the validity of my father's formula appealed to all. At times men and women discussed earnestly with each other and with themselves as to whether their own relation was ascending or descending; a query whose answer might bring them face to face with the dilemma of self-denial or an uneasy conscience."[41] Following the dictates of ascending fellowship required self-discipline and encouraged humility in every Oneida Perfectionist.

Although mutual criticism and the evening meeting had their roots in Putney practices, both were developed to a much higher extent at Oneida. Ascending fellowship, on the other hand, illustrates a pattern that played out in other aspects of communal existence. From the vantage of Brooklyn, Noyes suggested his followers do something. People in Oneida took it up and made it work. Noyes proposed; the Oneida Community disposed.

The Tenor of Life at Oneida

Improvement was the watchword of the Oneida Community. Spiritual advancement aside, the improvement held in the highest estimation was perfecting the mind by acquiring knowledge. All Oneidans furthered education by reading—privately or out loud in the course of working in groups or meeting in the evening. As soon as a person learned some topic, he or she would then share it in a talk or teach it in a class. At first, book learning was touted for its practical benefits. "As indicative of its application in industry, and the learning of new arts, our members are accustomed, and cheerfully ready, to be shifted from one occupation to another, as convenience or their own profit seems to require," the Community's report for the year 1850 declared. "Nothing comes amiss that offers an opening for new truth, and new practice. The farmer goes from the plough to the mechanic's shop for a few month's diversion, and some one else takes his place at the plough."[42] William Hinds explained that their goal was a universal education that "comprises a knowledge of all trades, as well as mere book-knowledge. No one here thinks of making some one or two things the business of his life. By rotation of employment, persons learn to do a great many things. This system has also entirely displaced the feeling that one kind of business is more honorable than another, and tends to cultivate unity and love between the different departments."[43] "Improvement is the motive power here," he enthused, and he claimed it to be present in every department.

But Hinds also extolled the sheer joy of learning, proudly noting that the evening meeting was "becoming more and more intellectual." With time, intellectual improvement for its own sake was increasingly emphasized. They devote "a certain portion of each day to intellectual cultivation," a visitor marveled. "Think of living always in such a school! Shall we not reap advantages which the world knows nothing of?" Many Bible communists thought so. "This spirit of improvement that reigns here has taken possession of me," as one of them put it, "and incited me to obtain such an education as is destined to be the lot of all this happy people."[44]

By early 1853, the Oneidans expanded their notion of improvement to include music, which "now became an acknowledged source of pleasure," according to Perfectionist Harriet Worden. "A small organization, consisting of a dozen members, was formed at this time, and a systematic course of drill attempted. The noon hour was chosen as most convenient, and for the succeeding eight or ten years the family spent the half hour after dinner agreeably, in noting the progress of this orchestra, as it grew in size and ability."[45] Shortly after, they took up playacting and theatrical entertainment. "Whenever the *whole Community* become interested in a matter, inspiration and enthusiasm seem to surround it with a peculiar charm, making it an ordinance of health and pleasure," Worden observed of the thespian activities.[46]

Intellectual, musical, and theatrical improvement, then, came to fruition early on, as did mutual criticism, daily meeting, and a number of other traits characteristic of Oneida. Those practices that originated with Noyes were made to function in his absence. Whatever the specific source of the custom, however, *all* the quotidian habits and rhythms of Oneida life developed in the course of living together at Oneida, including routines of work.

Labor was undertaken voluntarily or assigned by committees chosen by the commune to serve in that capacity, typically for a year. Committees and departments organized and ran Community businesses and, with time, an increasing number of Community activities.[47] The ideal, as we have seen, was that all should be able to perform all tasks, and rotate from one to the next. The reality was that people especially valuable to the commune for their skill and experience tended to be kept where they would do the most good.

The only formal structure to work was the marking out of time by a bell, attached to the outside of the Mansion House, rung seven times a day. Something of the feel of daily life is conveyed in the following passages drawn from numerous examples published in the commune's weekly newspaper. Such descriptions were attributed to "a member's log" or to "the journal of an Oneida friend," or, most frequently, to no author at all.

Mornings:

The first salute to my senses this morning was an excellent smell of breakfast cakes. The next was a charming strain of music. Then came the rattle of the big bell. Conscious of ability to dress in one minute, I waited for the second bell, at the ringing of which I jumped out of bed and into my clothes as promptly as usual; but the smell of the cakes, and the music had called up so many that all the tables were filled before I reached the breakfast room, and I had to wait for the second table. Had a good time after breakfast, reading about Joshua and Jericho, and attending the Bible-game. Then went to the barn and milked four cows. . . . At 8 o'clock went to the shop and took hold of the hammer and tongs with a good appetite. Had nothing but an "odd job" to do, in which I [man speaking] could not well employ a help-meet; so worked alone. At 20 minutes past 11, having pretty well moistened my shirt, I quit work and went home to my reading corner, and enjoyed reading Macaulay's History of England till dinner, or rather, as it proved, till the Johnny-cake luncheon.[48]

The "first bell" was rung this morning at a quarter before five o'clock A.M. At five nearly the whole family, young and old, were astir, and on their way in groups to a variety of "bees." First a number of men and women assembled in the ironing-room to do up a part of the family ironing. Then a group of men started with their pails for the barn to milk. A third detachment of men and women commenced taking up carpets and carrying out furniture preparatory to house-cleaning. A fourth group busied themselves in getting the family breakfast. The fifth and last company was much the largest, and embraced all ages, from sixty to six. The field of operations was the plot of ground across the road.[49]

Afternoons:

[After dinner] gave a lesson on the piano from 1 o'clock to 2, another from 2 to 3; then practiced myself from 3 o'clock till 4. Then read in "Plurality of Worlds," took the evening repast, worked a short time; read a Home-Talk on keeping accounts. Listened to a lecture on grammar, in which an independent spirit of inquiry was recommended, and the simple doctrines of common sense were held up in preference to the mere words used in the science. Attended evening meeting; worked a little at knitting, then retired, grateful for being permitted to enjoy the benefits of this school.[50]

Dinner; Read *Cultivator and Times*; Carpet-bag bee, one hour; Went to the wood-lot, two miles, and helped in getting home a load of wood; Loitered unprofitably, and took a nap; Supper; Looked over the news for the evening's report; Attended a committee session; Greek class, three-fourths of an hour; Evening meeting; Rest, with an invitation to help get breakfast to-morrow morning.[51]

Sunday:

Sunday is by no means a day of inactivity with us. Considering ourselves at work for God, and reckoning our labor as one form of worship, and as such, acceptable, we are conscious that we serve our master more to his satisfaction by making ourselves practically useful, than by the old-fashioned method of industrial abstinence and church-going. Our exercises for today are as follows: A group of twenty-five or thirty persons rise at four to commence washing. Breakfast at six; Bible-game at a quarter before seven. Then the washing is continued, lasting generally till nearly noon. Business meeting at eleven: in which various details of business, new propositions, &c., are discussed and decided upon. Dinner at twelve, and music by the band till one. Singing school at two; bag bee at three; a bee at the barn for husking corn from four to five, then milking, supper, an hour's reading in the parlor, meeting &c. Evening: Financial report by our book-keeper, shows an encouraging state of business prosperity. Criticism, at his request, of a young brother. . . . [Beneath his superficial coating,] there lies a really kind and loyal heart, good intelligence, and all the subjective qualifications necessary to develop a cultivated and attractive person.[52]

In addition to its normally scheduled soundings, the Mansion House bell could be rung anytime for bees: "This morning, precisely at 4, it heralds us forth, young and old, to pick the last of our strawberries for this year. . . . Then there are peas to pick for market, or weeding in the garden, or some

extra gathering in the parlor, a singing school, a march, or perhaps an outdoor dance."[53] This last passage illustrates the sense of contentment that
pervades these descriptions of daily life. One anonymous Perfectionist tried
to express the enjoyment felt in working outside in this fashion.

> Our people obey the inviting influences of the sun instinctively, as the
> bees do. Standing in the center of the garden, with a group who were
> thinning out the strawberry beds, clusters of busy workers could be
> seen scattered here and there all over the domain. One was spreading
> ashes over a ploughed field, another on the verge of the woods making
> fence, a third in the nursery taking up trees, others ploughing, and still
> another of men and women raking and weeding a strawberry bed on
> the western side of the garden.[54]

Harriet Worden described the satisfaction felt in working together indoors.

> The [washing-room] is brightly lighted, the tubs filled with water, and
> every preparation made for the morning's event. An odor of soap-
> suds, emanating from two large caldrons of boiling clothes, fills the
> atmosphere. One by one the washers come in, some looking rather
> sleepy, others wide-awake for the work. Finally, the wash-boxes are
> surrounded, the partners standing vis-a-vis. In a few moments all are
> busily washing—a pleasant hum of voices can be heard, despite the
> thumping of the one washing-machine in the corner. A few of the men
> are discussing the latest political news; another group are absorbed in
> topics nearer home; others are rehearsing, with comments of their
> own, the play enacted the previous Saturday evening. Anon, the whole
> group are formed into a grand musical chorus; now singing snatches of
> an old anthem, and now divided into sections, the air is soon resonant
> with such rounds as, "Scotland's Burning," "Merrily, Merrily Greet the
> Morn," "Glide along my Bonny Boat," etc. . . . Before another song can
> be produced the breakfast bell sounds, announcing to the astonished
> company that they have washed an hour and a half.[55]

An anecdote about Community work was told of an English visitor, John
Trevor, who encountered one of the Perfectionists "leisurely weeding a garden path." When asked how many hours he had to work, the Community
member replied "he did not have to work. Mr. Trevor then asked what time
he began and what time he quit. 'I begin when I want to and quit when
I want to' was the response. Mr. Trevor in describing the incident said that
he felt up to that moment he had been a fool. He felt that he had at last been
confronted by the man who had solved the problems of existence."[56]

The food that fueled all this activity was bland, simple, and largely veg-
etarian. Their diet was dominated by milk, potatoes, bread, baked beans,
apple dishes, and—after the first lean years—butter.[57] They agreed with a
basic assumption of Sylvester Graham's then-fashionable health regimen,
that the state of one's passions is determined by the food one eats. On the
one hand, "those who eat swine's flesh will be gross and swine-like." On the
other, "certain kinds of vegetable food may have a tendency to reform and
purify the life, causing it to repel some forms of grossness." They also agreed
with Graham that substances stimulating the passions should be avoided. In
accordance with this, they gave up "stimulants" including tobacco (mostly
they were chewers who also deplored the mess caused by constant expecto-
ration), medicine (mostly patent concoctions of problematic benefit), and
the caffeine-laden drinks of coffee and tea.[58] The most "ardent" stimulant
they knew was alcohol. While they avoided drinking it in any quantity, they
also tried to avoid zealotry on the subject. A distaste for polemics set them
apart from Grahamites, as did their religious orientation. What was effica-
cious about diet was the result, after all, of divine agency. Faith in Christ, they
averred, was the surest road to health, happiness, and longevity.[59]

Believing their cause was not of this world, Bible communists held themselves aloof from political activity. Nevertheless, they followed current
events closely and were particularly well posted on a subject they detested:
slavery. Noyes had some background in antislavery sentiment, having helped
to found one of the country's earliest abolitionist organizations, the New
Haven Anti-Slavery Society, in 1832. In 1837, he was communicating with
the fiery abolitionist William Lloyd Garrison. In 1850, he demonstrated the
basic arguments for abolitionism by applying them to the state of women in
marriage in a brochure called *Slavery & Marriage*.[60]

The Oneida Community started up against the backdrop of the Mis-
souri Compromise and the Fugitive Slave Act, political developments that
galvanized abolitionist sentiment in the Northeast to extreme measures.
The Perfectionists were impressed by the novel *Uncle Tom's Cabin*. Their
neighbor Gerrit Smith agitated for abolition of slavery in Congress during the years 1853–1854, and his legislative career was closely monitored in
the Community. They discussed African American bondage with the famed
antislavery activist Frederick Douglass when Douglass lectured at the Mansion House.[61]

The Oneida Community was very interested in fellow communitarian
ventures and reprinted notices in its own newspaper of such groups as the
Icarians, Hopedale, and Raritan Bay.[62] Some personal interchange occurred.
Oneida Perfectionist Amasa Carr observed the Ebenezer/Rappite group then

in western New York. The leader of the French Fourierists, Victor Consider-ant, visited Oneida.[63] The Oneidans were dismayed by Nathaniel Hawthorne's novelistic satire of life at Brook Farm (*The Blithedale Romance*), believing the author had exploited a noble experience for personal gain.[64]

But the strongest ties existed with the longest lasting (1843–1856) of the American Fourieristic ventures, the North American Phalanx in Red Bank, New Jersey.[65] Articles about this commune from other newspapers frequently were reprinted in the *Circular*. Members of Oneida and the North American Phalanx called on one another. And the North American Phalanx shared a knowledge of fruit-preserving technology that made possible Oneida's can-ning industry described in the next chapter.[66]

In addition to avoiding political entanglements, the Oneidans tried to maintain a general independence of the world. As an exclusive enclave, they were suspicious of the outside environment and regarded it as a source of spiritual contamination. Nevertheless, they were hardly isolated from con-temporary America and often had to interact with it. Locally, the Perfection-ists were good neighbors who always volunteered aid to those in need. The Bible communists helped everyone in distress around them, including those who bore them ill will: the Hubbards to the north and a family named Olm-stead to the south. In both instances, Community people turned out in force whenever there was a fire to fight or a barn to raise.[67]

Interchange was frequent with Oneida Indians living in two nearby settlements, each clustered around a Methodist meetinghouse. The Bible communists remarked on the Indians' appearance—the men dressed in Euro-American fashion, the women wrapped in blankets. The Perfection-ists were sympathetic to the Native Americans as folk who had been badly treated. "It is impossible not to feel a certain respect for this people," a communard observed. "They comport themselves with admirable dignity and order—are not curious and intrusive—yet are affable and susceptible to friendship, so far as we have had intercourse with them." Oneida com-munists and Oneida Indians visited back and forth, regaling each other with hymns sung mostly in the native language of the singers. As they were separated by mutually unintelligible languages, however, relations between the two peoples were formal and limited. That may have been fine with the Perfectionists who, on one occasion, rebuffed an Indian invitation to play baseball: "We thought we could not afford the time, and that we could meet the Indians in better ways than in sports of this kind, as they need sympathy with us of the white race, in our habits of thrift and industry, more than in gaming and pastime. Besides, to receive their proposal as a kind of chal-lenge, we did not like. We should prefer to mix the parties and not play one people against the other."[68]

Meanwhile, people from the outside world were pouring into Oneida, perhaps several thousand visitors a year during the 1850s. The majority must have been locals, because they arrived on foot or by horse, the nearest railhead and Erie Canal stop being some five miles away. The Perfectionists maintained a friendly demeanor toward the uninvited strangers while trying to avoid having their lives disrupted. "We have learned to show hospitality without the assiduities of the world, to give the freedom of home without costly attention," they said.[69] Some visitors came to sample the Community's fare: "This serving of strawberries and cream, commenced with complaisance to occasional visitors who asked if we would favor them, which went on, till it grew to be understood that they could be had here, and now we expect from twenty to thirty calls a day."[70] Most were drawn by curiosity about Community life and, especially, the Community's sex life. "The atmospheric opinion of us . . . is bad. We are thought to be a set of Mormons, or worse than Mormons—to be guilty of Convent cruelties." The Perfectionists often found themselves lumped with Mormonism in the public mind, although, in the Oneidans' view, complex marriage had nothing in common with polygamy—multiple spouses for a man but not a woman. How could a Mormon "claim the right to possess twenty women and not concede any corresponding liberty to them?" they wondered. "If plurality is right in one it is right is the other."[71]

The Oneida commune Noyes left behind was nearly destroyed by legal action directed against one of its members for whipping a young woman. The lawsuit, brought by the woman's father, was prosecuted in nearby Utica by a district attorney antagonistic to the Perfectionists. From Brooklyn, Noyes recommended the Oneida Association disband. Instead, the Oneidans enlisted local sentiment and won a victory that surely strengthened their resolve.

Oneida Perfectionists were deeply religious folk who found meaning and inspiration in Noyes and his doctrines. When Noyes, from afar, suggested specific courses of action, the Bible communists in Oneida tried their best to carry them out. Early on, for example, Noyes proposed a doctrine of spiritual ranking with himself at the apex. At Oneida, they took the measure of the concept, then administered its logic to one another.

More generally, the Oneida Bible communists worked out the essentials of communal existence in Noyes's absence. They developed effective social arrangements, including mutual criticism and the evening meeting. They promoted intellectual, musical, and theatrical improvement. They crafted a system for labor in which committees assigned tasks on a rotating basis, for work that brought satisfaction and contentment. They established a diet of mostly vegetable foods and formulated a visitation policy tolerant of tourists. Some of these practices grew out of precedents originated at Putney; but whatever the antecedents, at Oneida they were worked out and developed in local circumstances by a dedicated group of people much larger than the Putney Association. The innovations most clearly autochthonous to the Oneida setting included the subject of the next chapter: gender relations more equal than they had ever been at Putney and group marriage that worked on a scale unimaginable at Putney.

CHAPTER 5

Gender and Sex

Noyes recommended, in *Bible Argument*, that the new commune should live off fruit grown by the communards. A short time later, the founders of Oneida pioneered working in bees. Out of trees and bees and in Noyes's absence, the Bible communists of central New York developed a horticultural mode of subsistence that proved to be spiritually gratifying. And, in spite of theology defining females as inferior, interaction of this sort encouraged a state of practical, emotionally satisfying equality between the sexes. Horticulture and mingling men and women in common endeavor may have brought the Bible communists as close to realizing utopia as any group has ever come.

Also in *Bible Argument*, Noyes defined group marriage as the center of his religious outlook, as well as the engine that could run a utopia. Following the instructions of their Brooklynite leader, the Oneidans moved beyond theory to fashion a collective life of free love—and actually made it work.

At Oneida, they wrote new chapters in the history of gender and sex relations during the 1850s.

Horticulture

In *Bible Argument*, Noyes suggested that the coming association would subsist on tree fruit. "As society becomes vital and refined, drawing its best nourishment from love, the grosser kinds of food, and especially animal food, will go out of use. The fruits of *trees* will become the staple eatables. Gen. 2:16. The largest part of the labor of the world is now spent on the growth of annual plants and animals. Cattle occupy more of the soil at present than men. The cultivation of trees will be better sport than plowing, hoeing corn, digging potatoes, and waiting on cows and pigs."[1]

While the diet of the Putney Perfectionists certainly included nuts and apples,[2] the doctrinaire emphasis placed on tree fruit in this passage sounds like Fourier, who loved pears and hated wheat. The communes envisioned by the Frenchman were rural, agricultural enterprises especially devoted to fruit growing.[3] Noyes's sentiments in this regard probably were derived from Albert Brisbane's American writings on Fourierism, published in 1843 after running in the pages of the *New York Tribune*. This source indicated that an association—especially a small one, especially at the beginning—should favor fruits and vegetables over the heavy branches of agriculture. The examples recommended were apples and pears, which the author sometimes called horticulture. "The association should raise large quantities of fruit, for its cultivation is both attractive and profitable," Brisbane concluded. He also stressed how men, women, and children could work productively together in this line of work.[4]

At Oneida, the word "horticulture" meant tending fruit trees, berry bushes, and vegetable gardens, in contrast to "farming," which referred to the keeping of domesticated animals and the raising of grain crops. Horticulture, also called gardening, was more desirable than farming and, according to their annual report covering 1850, was to be the Community's chief source of food. "The instincts and tastes of the Association, from the commencement of operations at Oneida, have led steadily to a revolution of the practices and notions, commonly associated with the idea of *farming*. Motives of *policy*, as well as good taste and the habits of community life, invite our efforts in the direction of making our domain a *garden*, rather than what is usually understood by the term *farm*. . . . It is not in the line of our ambition or attractions, to make a main business of waiting on animals."[5] The Bible communists claimed horticulture would take one to a higher spiritual plane and bring about a more advanced state of civilization.[6] Horticulture, furthermore, was both the original way of Eden and the way things would be again in the coming heavenly state on earth.[7]

A prominent nurseryman, Henry Thacker, was recruited to the Community—along with his tree nursery in Owasco—in 1850. By 1853, the Oneidans judged that the horticultural regime was successfully established.[8] They credited the success to Noyes, whose theory of tree fruits, one of them wrote, "may have been thought a Utopian speculation. But the Association, without much reference to theory, have naturally slid out of *farming* into *Horticulture*, as a means of subsistence."⁹ The same year, as earlier remarked, the phrase "Horticulture the leading business for subsistence" began running on the first page of almost every issue of their newspaper as a statement of a key belief. It would continue to be featured in that capacity for the next eleven years. It still seemed, in 1866, that it was in the minds of God and Mr. Noyes that "fruit-growing should take the precedence of farming."¹⁰

Subsistence aside, the Perfectionists were not averse to making money from horticultural efforts. They sold produce and nursery trees. Inspired by the canning precedents of a Fourierist commune, the North American Phalanx, they turned to developing the technology of vegetable preservation in 1854.¹¹ In 1856, the Oneida Community test marketed tomatoes preserved in cans and jars. What came to be called the fruit business began in earnest in 1858 with retail sale of foods hermetically sealed in glass jars. Over the course of the next decade, the Community would sell preserved cherries, corn, grapes, peas, strawberries, tomatoes, and many other fruits and vegetables packed not only in glass but also in tin cans.¹² The fruit business resulted from men and women working together in horticultural pursuits.

Mingling and Gender Relations

Bees, the volunteer task groups invented by the Oneida Community in the early days, occurred inside and out but were chiefly appreciated for encouraging the sexes to mix in activities out of doors (see figures 6 and 7).

"For women," Charlotte Miller enthused, "the Bee is an unparalleled opportunity for exercise in the open air—and in companionship with men, too, which is of itself invigorating—and for men it takes off the ruggedness and drudgery of labor, by association with those whose presence naturally calls out the refinement and chivalry of their nature."¹³ By the early 1850s, the practice of men and women working together had become intertwined with the Community's interest in horticulture. "As horticulture supplants farming, and advancing civilization modifies man's business in many respects, the association of the sexes in work, will of course be more agreeable as well as practicable," explained one Bible communist. Gardens and orchards, said another, provide a wonderful opportunity for the aggregation of men, women, and children in "the industry of Horticulture," a mixture that transforms work into an occasion for social festivity.¹⁴

Finding that they enjoyed it immensely, mingling raised the Perfectionists' consciousness about gender equality. Noyes caught the enthusiasm for

FIGURE 6. Bible communists gather for a bee to hoe and rake, 1867.

FIGURE 7. Bee to make traveling bags, 1865. Community members thought this scene would "be interesting to some as indicating how Communism renders labor attractive" (*Circular*, June 19, 1865). Note the man reading from a book.

the change in distant Brooklyn. In 1850, he was saying that a woman's life in marriage was like a slave's bondage in the South. "I vow to the Lord before you women in the name of all the men," he declared in 1853, "that we will do the fair thing by you. We will try to understand and appreciate you, and remove the torments and encumbrances between you and the men. We will make room for you and you shall have all the chance you want. Before God here tonight, we give you free papers."[15]

As they realized how much their lifestyle improved women's lives, the Oneidans were inspired to lighten domestic drudgery further with such labor-saving gadgetry as the sewing machine. "To relieve them [the women] some-what from the exclusive and unhealthy occupation of sewing," the association, in 1852, "furnished itself with one of Singer's celebrated Sewing Machines, which is found admirably adapted to the economies of Community life." A second machine purchased a few years later was described as "an iron arm" coming to the aid of women.[16] At one Community meeting in 1857, "a consci-entious brother wished to know whether woman had her full rights here. . . . He wanted to know if any of our women felt themselves limited or oppressed, or in any way deprived of their natural rights." The reply was no. The women said they "felt no oppression, but *help* every way from the men, and that they saw no distinction of privilege in the Community; women enjoy all the advan-tages for personal improvement and expansion that men do."[17]

However sympathetic men in the outside world might be to women's equality, they never put their hands to "women's work." In the Oneida Community, in contrast, men participated in such traditionally feminine tasks as cooking, waiting on tables, and performing housework, including housecleaning. To do laundry, probably the most onerous domestic chore, they assigned fifteen men to work with fifteen women washing, ironing, and folding the clothing.[18] At one point, they discussed whether it wouldn't be fair for the men to adopt new costumes the way women did—apparently an inconclusive discussion.[19] Lawrence Foster, the researcher who has studied these developments most closely, was impressed "by the extent to which the Community broke down or undercut traditional male and female occupational patterns and authority relations."[20] At Oneida, men and women worked together "not only more than in Fourier's books, but more often than at any contemporary commune," historian Carl Guarneri concluded.[21]

Perfectionists understood that their way of life flew in the face of gender segregation in the outside world, which increasingly consigned men to the workplace and confined women in the household. They were sincere in their goal to correct the injustice of such relations and consciously integrated men and women in most forms of work. There was, however, a countertendency for women to prefer occupational roles prescribed by custom as appropriately feminine. Throughout the existence of the Community, for example, traditional household work was mostly performed by women. The Oneida Community perception of the problem was that women resisted leaving the domestic sphere and held themselves back by not being assertive. "We notice that the women are the last to acquire and the slowest to use their liberty in our meetings," a Community member noted in 1859. "They are exhorted to speech rather than to silence."[22] Women, another thought, seemed to prefer "their sewing, knitting, braiding and other womanly industries" to contributing their thoughts to Community discussions. "Several years ago," one Perfectionist wrote in the *Circular*,

> the men of the Community were fain to quarrel—good-naturedly of course—with the women, because of their habit of taking sewing to the evening gatherings in the Hall. "We wish," said the men, "that the women would lay aside this work which must take so much of their attention, become freer of speech, and join equally with us in discussing whatever subject may be introduced." To please their brothers the women now and then consented to this change, but the wished-for freedom was not so easily gained. The women did not feel at home; they scarcely knew how to dispose of their hands; so, very soon they fell into the good old way. "If our fingers are busy," said they, "our heads and hearts are busy also, and we can pay even better attention to the subject of your conversation, though we have the appearance of pre-occupation." The men not only gave up the contest, but some of them have actually gone over to the enemy, and may be seen in the evenings enjoying themselves quite skillfully in such feminine accomplishments as knitting, crocheting and darning.[23]

An anonymous writer complained, in 1859, that women were not embracing outdoor labor with sufficient enthusiasm because of what they called the "tire-lady spirit,"

> which would always be glad to creep in and install itself in the place of our principle that it is good for woman to associate with man in his work outdoors. We started here with the principle of mingling the sexes in labor, and cultivating a robust race of women; but the law of habit and worldly fashion resist our purpose with great force and pertinacity. The love of dress is the natural rival of this principle. If we are dressed very nicely, we are disinclined to work out-doors, and on the other hand, if we forsake manly industry, the vanities of dress are likely to employ our hands.[24]

Women were disposed to love of dress to appear well in the eyes of others, reasoned the Bible communists. That required considerable sewing, which in turn prevented them from asserting themselves in family meetings. Hence, their priority in mingling the sexes in daily labor was to get women out of the domestic sphere and into the male world, to make women more like female men, as Noyes put it in *Bible Argument*.[25]

"The amelioration of woman's lot in our manner of life is too manifest not to be seen by all" was a sentiment frequently expressed in Community writings.[26] It was true. In the Oneida Community, women supposedly were liberated from marriage bondage. Almost certainly, they were relieved from propagative and domestic drudgery to an extent unmatched in the outside world. Going further, the Community redefined the ideal of gender relations around the practice of bees in which men and women cooperated happily in horticultural pursuits. Mingling, as a result, paved the way for practical advances in female standing and for the development of gender relations astonishingly progressive by the standards of their day. Relations between the sexes were more truly equitable in the Oneida Community during the 1850s than they were elsewhere in Victorian America.

Victorian Sexology

As they redefined gender relations, Oneidans also established complex marriage as a living practice. In Putney, sexual communism was a small-scale affair involving several couples swapping spouses. In Oneida, heavenly matrimony embraced the sexual activity of hundreds. How the emotional volatility linked with sex was enlisted to the cause of the whole and how it was constructively channeled is a topic, like gender, grounded in Oneida's formative years. Discussion of the subject, however, must draw on information that will take us into the commune's later period.

Before describing the Community's career of complex marriage, a caveat is in order. The Oneida Community was—and probably still is—best known for its unconventional sexual mores. However, some Community assumptions about sex that seem to us exotic and even bizarre were characteristic of the age. Oneida notions about interpersonal electricity, ejaculatory danger, and masturbatory evil, for example, would have seemed perfectly sensible to other Victorian Americans. These will be noted, then set aside to focus on what was more purely Oneidan about sex.

All human interaction, it was generally supposed, involved some sort of magnetic connection between the parties involved. The term "magnetism" derived from the popular fields of animal magnetism and mesmerism, which held, as Noyes explained it, that "there is a subtle fluid in the human body, in some respects like electricity, which may be transmitted in divers ways, from one to another, and under certain circumstances, may produce astonishing and beneficial effects of various kinds." This "nervous fluid" was stored in the heart, which Noyes believed was an invisible organ in the middle of the chest.[27] Some people, "magnetizers," had a much higher charge of magnetism than others. Such folk could, in some fashion, project their magnetic "effluences" outward to influence others of lesser will and magnetic potency.[28] Noyes was thought to be a magnetizer. A disgruntled apostate, for example, described Noyes's power in these terms: "In February, 1843, Mr. Noyes began to try his skill in Animal Magnetism. Being impressible, I was the subject of many of his experiments. By reason of their continuation for some weeks . . . a diseased state of mind and body was produced. For many months I suffered a very great depression of spirits. I felt myself in connection and rapport with influences which caused the keenest mental anguish."[29] Far from being considered eccentric, theories about magnetism were thought to have great explanatory power.[30]

Personal magnetic power played an important role in sex because coitus supposedly involved the transmission of magnetic energy—having nothing to do with semen—between the partners. In *Bible Argument*, Noyes explained that "sexual intercourse, pure and simple, is the conjunction of the organs of union, and the interchange of magnetic influences, or conversation of spirits, through the medium of that conjunction."[31] One of his lovers, Tirzah Miller, illustrated how this worked: "Slept with J.H.N. I dreaded to go, because he must discover my unmagnetic condition. He did fast enough. In the night he said: 'Would you like some criticism?' 'Yes, I should very much.' 'Well, there is no disguising the fact that you don't attract me. You impress me with the feeling that your sexual nature has been abused by your entering into sexual intercourse without appetite. Spirits of men which are indigestible to you have come between you and me.'"[32]

Another sexual belief of Noyes was that a man's supply of seed was limited. The male should hold on to it because seed, in Noyes's view, "has an *immanent* value, and is in its best function while retained. It is the presence of the seed, and not the discharge of it, that makes the bull superior to the ox." Keeping seed inside is good, Community member George Miller explained, because the seminal secretion "is reabsorbed by the blood and adds enormously to a man's magnetic, mental, and spiritual force." Losing seed is bad because ejaculation drains a man's life and renders him vulnerable to disease.[33]

This sort of thing also was not unusual and in fact accorded with the popular ideas of Sylvester Graham, whose health crusade in the 1830s–1840s did much to influence American attitudes not only toward diet (see chapter 4) but also toward sex. The key to health, according to Graham, was restraint in all expressions of emotion and passion. While emphasizing nutrition as important to well-being, he also had much to say about the negative effects of sex and masturbation. The emission of male seed was injurious, Graham insisted, and should be avoided as much as possible.[34]

If the seed is not expended to impregnate, the emission is wasteful, useless, and, according to Noyes, "the useless expenditure of seed certainly is not natural." Noyes regarded most male ejaculations as examples of "the same seed-wasting business," whether occurring in ordinary matrimonial intercourse or as the result of masturbation, which Noyes, in company with a great many of his Victorian contemporaries, particularly deplored.[35]

Ideas about magnetic exchange, retention of seed, and abhorrence of masturbation did not set the Oneida Community apart from the outside world. What was distinctive about Oneida was the affirmation that coitus was spiritually uplifting and fun.

Sex at Oneida

Oneida sex was a means of uniting with God.[36] In *Bible Argument*, Noyes emphasized what he saw as the religious aspects of sex as both heavenly practice and a means to hasten Christ's return. Heterosexual activity in pairs was a form of worship re-creating the godhead and bringing the participants closer to God. Noyes's aim, according to Robert Parker,

> was to integrate sexual love with the life of the spirit, to make a sacrament of physical love, the outward and active sign of inward, spiritual grace. Love should be a science as well as an art—the deepest and most engrossing of all sciences. Only through this function, so long abused and misunderstood, could men ever truly experience unity with God and Humanity. Its value was not merely in a rite sacredly fulfilled, but in its power to awaken complete realization of divine unity—the knowledge that all love is one and indivisible. Sexual love, transcending individual consciousness, Noyes explained, provided the experience through which we, as members of the human race, are enabled to experience the ecstasy of true communion, to break through the dark isolation of egotism and self-hood.[37]

As one Community member put it, the Perfectionists considered their sexual organs to be "the highest instruments of praise and worship in the Heavenly world."

But, that person added, the Oneidans claimed liberty "for the free use of our sexual organs as a means of social enjoyment."[38] What he meant was that, in addition to its spiritual value, sex at Oneida was celebrated as pleasurable. In the bigger picture, Noyes insisted that life was meant to be enjoyed. People should be happy and, if necessary, work hard to be happy because human joy pleases God. Oneida Perfectionism "was a happy religion, never a gloomy one," remarked one who grew up in it. "The grown folks seemed almost as bent on being happy as they did on being good." God, in Noyes's opinion, was "not on the side of asceticism . . . God made our bodies to rejoice and be happy in his creation." As a part of life, sex was something given by God and intended, by God, for people to enjoy to please him.[39]

Oneida sex was said to vastly increase the satisfaction of both lovers, who, thanks to male continence, "may enjoy the highest bliss of sexual fellowship for any length of time, and from day to day, without satiety or exhaustion," as Noyes thought.[40] The male was supposed to experience elevated spiritual pleasure, the result—apparently—of suppressing ejaculation, thereby subordinating his interest to that of his lover. The female's amative nature was "developed to its fullest extent" in the estimation of Perfectionist George E. Cragin, who also reported that women experienced orgasms. Medical doctor and Community child Hilda Herrick said some women welcomed the variety of lovers made possible by complex marriage. That diversity, in one known instance, amounted to having four sexual partners in the course of a month. A popular woman, according to a popular woman, might have intercourse two to three times a week.[41]

Having longer and more enjoyable sex experiences meant that married life in the Oneida Community was, as Noyes enthused, "permanently sweeter than courtship, or even the honey-moon"—the high points of romantic excitement in matrimony of the outside world. "A state of continuous courtship," Community member Abel Easton agreed, was an accurate characterization of the communal experience. Pierrepont Noyes fondly recalled the romantic atmosphere that seemed to emanate from the adults. The sexual dimension of Community existence rendered life more colorful there than elsewhere, in the memory of that writer, and enlivened the elderly with "a vivid, youthful interest in life that looked from their eyes and spoke in their voices and manners."[42]

The Bible communists, in contrast to the Shakers, had nothing against reproduction. Indeed, they said they wanted to have children but awaited more comfortable circumstances to do so. In the meantime, they practiced male continence as birth control and as a means to free women from propagative drudgery. Avoiding ejaculation may not be a certain way to prevent conception, but it seemed to work reasonably well. Over the first twenty years, Community women bore about thirty-five children, a birth rate they thought was very low. Many, perhaps even most, of the children were regarded as intentionally conceived. Noyes, for example, claimed in November 1849 that not a single involuntary impregnation had occurred for two years, a period including at least nine conceptions.[43] If a policy existed for having children, it was that they would raise a pair of children annually, "just enough for playfellows." Some births may have been authorized by the Community in cases of women wishing to have children but approaching menopause.[44]

Those joining the Oneida Community were expected to enter into the holy ordinance of group matrimony or pantogamy in which heterosexuality was taken for granted, monogamy was forbidden, celibacy was discouraged, and free love was strongly encouraged. Each individual was to love all family members of the other sex as a spouse and without jealousy or selfishness. There was to be no exclusiveness in love that would encourage the formation of couples. This did not mean that one could not find particular enjoyment in one partner—so long as it increased one's capacity to love everyone more and nourished love for all. If it did not, it was classified as a relationship exclusive to two egos focused solely on themselves. Contemptible and selfish, that kind of bond was a sin called "special love."[45]

Such was theory; the reality was more daunting. Oneida Perfectionists taking up complex marriage were venturing into unknown and dangerous territory. The early years of sexual adventuring were turbulent, a time when—as Noyes put it—the Bible communists were beset by "gales and icebergs and elemental perils."[46] Most came into the Oneida family as conventionally married couples supposed to engage in sex with new partners and to overcome jealousy and all negative sentiments. They thought of themselves as respectable, sober folk of good character. None was connected with the radical sex avant-garde of New York City. Few joined (or were allowed to join) seeking sex.[47] It is difficult to imagine these rather straitlaced people as sexually adventuresome and libidinously motivated. What was their reaction to the doctrine of group sex?

Sewell Newhouse, the blacksmith who brought animal traps to Oneida, attacked a man he saw walking in the garden with his wife. On first learning of complex marriage, Joseph Ackley "came under sore trial, but my past acquaintance with what I had believed to be truth convinced me of the truthfulness of [Noyes's] doctrine." Invalid Hettie Macknet was deeply shocked to learn of Noyes's heavenly system of matrimony. But believing her malady was cured by Perfectionism, she bought into Noyes's teaching wholeheartedly. When Catherine Hobart of the Putney Community married James Baker, she helped to reconcile her husband to the idea of complex marriage by "prayer and supplication."[48] Many who joined probably were of this sort: they took up the practice at a spouse's behest. While all were initially taken aback by the idea of free love, almost all made the transition into acceptance.

Noyes conveyed enthusiasm for embarking on complex marriage as an adventure. Early on, for example, he addressed several young men in these terms. "I propose," he wrote to them, that we

> maintain our freedom from the favoritism in which many of our married brethren are entangled, and study to be liberal and diffusive in our love and attention to the other sex. Let it be in our ambition to hasten the grand consummation of the courtship which is going on in this Association between all the men as one man and all the women as one woman. To this end let us consider whether we may not do good, get good, and feel good by drawing nearer than we have to certain worthy young ladies whose charms have not yet been fully appreciated. . . . Let us also be heroes in love, and train our hearts to scale the heights above us as well as to enjoy the beauties of our own level.[49]

The transition in Oneida was furthered by the force of peer-group pressure. The more difficult cases, Foster observed, could involve "the suspension or limitation of sexual privileges until the ostracized individual began to shape up to Community standards."[50] And the transition was structured by rules. Noyes, from the distance of Brooklyn, proposed guidelines for institutionalizing amativeness on two occasions. On one, in 1852, he recommended a formal protocol for lovemaking. First, "the sexes should sleep apart," he counseled. "Their coming together should not be to sleep but to edify and enjoy. Sleeping is essentially an individual function that precludes sociability." The sexual encounters or "social interviews" should be limited to an hour or two. Avoiding satiety would encourage the partners to "think of each other with pleasure afterwards." Since "the tongue has its field to itself all day," the partners should avoid excessive conversation in favor of "sagacious, reflective observation."[51] Second, a man's proposal for a love interview would be conveyed to a woman by a third party, an older woman superior in spirituality to the potential lovers. "This method is favorable to modesty and also to freedom. It allows of refusals without embarrassment." Such an intermediary advises the lovers, prevents "inexpediencies," "excludes selfish privacy and makes love a Community affair." Having an intermediary brought the matter "in some measure under the inspection of the Community."[52] "So shall the

spirit of truth go with you and perfect you in the heavenly art" was the blessing Noyes dispatched to Oneida along with these instructions.[53]

Central members—Noyes and his closest associates—were well informed
on who was sleeping with whom, according to George E. Cragin. That group
monitored sexual couplings within the family to head off and to discourage disruptive love affairs. The diary of one Community woman spanning
the late 1860s to the 1870s indicated how her intimate bonds with various
Community men were influenced by her long-standing lover—John Noyes.
Another Community diary documented how a man and a woman, drawn to
one another, were pressured to mate with others in the interests of the Community's later eugenics program. And one "proud fellow," it was remembered, "committed the double sin of loving one girl too much and another
too little. Since his feelings were obvious from his conduct, the young man
one day learned that his loved one was in Wallingford and that the Committee recommended, as a sort of punishment for his sin, that he become a
father by the girl whom he did not like. So strong were the sanctions of the
Committee that the young man did not demur."[54]

On the other hand, during the nearly two years of time chronicled in the
Community Journal, only a single instance is recorded of Noyes intervening in
Oneida's love life. On that occasion, Frank Wayland-Smith and Tirzah Miller
were criticized for continuing their affair after being "pointedly censured by
Mr. Noyes and the family." There is, in fact, little to indicate that most Com-
munity members living the life regarded sexual arrangements as coercive.[55]

The Oneida Community was not a totalitarian state structured to compel
obedience. Compliance depended on the consent of the governed, which
was based on faith in the rightness and wisdom of Noyes's inspiration. In
matters of sex, that meant edicts about partners had to comport with an
accepted principle of justice. It was a matter of Perfectionist pride that, unlike
monogamous marriages in the outside world, sex at Oneida required mutual
consent. Their fundamental rule, according to a Community handbook of
1867, was that *"persons shall not be obliged to receive under any circumstances the
attentions of those whom they do not like* [emphasis in the original]." The Perfectionists would not permit rape, participant Abel Easton stated, and, on the
contrary, were "pledged to protect all their members from disagreeable social
approaches. Every woman is free to refuse every man's attention." There
was no compulsion for anyone to have sex, Perfectionist George E. Cragin
claimed. Community member Martha Reeve agreed that the Oneida system
accorded women control of their own bodies. The most basic principle—
"well known and carried out," was that no one be forced to receive the amorous attentions of another. "We abhor rapes, whether committed under the

cover of marriage or elsewhere." And when we say this, Reeve added, "we mean it, without any reservation or exception, and we mean to live by it both in spirit and in the letter."[56]

Sex and Ascending Fellowship

A second instance of rule making occurred in 1849 when Noyes introduced the principle of ascending fellowship. This concept earlier was noted as Noyes's assertion of authority, in absentia, over Oneida (chapter 3) and as a socially integrative mechanism taken up at Oneida (chapter 4). Additionally, ascending fellowship was relevant to complex marriage. The rule promoted widespread participation in sex and defined authority over choice of sexual partners. It could be administered hierarchically from Noyes down, and it could operate horizontally through the action of peer-group opinion. Ascending fellowship, they thought, was their most effective measure for domesticating sex, for channeling its potentially divisive tendencies toward cooperative results.[57]

Ascending fellowship also encouraged younger people to associate with older and, as they thought, more spiritually endowed partners. It supplied the rationale for initiating the young into the family's love life and, beyond that, for educating and socializing them in the sexual mores of the Community. "The principle which lies at the foundation of our social system," Noyes wrote in 1851,

> is that in all safe, healthy fellowships the ascending fellowship must prevail. Though we may be baffled, slandered and abused, we shall at last establish the principle that the way to induct the young into a true state of amativeness is to have them mate with older persons. There is a natural attraction between superiors and inferiors, the old and the young, the spiritual and novices, and it is an attraction that is necessary and desirable for both. The time will come when a young person, with no forcing, will naturally be led by the hand of some older person in matters of love; when the idea of persons that are not spiritual embarking on the tempestuous ocean of amativeness without a pilot will be regarded [as] absurd.[58]

The arrangement of ascending fellowship was applied to young males needing to learn the technique of male continence, which at first was a challenging task. A plan to introduce "the young men to the freedom of the Association through the more spiritual women has been attended with difficulties," Noyes noted in 1850. "Mrs. Cragin has lost her equilibrium in the attempt to carry it out."[59]

When the principle was applied to young women, Noyes was in the ascendancy. It was he who usually initiated the young women at puberty, an arrangement his son Theodore regarded as the keystone of the social fabric. "In our society, the consequences of the first sexual experience were to lead the women on to an honorable position, in every respect as desirable, from our point of view, as in hers in a monogamic marriage. . . . It eliminated the whole mass of sentiment and passion which, in the world, revolves around the question of virginity."[60] In performing the office of "first husband," Noyes came to enjoy the trust and love of many young girls as expressed by one of them (perhaps Harriet Worden) in a letter to Noyes:

> Last evening there was a call for volunteers to give a little extra help in the trap-shop, at putting together traps; and as I *used* to work at that, I thought I would volunteer. . . . My work—the noises and the odors of the shop,—everything around me—reminded me of old times; and when not looking up, I could almost imagine that you were standing at the bench with me. And so my thoughts went gliding down the gulf of time, and I saw myself at your side, heating springs for you to hammer out, a girl of fifteen just waking up to the idea that this world contained many things not dreamed of at the children's house. Then I found myself weighing steel for you, and could see your every attention to detail, and myself grown a little older, having just launched out in the great ship of experience, and met one or two icebergs; confiding in you for guidance, yet wayward and thoughtless. Again, the trap-shop was enlarged, and you and I were putting together traps with the greatest zest. I could see you screwing the posts so carefully, and inventing little improvements until we reached the maximum of speed. With every little improvement and incident in the trap-shop, my own life seemed intertwined; for thinking of one brought up the other; and at this stage, I could see myself wild with youthful excitement—having seen the end of several flirtations, but under new fascinations, and still clinging to you as my guide and refuge. And with this reminiscence, I was truly astonished at your patience with me. I cannot imagine what encouraged you to hold on to me, for I was indeed very wayward, but God alone put it into your heart.[61]

The extent to which youngsters agreed to be initiated is unclear. And inherent in ascending fellowship was a potential for abuse in which some—especially young women—might be pressured into having sex with partners they did not desire. "Always," Jessie Kinsley remembered of her youthful love life in the Community, "there were the changing and the steadfast lovers—some heartache, much happiness. What seems now to have been a strange experience was then but natural. One formed no habits to dull the edge of love except, perhaps, as one was obliged to maintain too rigidly the principle of Ascending Fellowship."[62] But when it came to maintaining the principle too rigidly, Martha Reeve vehemently insisted:

> We do not say that the members of our Community have always been so free from selfishness that no instances or departure from, or violation of this principle [i.e., no one obliged to have sex] have ever occurred, nor do we say that it has been an easy task to subdue and tame our passions, and in respect to them to "put on the Lord Jesus Christ," nor do we claim that it has yet been fully attained in every case, if it has in general; but we do say that no known instance of such departure or violation has occurred without faithful criticism, and that we are aiming steadily, and working heartily for full attainment in a social state where the "members shall have the same care one for another."[63]

In successfully practicing free love for thirty years, the Oneida Community provides, in Foster's view, "one of the very few examples in history of a long-lived system of group marriage."[64] But how well did it work? One approach to answering that is to consider what was going wrong as indicated by the sexual problems addressed in mutual criticism. In the 1863–1864 record of public criticisms, only about a third of the sessions focused obviously on difficulties of this sort (12 of 34). The issue, overwhelmingly, was one of pleasure-seeking in love (5 instances: 4 men, 1 woman), or of exclusivity in love (5 instances: 3 men, 1 woman, and 1 couple).[65]

Admittedly, what the Community found objectionable in the attitude or behavior of a few individuals is an indirect measure of communal satisfaction with complex marriage. More to the point is what Perfectionists said when asked how they felt. In 1861, the Community conducted a survey to ascertain: "Has your social expression for the last year been encouraging, or otherwise?—and in what particulars?" Of 130 respondents, 49 answered affirmatively and 26 answered "affirmatively in part" (a combined 58 percent). "In commenting on social matters in the Community," it was noted, "criticism is given by some on pleasure-seeking or insincerity in love. One or two speak of observing a spirit of exclusiveness, or what is called the marriage-spirit, leading to the pairing off of persons under the influence of special attractions, by which social benefits are not equally distributed. Several writers join in expressing the wish that there might be more free, full and systematic discussion of social relations in the evening meetings."[66]

How smoothly did complex marriage function at Oneida? It probably worked about as well as marriage elsewhere and to the extent its participants made it work. What Jessie Kinsley recalled of marital existence was that "all Community women were conscientious—by this I mean that they all *tried* to be unselfish. The *marvel*, though, in Community life was the unselfish spirit of the men toward one another, and their freedom from the instinctive desire for sole possession. I know how unselfish they were."[67]

By the early 1850s, the practice of men, women, and children working together outside became bound up with the Community's interest in tending fruit trees, berry bushes, and vegetable gardens. Horticulture, it was thought, would take the Community to a higher spiritual plane and bring about a more advanced state of civilization. Since women seemed especially valuable in gardening, horticulture came to be regarded as the fundamental activity for drawing the sexes together in labor.

Noyes never envisioned mingling as a measure to promote equal rights for women, nor did he elaborate a theory of horticultural subsistence. He never proposed—and probably could not have imagined—that such a lifestyle would elevate the standing of women. Nevertheless, all of this came about when a horticultural regime was invented in real life. Oneidans discovered that bringing men and women together in outdoor work was socially satisfying and spiritually enriching. It pleased them to realize they were advancing female standing in practical ways. In effect and in Noyes's absence, the Oneida Community fashioned gender relations that were essentially egalitarian.

And it was people in Oneida who translated radical new mores of sex into reality. During the early years, Community members worked out the emotionally challenging terms of sexual communism well enough to establish a functioning system of group marriage. Sex at Oneida was supposed to be a spiritually uplifting experience in which the partners recreated and drew nearer to God. It was a pleasurable, unselfish act in which the male suppressed ejaculation to relieve the female's fear of pregnancy and to heighten her enjoyment.

There were hierarchical regulations at work in the Community's sexual arrangements. Noyes and his inner circle monitored romantic couplings to discourage amative selfishness and head off socially disruptive affairs. The system of ascending fellowship encouraged the young to have sex with older partners. Strictures of control were softened and ameliorated, however, by a deeply engrained notion of justice: sex in the Oneida Community required the consent of both partners. No compulsion, the Perfectionists claimed, was permitted in love.

CHAPTER 6

Buildings, Landscapes, and Traps

Dedicating themselves to building up community infrastructure, the Bible communists realized substantial works projects during the early 1850s, which included horticultural facilities, an irrigation system, and a large mill. They also went well beyond functional necessity to beautify their surroundings. In the mid-1850s, Brooklyn and other branch communities were abandoned, and their personnel, including John Noyes, were brought back to a now overcrowded Oneida. The Perfectionists enthusiastically planned a new Mansion House together during the ensuing years. When it was finished, the communards transformed the surrounding grounds in accordance with the most discerning standards of their day.

The Oneida Community had long been exploring ways to raise money. The most promising product available to them was a steel-jawed animal trap brought into the Community by blacksmith Sewell Newhouse. Noyes encouraged the Community to concentrate on traps and promoted mechanization in their production. Commercially successful, the making of traps became the main business of Perfectionism.

Creating Eden

Architecture, considered as belief translated into reality, provides an obvious opportunity to look beyond Noyes to see what the Perfectionists accomplished together. The commune on Oneida Creek was, as we have seen, begun by people dedicated to doing God's work and to building a new world. After the erection of a residence and a home for the children, the pace of construction actually accelerated as Oneida took form as a functioning settlement during the early 1850s and in the continued absence of Noyes.

The first Mansion House put a roof over 87 people. More residential space was needed immediately, however, because the commune grew to over 205 members by the end of 1850. Two two-story extensions were built onto the west side of the home, followed by yet another wing, a one-story affair sixty feet long, added in 1851.[1]

In 1849, the Perfectionists erected a two-story building just south of the Mansion House to house the printing press. The structure reflected Noyes's idea that the Community should be printing religious tracts. It also contained a general store selling goods to outsiders.[2] When the building burned down in 1851, the press was moved to Brooklyn. The retail store, continued at various locations over the ensuing years, would prove to be an important site for neighborly interactions. Other construction projects included cattle and horse barns and a blacksmith shop. Christened the Circularium, a new mill standing two-and-a-half stories high permitted the grinding of flour as well as the sawing of wood. It also contained shops for carpentry and mechanics. As horticulturalists, the Bible communists were particularly enthusiastic about laying out large beds for produce on the knoll above the Mansion House. Henry Seymour's strawberries were irrigated at that location by means of a steam-powered system that pumped water uphill from five hundred yards away. A greenhouse, a preserving building, and a toolshed went up nearby.[3]

Though practical in outlook, the Perfectionists looked beyond immediate necessity to beautify their surroundings. By 1849, they were planting trees and flowers for aesthetic reasons. Noyes thought this was frivolous. From his vantage in Brooklyn, he irritably recommended that the Oneidans "turn their attention from the ornamental to the profitable enterprises. Let the ornamental come in as incidental." Ignoring his advice, the upstaters persisted in creating flower plots, including the star-shaped South Garden still in existence.[4] Walkways for leisurely, contemplative strolling were laid out. "I have been engaged the last two days in marking out and working the wide paths for our new garden-ground," Jonathan Burt reported. "I confess that in this approach toward a scientific and artistic arrangement of our gardens, I find a relish which I have not been wont to have in tilling the ground." The landscape they fashioned included rustic furniture—"sofas, divans, and settees"—made from gnarled roots of white cedar by Community member Charles Ellis.[5]

These landscape embellishments could have been inspired by the Fourierists who thought that the destiny of humankind was to cultivate the planet and make it attractive. Alternatively, the Bible communists simply partook of the common outlook of the day, which called for beautifying the surroundings. Agreement was widespread that landscape gardening, also referred to as ornamental horticulture, was desirable. Unquestionably, however, the Perfectionists were reading works by the leading theorist in the emerging field of landscape architecture. A. J. Downing taught that a park ground around one's country home rendered the property attractive, made domestic life more enjoyable, and increased local attachments. A properly embellished lawn, he also maintained, elevated the moral character of the neighborhood.[6]

Henry Thacker, the Oneida Association's fruit tree specialist, may have been influenced by Downing when he planted a tulip tree (still standing) in 1851, the same year Downing recommended planting such trees.[7] Others articulated Downingesque sentiments more explicitly. A gardener named Lemuel Bradley, for example, called attention "to the beauty of the landscape. We do not always want to look abroad with the *farmer's* eye. We have a human eye to please, an eye for the beautiful and the picturesque; and the naked field is less pleasing than one dotted here and there with trees." Another, Alfred Barron, echoed Downing's sentiments when he described the garden and flower grounds as deliberately created sources of delight to the refined person capable of appreciating beauty.[8]

The 1862 Mansion House

Noyes's establishment in Brooklyn in early 1849 proved to be only the first of several Perfectionist communities outside of Oneida. Collectively styled the "Associated Communities," they were small groups residing in Manlius, New York; Cambridge, Vermont; Newark, New Jersey; and Wallingford, Connecticut—as well as the Oneidans who had moved to Brooklyn or a few who had reoccupied their old stomping ground in Putney, Vermont. These communities seemed to accrete haphazardly when a handful of people, staying where they lived, declared allegiance to Noyes's movement, or when people joined established communities and gifted their farms to the association. The largest of these was the Wallingford, Connecticut, property of Henry and Emily Allen donated to the cause in 1851. None of the small centers was self-supporting. The maintenance of Brooklyn, which must have required

thousands of dollars, was an especially heavy drain on the original association in central New York.[9]

The passing of John Miller, the association's financier and treasurer,
brought Oneida's period of communal development without Noyes to a
close. Harriet Worden credited Miller with "the successful management
of our finances, and the toleration gained for our movement in this State."
His death—ascribed by some to overwork and worry—focused attention
on the organization's financial health.[10] Oneida, under Miller's stewardship,
had borne the weight of the Associated Communities. With Miller gone,
with anemic income, and with assets rapidly dwindling, the folly of Oneida
struggling to support Brooklyn and the other colonies could no longer be
denied. The time had come, Noyes conceded, to contract and consolidate.
Accordingly, Perfectionists closed up the various outposts in 1854–1855 and
assembled at Oneida to concentrate on fiscal responsibility. Noyes himself
returned at the end of 1854. The only satellite community allowed to continue was the one at Wallingford.

The ingathering created a housing crisis. "We need more room," a Perfectionist wrote in 1855. Never were so many persons "found before living
in one family under so small an amount of roof as ours." They determined
to build a new family residence as soon as they could afford it. "We take this
as a hint from the Lord to go to work vigorously and make money, which
we shall endeavor to do. In due time we are confident that the interior life
that is given to us will also have the means of clothing itself in fitting forms
of external excellence and beauty."[11] Discussing a future home became one
of the Community's favorite activities over the next few years. Everyone had
a hand in the planning, which, according to architectural historian Dolores
Hayden, was an important participatory activity contributing to group cohe-
sion and identity.[12] What resulted—the second Mansion House and mani-
cured grounds—was a tangible expression of collective will and action.

The 1848 Mansion House nestled at the base of a knoll, supposedly the
most commanding topographical feature in the vicinity. The Community's
first decision was to site the new home on the crest of that knoll, a location
that, according to a notice appearing in 1857, was suggested by Noyes and
unanimously seconded by the Community.

The advantages of this spot are its conveniences of access, its nearness to
the existing buildings of the Community, its dry situation and good prospect. The most apparent objection that rises against the locality, is the
fact that the building and its surroundings will occupy some of our choic-
est garden ground that is now used for the production of strawberries,

grapes and vegetables. But on the whole we want just such land for our site, and all the associations connected with this spot are home-like and loving. It will be in the center of what has been the favorite promenade of old and young since the beginning of the Community.[13]

The Perfectionists wanted a better and bigger home, but one that was still eminently practical. "We are convinced that simplicity, absence of pretension, and the straightforward adaption [sic] of means to end, will ultimately prove, in architecture as in all things else, to be the truest standard of taste," one of them wrote. At the same time, the new home would exemplify what a community dwelling should be. "We expect," added another, "that like the society it is intended for, it will be original, expressive of new ideas, and we shall seek to have it combine all that is best in material, form and arrangement."[14] Although many possible models were discussed, published accounts say little about what the building would actually look like. With respect to style, for example, one can learn only that the Perfectionists were considering various looks, including one they thought was rather stylish.

"The Italian style, with its broad, nearly flat roof, its verandas and arcades, and more prominent campanile or tower, has become quite popular," it was reported in 1858. "There is much in this style adapted to the wants and tastes of this country and wealthy men of the world, and consequently it is quite a favorite, and no doubt is an improvement; but we do not think that even this style is alone adapted to characterize a Community home."[15]

In fact, the 1862 Mansion House turned out to be an "Italian Villa" building featuring a tower, a low gabled roof with cupola, and a porch described as arcaded (see figure 8). Architect Erastus Hamilton's design probably was inspired by examples of villas in Italian style illustrated in the most popular architectural handbook of the day, *The Architecture of Country Houses*, by the day's most eminent theorist of landscaping, A. J. Downing.[16]

Little is said in Community accounts about the collective process of decision making. A good example of what probably took place is afforded by discussion concerning a later wing intended to house the Community's children. After making the decision to build it, the Community directed Hamilton to prepare a set of architectural suggestions for the new construction.[17] After due consideration, the commune rejected most of Hamilton's proposal. For one thing, the architect's idea to continue the Italian Villa style of the existing building into the addition was unacceptable. Most Perfectionists, it turned out, preferred the newer Second Empire look. More importantly, Hamilton was not thinking big enough to suit Community tastes. The Children's Wing realized in 1869 was at least three times the size of what Hamilton first illustrated.

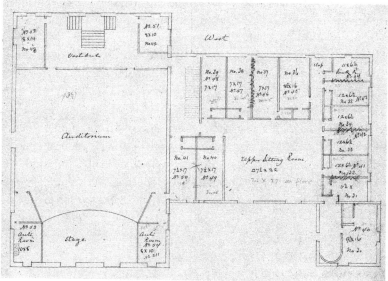

FIGURE 8. Architectural drawings of the 1862 Mansion House: elevation view of the front facade and plan of the second floor. The Italian Villa exterior projected respectability, substance, and success. The interior facilitated comfortable Perfectionist living with a communal meeting space for shared entertainment ("auditorium"), a common area for sociable mingling ("Upper Sitting Room"), and individual bedrooms reflecting a preference for sleeping alone.

As regards deliberations for this, the second Mansion House, we know there was considerable debate over construction materials. The advocates for the leading contenders—brick and stone—agreed, at one point, to settle the issue with a game of chess, which, ending in a draw, resolved nothing.

Those in favor of brick set up a brickyard northwest of the Mansion House, where in 1860 they fashioned a 40,000-brick kiln. The product, however, was defective, and in the end the Oneida Community had to purchase about 330,000 bricks. Meanwhile, Jonathan Burt and others began drawing stone from a nearby quarry. Their limestone ended up as the basement foundation, in which a cornerstone was laid in April 1861.[18] These questions were debated heatedly, and, looking back, the Perfectionists were proud to have overcome contentiousness. "When we built our new house," Erastus Hamilton recalled, "how many were the different minds about material, location, plan! How were our feelings wrought up! Party-spirit ran high. There was the stone party, the brick party, and the concrete-wall party. Yet by patience, forbearing one with another and submitting one to another, the final result satisfied every one. Unity is the essential thing."[19]

The Perfectionists had built the first Mansion House themselves. The second was put up by hired labor. When the brick walls were completed, the Community celebrated the occasion with the workmen "who have labored on them so faithfully for the last four months. . . . A supper was prepared with wine and ice-cream for extras. The table was decorated with flowers, and at the head of it was exhibited, encircled by a wreath, the words, 'Honor to Labor.' The whole family joined in the party, with the hired masons and laborers as guests. Among the sentiments offered at the close of the meal was the following by Mr. Hamilton: 'A health to workers—honest, faithful, industrious workers. May they realize that their calling is an honorable one. God bless them and their families and build them up in all good ways.'"[20]

The Mansion House they ended up with reflected their values, of course, but also provided a physical setting facilitating the collective life they wished to live. How the Oneida Community translated years of discussion into architectural space can still be seen today in a series of three rooms laid out along an axis on the second floor (see figure 8).

The first was the Family Hall, in which the entire Community gathered to enact what came close to being a sacred ritual for them: the daily meeting. This large room was patterned not after a church but after a public theater—the "opera house," it was usually called—typical of virtually every town of the day. Its ground floor and balcony together provided seating for about six hundred people directing their attention not to a pulpit but to a stage. As a space for sharing entertainment, the Family Hall exemplified the Community's dedication to celebrating life as pleasurable for themselves and their neighbors. The Bible communists frequently staged free musical and theatrical shows for the local populace, one of which attracted eight hundred visitors.[21]

The visitor of today can inspect, next to the Family Hall, a bedroom measuring about eight by twelve feet. It was typical of the 1862 Mansion House, which provided many of the Perfectionists with a private sleeping space. That was done, presumably, to enact Noyes's advice that lovers not spend the night together. "Short interviews will be found the best. Lovers should come together for an hour or two, and should separate to sleep," because "sleeping is essentially an individual function that precludes sociability."[22] The consequence of reifying Noyes's idea was a collective accommodation to individuality and privacy unprecedented in secular communal arrangements then and perhaps now. What the Bible communists hoped was an antidote to the personal exclusiveness of bedrooms can be seen a few feet farther on. The Upper Sitting Room, one of them said, made associative life "easy and attractive."[23] It was an intermediate-size, salon-like space designed to encourage informal sociability.

All of this added up to a surprisingly comfortable and friendly environment. Inside, the building was an enlarged, bourgeois American family home, "a sort of palace of plain comfort," as one visitor remarked.[24] From the outside, it struck most as rather elegant, and all agreed it was physically impressive. As the biggest building for miles around, it broadcast a powerful message to the outside world about Victorian respectability, substance, and success. In the Civil War year of bloody battles at Antietam and Shiloh, it also connoted harmony and peace (see figure 9).

A public ceremony inaugurating the new house that summer was largely given over to martial enthusiasm and patriotic music. Expressing pro-war sentiment was not hypocrisy, the Perfectionists thought, because the cause was just. The removal of slavery would mean "the casting out of a devil from the nation—the conversion of a people from barbarism to at least a higher kind of morality." The standing-room-only crowd sang "My Country, 'Tis of Thee!" and the "Battle Hymn of the Republic." A speaker brought in from the outside declaimed on the "great struggle in which the country is now engaged." The program closed with Perfectionists and local residents together belting out "The Star-Spangled Banner."[25]

The pacifistic Perfectionists had the good fortune ("damned good luck," the townspeople called it) to escape having their men drafted during the Civil War. The Community donated money to support families whose men had been drafted and advanced more money to the county toward the payment of bounties for volunteers. "We have responded to repeated calls for aid to the poor soldier (just how often and how much we cannot state, not having kept account)," noted Community member Amasa Carr. "Our direct United States war taxes have amounted to more than $10,000," he added. "Besides

FIGURE 9. The main Community buildings, 1865. Visible (*left to right*) are the first Mansion House (1848), the Children's House (1849), the permanent Mansion House (1862), and the "Tontine" (1863).

this, our State and County taxes have more than quadrupled, in consequence of heavy bounties paid by the State and Counties for volunteers."[26] Altogether, the Bible communists contributed to Northern victory by paying, as they thought, their fair share—a business-sounding sentiment hinting at changes taking place in Community attitude.

Mansion House Grounds

Beauty in architecture and landscape were complementary and inseparable, according to A.J. Downing, who also preached that the aim of landscape gardening was to embody the ideal of the home. Downing had students among the Perfectionists who knew this, and it was they who provided the new residence with a new setting. "A plan for laying out and planting the grounds about our house, was presented and explained during the past week," it was reported in the *Circular* on March 13, 1862. "This naturally led to the subject of Landscape Gardening, and a lecture occupying nearly an hour on two meetings, historical and explanatory of the art was given by Alfred Barron." Barron's talks conveyed Downing's final word (he died in 1852) on the subject. For Downing, Barron explained, the purest embellishment resulted from choosing the finest in nature and artistically enhancing it. "The earth," Barron expiated, "is a great repository of wealth and beauty, of that which is calculated to please the eye, and minister to the happiness of man; and a great part of man's happiness lies in his power to develop and reveal these hidden treasures."[27]

Warming to his subject, and quoting the master, Barron proclaimed that knowing what to choose and how to apply it required the sensibility of a fine-arts painter. "'Our art,' says Downing, 'to appear to advantage, requires some extent of surface; its lines should lose themselves indefinitely, and quite agreeably and naturally with those of the surrounding country.'—Although nearly every man thinks himself competent to undertake rural embellish-ment, it really requires a high order of talent—even genius—to produce results really artistic."[28] Barron invited the Community to imagine that he was such an artist and that his artistry adhered not to the geometric, but to the natural school of landscaping derived from "the genius, enthusiasm and fine writing" of Downing. Even though Downing was gone, his precepts still could be studied firsthand in New York's recently completed Central Park.[29]

The natural approach to landscaping was supposed to rely on the free and flowing nature of the natural world. Yet, at the heart of a Downing pleasure park was something wholly unnatural: a perfect green lawn. In and around the greensward, gravel paths glided "in gentle sweeps and undulations," Barron enthused, "like the rich curves of beautiful women." Along the paths were clumps of such shade trees as "the noble oak, the melancholy pine, and trees from every clime that will send representatives to lend a charm by their quaint and beautiful presence; all these trees have arrayed themselves in artistic *pose*, as if standing for their pictures." This latter was a reference to Downing's con-cept of a type-form in which each species possessed its own ideal beauty. Oaks, for example, branched boldly and grandly; elms were drooping and elegant; chestnuts were broad with stately tops.[30] Barron also followed Downing's pref-erence for local plants environmentally suited to the project area.[31]

At summer's end, the results of the landscaping campaign were reported in the *Circular* in this wise: "Our new lawn, for the first time close shaven, begins to have the carpet feeling and finished reflection which is required; and notwithstanding the lack of shade, which only years can supply, with its paths and verdure pleasantly environs our Community dwelling. What-ever may be true of other objects of human art, a lawn may be watched for increasing beauty for many years."[32]

Barron's landscaping scheme centered on a graveled walkway winding around the periphery of the lawn north of the Mansion House (see figure 10).

In the near future, flower beds would be created, and Henry Thayer and a workman would build a gazebo.[33] However, the campaign to beautify the

Figure 10. The north lawn of the Mansion House, 1865. Visible here is the scope of the 1862 landscaping program.

surroundings of the Mansion House was essentially carried out by the Perfectionists in one summer.

They themselves said little about how they created the physical milieu around them. In retrospect, much of the work seemed to have been done on an impromptu and individualistic basis. "We have spent 30 years in developing the form of our estate, until it offers the eye a pleasing view," one of them mused. "There was no settled plan at the beginning; but gradually the arrangement of our grounds fell into the hands of those among us who have the most taste in landscape culture." Writing little about design process, they preferred to emphasize finished product, which they often attributed to Mr. Noyes. Nevertheless, their collective skills in defining and creating a home and a coherent physical environment around it were undeniable.[34] What they accomplished remains impressive today.

The Newhouse Trap

Back when Noyes was preparing to sail to Europe in early 1851, he sounded an alarm about running out of money.[35] The Oneida Association took the warning seriously because they, after all, paid for everyone else. Experimenting with raising money in various ways, the Oneidans discovered that trap making offered the best potential to prosper in a capitalistic economy. On Noyes's return to Oneida, trap making was developed into an enterprise that underwrote the Community's existence.

Bible communists in Oneida investigated the making of various products, including rustic furniture, brooms, and containers for travelers—carpetbags and leather satchels. They also sent out teams of peddlers to sell sewing thread (purchased elsewhere) door to door. Their most important offering, however, was steel-jawed traps for the taking of fur-bearing animals.

This seemingly odd commodity originated with Sewell Newhouse, the village blacksmith of nearby Oneida Castle. During the 1830s and 1840s, Newhouse had developed a trap superior to anything else at the time in strength—its jaws held the animal after being caught—and durability—its spring resisted brittleness and breaking in the winter cold. Newhouse could hand-forge about fifteen hundred traps a year.[36] Newhouse was a colorful character to whom attached every local anecdote about European American manliness in the outdoors and in dealings with Native Americans. While one cannot separate legend from fact, it is certain that Newhouse was well acquainted with the local Oneida Indians. Years later (1869), for example, Chief Daniel Bread—a man who led an emigration of Oneidas from New York to Wisconsin in the 1820s—called on Newhouse at the Oneida Community. For hours, the two sat together reminiscing about old times—in the Oneida language. An odd mix of talents and interests, Newhouse restocked the local creeks with salmon and designed a new cartridge for the Remington Arms company.[37]

Newhouse, then in his early forties, joined the Oneida Community in December 1848. Initially, he was put to work clearing brush in swampy areas, working in the tree nurseries, and blacksmithing. In the latter capacity, he was prohibited from making traps, apparently to test his commitment to the communal order. The idea that Newhouse's time might be best spent doing precisely that resulted from an order for five hundred muskrat traps arriving unexpectedly in December 1851. Newhouse and two assistants filled the order by the end of January 1852, then set to work to make five hundred more.[38]

It seemed obvious from the start that this was where money could be had. As noted earlier, Henry Thacker reportedly told Noyes in Brooklyn, "Why you have a perfect gold mine in that Newhouse trap. You can drive every other trap clean out of the market."[39] John Miller, the Community's treasurer, told Noyes the same thing: "I think we shall have some very nice traps . . . I think we shall make this a very profitable business." And, even with this first batch, Miller thought the Community had introduced significant improvements on Newhouse's original design. In late May, Henry Burnham, commercial agent for the Oneida Community, reported he had sold a batch of traps in Chicago "at $4.50 per dozen, and the prospect is that we can sell there at that price all we can make." Noyes approved. In March, it was reported that he "was pleased with it [the trap business] on the principle of exterminating wild beasts." The letter containing this passage goes on to explain that the wild beasts Noyes had in mind were the rats driving him to distraction in Brooklyn.[40]

Newhouse continued to make traps, and by 1853, four men were assembling them in the blacksmith shop. Producing traps already was one of the Community's larger businesses, exceeded only by the making of brooms and rustic furniture, each employing five.[41] Brooms and benches, however, offered no obvious solution to the economic crisis looming over the Associated Communities.

Not surprisingly, then, Noyes returned to Oneida with the conviction that survival depended on intensifying trap production. At that point in late 1854, he was said to be "more realistic, less visionary, more practical."[42] The apparently chastened leader declared himself ready to roll up his sleeves and get to work. He became a trap maker, mastering every aspect of the craft. Noyes personally domesticated Sewell Newhouse by getting that individual to accept the notion that traps belonged to the association and not exclusively to one blacksmith.

Turning serious collective attention to traps meant the business had to be "communitized," because trap making had been the exclusive domain of men. Integrating it into family life required softening the hard-edged male character of the enterprise. This was done by subjecting the workers to a healthy dollop of mutual criticism, then by mingling women with men in the fabrication process. People working in the trap works were encouraged to have more fun by dancing together on their breaks. Communal dancing, in fact, was begun to draw trap makers more meaningfully into the fabric of family life. At the same time, pleasurable music activities, both instrumental and vocal, were enthusiastically intensified, and theatrical projects were initiated.[43]

In the process of consolidation, an expert machinist named William Inslee was brought to Oneida from Newark, New Jersey. Noyes encouraged him to design machines that would mechanize the production process of traps. The devices Inslee built were installed in the Circularium and started up, late in 1856, with dramatic results. In 1857 the Oneida Community made twenty-six thousand traps—some five thousand more than in the first five years combined.[44]

Trap making had its scheduling difficulties. It was a seasonal industry (orders were concentrated in the late summer to fall) also subject to market fluctuation. Driven by the whimsical tastes of clothing fashion, demand for furs varied considerably. In 1858, for example, orders for traps plummeted, and only eighty-five hundred were made. That year aside, the Oneida Community manufactured roughly forty-five thousand traps annually into the early 1860s.[45]

Keeping pace with the escalating output, the Oneida Community developed new methods to publicize and sell the devices. Newhouse had been basically a one-trap person, his product being the muskrat trap—a small, single-spring affair. This model and size of trap was called the "No. 1," because there came to be a No. 2 and so on. By 1858, the Oneida Community had developed a comprehensive offering for a wide range of animals, a standardized line of traps numbered 1 through 6. By early 1861, the products were being marketed as "Newhouse's Traps"—that is, the name "Newhouse" was applied as the brand name (see figure 11).

Earlier, they had been described as Oneida Community traps or as traps made in the Community under Newhouse's supervision. Now they were simply "Newhouses." By early 1864, the name was stamped on the round, central pan of each trap: "S. Newhouse Oneida Community."[46] The Oneida Community published *The Trapper's Guide* in 1865, a book providing information about catching different animals, along with chatty articles about camping and outdoor life. Generously illustrated with wood engravings, it sold well and remained in print for fifty years. Luster was added to the Newhouse name by citing him as author.

Overall, trap making was a resounding success. By the early 1860s, the reliable traps of the Oneida Community dominated the market. "No professional trapper would look at anything else," Community member George Cragin recalled, "and its adoption by the great Hudson Bay Company placed it apparently on a safe footing. There was but one trap in the market and its name was 'Newhouse.'"[47] Traps were now the Community's financial mainstay.

In retrospect, the Oneida Community's entry into trap making could hardly have been better timed, because every aspect of the trap business began to change about 1850. After that date, the primary demand of fashionable clothing was not for beaver, whose under-fur provided the felt for men's hats. It was for smaller animals—muskrat, otter, mink, weasel, skunk, opossum—whose pelts often were used as decorative trim on the clothing of both men and women.[48] Smaller animals dictated smaller traps, and that, of course, was Newhouse's specialty. His No. 1 trap was the biggest

DESCRIPTION OF THE NEWHOUSE TRAP

There are eight different sizes of the Newhouse Trap, adapted to the capture of all kinds of animals, from the house-rat to the grizzly bear.

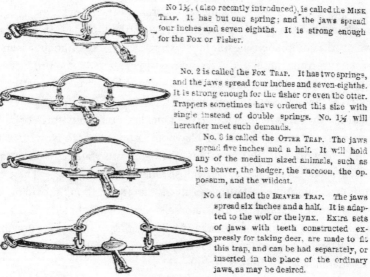

The smallest size having but recently been introduced into the series, is designated as No. 0, and is called the RAT TRAP. It has a single spring, and the jaws spread, when set, three inches and a half. It is designed for the house-rat, but is strong enough to hold the muskrat.

No. 1 is called the MUSKRAT TRAP. It has one spring, and the jaws spread four inches. It is adapted to the capture of the mink, marten, and all the smaller fur-bearing animals. John Hutchins refers to this when he says:—"I use the smallest size altogether for catching the fisher, and prefer them for that purpose. I have caught several otters, foxes, lynxes, one beaver, and one wolf in the small trap; and I use them exclusively for catching raccoons."

No 1½, (also recently introduced), is called the MINK TRAP. It has but one spring; and the jaws spread four inches and seven eighths. It is strong enough for the Fox or Fisher.

No. 2 is called the Fox TRAP. It has two springs, and the jaws spread four inches and seven-eighths. It is strong enough for the fisher or even the otter. Trappers sometimes have ordered this size with single instead of double springs. No. 1½ will hereafter meet such demands.

No. 3 is called the OTTER TRAP. The jaws spread five inches and a half. It will hold any of the medium sized animals, such as the beaver, the badger, the raccoon, the opossum, and the wildcat.

No 4 is called the BEAVER TRAP. The jaws spread six inches and a half. It is adapted to the wolf or the lynx. Extra sets of jaws with teeth constructed expressly for taking deer, are made to fit this trap, and can be had separately, or inserted in the place of the ordinary jaws, as may be desired.

No. 5.

No 5 is called the SMALL BEAR TRAP. The jaws spread eleven inches and three-fourths. The weight of each spring is two pounds and ten ounces, and the weight of the whole trap is seventeen pounds. It is adapted to the common black bear, the panther, and most of the large animals found this side of the Rocky Mountains.

All these traps are furnished with swivels, and if desired, with chains.

FIGURE 11. Newhouse traps depicted in *The Trapper's Guide*, published by the Oneida Community in 1865.

seller for many years to come. There were, at the same time, corresponding changes in production and distribution. Prior to 1850, most traps were hand forged by blacksmiths. Later in time, they were mass-produced in factories. Before 1850, traps typically were commissioned by the big fur companies, which then distributed them to trappers—native and non-native—in their employ, professionals who spent the winter in the bush trapping. After 1850, most traps were marketed by independent middlemen, the hardware dealers. In general, the traps were then sold to amateurs who were part-time trappers, many of them farm boys who set out a few traps near their homes.[49] These conditions—and the presence of Newhouse—presented the Oneida Community with a set of unique possibilities. Taking advantage of them would set them apart as the only communitarian group that became truly industrial.

But in taking that path, the Perfectionists must have wondered whether they could still aspire to a plane of higher spirituality on money raised by cruelly slaying animals. In describing the tour he was given of the Community's trap works, the visitor William Hepworth Dixon touched on this moral conundrum: "As I walked through the forges with Brother Hamilton, I could not help saying that such work seemed rather strange for a colony of Saints. He answered, with a very grave face, that the Earth is lying under a curse, that vermin are a consequence of that curse, that the Saints have to make war upon them and destroy them—whence the perfect legitimacy of their trade in traps! It is not in the State of New York, where every man is a pleader and casuist, that any one is found at a loss for arguments in favor of that which brings grist to his mill."[50]

The interchange, according to Erastus Hamilton, was purely imaginary. What the Oneidans actually claimed was that they were "the prow with which iron-clad civilization is pushing back barbaric solitude, causing the bear and beaver to give place to the wheat-field, the library, and the piano."[51] The Perfectionists made traps, they said, to help Americans conquer the wilderness.

During Noyes's Brooklyn years, the hardworking Bible communists of Oneida built Eden from the ground up. Exploring ways to make money, they then laid the foundation for economic security by learning to make metal animal traps.

With the death of the Community's financial coordinator, it became apparent that Oneida could no longer support Brooklyn and the other groups that had sprung up as the Associated Communities. All, excepting Wallingford, were duly shut down. Their personnel (including Noyes) returned to Oneida, where they contributed to another housing shortage.

Planning an expanded family home became one of the commune's favorite pastimes during the ensuing years. Eventually, they agreed to build it in the "Italian Villa" style popularized by A. J. Downing. Community members reconfigured the grounds into the kind of pleasure park that Downing also recommended. The Perfectionists themselves said little about how they created their built works. Nevertheless, what they accomplished remains today an impressive manifestation of collective will.

The Oneida Community had the great good fortune to have on hand a commodity desirable to the outside world. One Community member, blacksmith Sewell Newhouse, had developed a metal animal trap superior to anything then available. When Noyes returned to Oneida in the mid-1850s, he became a strong proponent of building up the trap-making business and mechanizing it to boost output. The financial success of the Newhouse trap was dramatic. Turning out over two hundred thousand units a year, the Bible communists dominated the national market by the early 1860s. But traps, now the financial mainstay of Perfectionist existence, were beginning to dominate the Oneida Community.

CHAPTER 7

Industrialization

John Noyes dedicated himself to traps—fashioning them, improving them, and diversifying them. He vigorously promoted mechanizing and increasing their production during a second period of residence at Oneida between about 1855 and 1864. As a result, the Oneida Community became proficient in making and selling Newhouse traps. By the early 1860s, a point was reached at which employing outside workers and expanding facilities seemed necessary to, as they said, keep their customers satisfied. Traps, along with concomitant building projects and the establishment of a second factory industry to make thread, required the hiring of increasing numbers of workers from the outside world.

Traps and thread effectively changed the Community's mode of production from one grounded in horticulture to one centered on the factory. The new economic order tended to separate men from women in daily work and to encourage materialistic values. For the individual Bible communist, the transformation was likely to entail moving from home and garden to the factory floor, and sacrificing family companionship for a world in which one worked by supervising the work of strangers.

This second phase of Community life was established by about 1865. While altering the fabric of collective existence, the system of factories and paid workers also brought a higher standard of living. The Perfectionists came to enjoy that—albeit with mixed emotions and perhaps a little self-consciousness.

Industrial Buildup

The 1862 Mansion House, it will be recalled, was built not by Perfectionists but by paid laborers. The Community must have found something to like in that, because ensuing construction projects were carried out in the same fashion. Indeed, the new residence seemed to touch off a building binge of hired help. One of the first projects realized with outside labor was a new water system. Whereas the earlier arrangement delivered water from the mill for irrigation and bathing, drinking water was drawn from a distant well by means of a suction pump requiring laborious pumping by hand.[1] Now potable water flowed by gravity underground over a distance of about three-eighths of a mile to an aboveground reservoir behind the Mansion House. It was a complicated system, which over the years committed the Perfectionists to various outside contractors, beginning with one hired to dig the ditch and another who agreed to furnish and lay the pipes consisting of hollowed-out pine logs.[2]

As soon as the Mansion House was completed, the Community hired workers to construct two substantial buildings near it. The first was a state-of-the-art barn for a newly acquired purebred dairy herd. Erected across the road a short distance northeast of the Mansion House, it was proudly christened the "Ark" and pronounced "in every respect a model of convenience." The second was a three-story brick building erected by workmen in 1863 just west of the 1862 Mansion House. Designed to solve the problem of laundry toil, the "Tontine," as it was named, was equipped with the latest steam-driven machinery for washing.[3]

In the course of shopping for a washing machine for the Tontine, the Perfectionists visited the closest Shaker settlement, in Watervliet, New York, a hundred miles to the east. This initiated a long-term relationship between the two groups of Christian communists. Both parties insisted they dealt with one another chiefly on business matters, and, to both, "business" seemed to mean fascination with the other's labor-saving gadgetry. For over a decade, businessmen of Oneida and Watervliet shuttled back and forth, bringing to their communities increasing familiarity with and respect for the other.[4] Following a visit of Oneida men and women in 1875, however, the Shakers pulled back. "We are not yet sufficiently liberal to acknowledge what is admirable in [your system]," a Watervliet elder explained to the Bible communists, "nor to meet you half way even to confer on the subject. I candidly believe you love us more than we do you."[5]

The extensive construction projects required more and more money from traps. Trap production, in response, surged from 42,000 to 226,000 units in 1863 and then to 275,000 in 1864.[6] It was a frantic level of output achieved by hiring, on a temporary basis, about fifty non-Community workers. Acknowledging their inability to make so many traps themselves, the Perfectionists committed to becoming permanent employers in 1863. "The Community have decided upon the very important move of hiring help to man our Trap Shop! Our Trap Business has increased so much that we are over-run with orders," it was explained in the *Daily Journal*, "and are unable with our own folks to fill them; so that it was a matter of necessity to hire help." In their own minds, they took up the hireling system so as not to disappoint their customers.[7] The alternative—make fewer traps, disappoint a few customers—apparently was not considered.

When Community members realized they had outgrown the trap-making capacity of the Circularium, they purchased a farm a mile to the north to gain access to greater water power.[8] The new location was named "Willow Place" after the address of the former Brooklyn Community. The site had the advantage of being close to the nearest pool of outside labor—a small settlement called Turkey Street. At Noyes's suggestion, they built, at Willow Place, the largest trap manufacturing facility in the United States and staffed it with permanent employees working in assembly-line fashion.[9] That allowed them to double the output of traps.

Immensely proud of the apparent material prosperity created by the industry, Noyes began referring to Oneida as "a manufacturing or mechanical Community" based on traps. Trap making was what built their houses, improved their surroundings, and placed the Bible communists before the world as a successful business community. That industry, it now seemed to him, should be credited to two mechanics. One was William Inslee, who, "as a machinist, and the educator of machinists, was in an important sense, the father of our success in trap-making." The other, he had to admit, was himself.

If you take up the lineage of the Community on the other side, as indicated by my connection with it, you will arrive at a very similar result. People may think I am a professional person—a mere clerical or college-bred man; but the true story about the matter is that I am a mechanic, and always have been so. . . . I took hold of the trap-business and went through every part of it, and had as much to do with the inventions which marked its history as any one. If you study my career you will find that far more than I was ever a clergyman, I have been a stone-layer, and a tinker. I say I have worked harder and more at those businesses than I ever did at preaching. . . . I have always had a mechanical spirit and turn. So the Community was born of mechanical parents on both sides, and is a mechanic in itself, in all its nature and history.[10]

The new Willow Place factory allowed the Bible communists to increase trap production but at the cost of putting them over $30,000 into debt. Faced with the necessity of raising more money and obligated to factory-level production, the Community initiated a second factory industry, one requiring even more employees. In 1866, the Oneida Community began manufacturing "Machine Twist" silk thread for the sewing machines just then coming into widespread use.

The industry of silk thread was suggested by Noyes, who could scarcely contain his enthusiasm to start it up. The fresh challenge reinvigorated the fifty-four-year-old man, who declared himself "eager for another campaign, and for a revival of the inventive spirit we had in making traps and the necessary machinery. A glorious time we had of it in those days; it was not work, it was not toil, it was glorious sport, and we made it true pleasure. The same God is over us now as then, and he has not lost any of his power or will to help us."[11] Noyes assumed thread making would be financially promising because it was predicated on employing relatively cheap feminine labor—the girls and young women who staffed textile mills throughout the Northeast. At the very least, thread manufacture would complement trap making by providing insulation from the marked seasonal fluctuations associated with making the metal devices.

Though no market analysis was performed, the Community went about learning the field of thread making in a systematic fashion. Machinist William Inslee studied the requisite machinery at several factories in New Jersey and Connecticut. The Community sent three young people—Charles Cragin, Elizabeth Hutchins, and Harriet Allen—to serve an apprenticeship in thread making at a factory in Willimantic, Connecticut. Eschewing industrial espionage, the Perfectionists openly indicated what they were doing and why. They were astonished to find that their potential competitors welcomed them and seemed eager to impart all they knew.[12] In the summer of 1866, thread manufacture commenced on the second floor of the Willow Place trap works. The enterprise required that tsatlee and Canton varieties of silk be imported from China and Japan via New York. The raw material was then processed in a series of operations including sorting, winding, cleaning, spin-ning, and dyeing. Most steps were performed with machinery built by the Community. The final stage was to wind the thread onto wooden spools for market.[13]

The success of the spooled product was immediate. Oneida thread estab-lished a reputation for quality "unrivalled in the United States and probably in the World." It was all the Oneidans could do "to supply the demand for our machine-twist, notwithstanding it is the highest-priced article of its kind in market." A downturn in business caused by the Panic of 1873 affected the Community's thread more than its traps.[14] For a short time prior to that, however, thread actually outperformed traps to become the commune's chief moneymaker. Silk sales in 1869, for example, amounted to $142,000, as compared to income from traps totaling $115,000.[15]

By 1872, the Oneida Community employed at Willow Place a feminine workforce of about ninety "silk girls" (see figure 12), in addition to perhaps forty workmen making traps.

By 1875, the Community of some two hundred adults supervised about two hundred employees.[16] Oneida had become the largest trap manufac-turer in the United States and one of the most successful thread makers

FIGURE 12. "The Silk Factory," from *Leslie's Illustrated Newspaper*, 1870. This picture captures the irony of a Bible communist woman as capitalist supervisor in the Oneida Community's thread works.

in the land. Paid workers provided the muscle that brought that about. Wage-driven production propelled Oneida into the mainstream of American industrialism.

Becoming Employers

But if employees now played a major role in Community life, that fact was hard to digest. "Stop hiring, and carry on your business by taking your workmen into your family," Noyes had thundered at the hireling masters of the world. "Let the employer, whatever his line of business, live with his men, and make them interested partners instead of holding them by mere bond of wages." Paid laborers, in the words of another Community writer, were "crushed down beneath the weight of drudging toil—toil which is a master, stern and relentless." Only nominally better than slavery, "the old vicious hireling system" required "a kind of driving, quite distasteful to Community people."[17] Yet now the Bible communists found it was they who were the hireling masters. As folk who led deeply self-examined lives, they could not help but wonder whether paid labor could be reconciled with the communal and socialist values of Oneida. "While the Community employs many persons for wages," the Community handbook informed visitors in tight-lipped fashion, "it does not wholly approve of the hireling system, regarding it as one of the temporary institutions which will in time be displaced by the associative principle."[18] The moral dilemma bothered them, and they never resolved it.

The Oneidans immediately discovered that employees were more than an abstraction posing ethical difficulties. Now that they were employers, Community members had to interact with outside people to an unprecedented degree. How should relations with workers proceed? Fraternization with them was frowned on, but on the other hand, the workers could hardly be ignored. Further, when the "world's people" entered the Oneida workplace, they brought with them the ways of the world, which included ethnic and racial bigotry. How should the Community react to that? The Community was forced to confront that problem immediately after deciding to adopt the practice of paying wages. Their initial reaction to such unpleasantness was to look the other way:

> In the meeting this evening [reported the Community Journal], a talk was had about the proceedings of some of the Irish workmen toward the colored man that we employ. There is some tendency among them to rather put upon him in a provoking way to gratify prejudice against

his color. Many were in favor of turning off any workman who should operate in this way, but Mr. Noyes counseled not to bring a direct issue with any of our workmen on account of their prejudices against color. If the Irish and colored men would not work together, then calculate to avoid hiring either one or the other of their classes. The proposition was generally agreed upon.[19]

On further reflection, this course of action must have seemed neither charitable nor constructive. Noyes acknowledged as much when he next addressed the family on the subject of "our getting mixed up with the Hireling System of the world." He now reasoned that "as the Hireling System is a step in advance of the Slave System of the South so we must rise a step higher than the Hireling System,—must introduce a new element into it—an element of civilization, refinement and liberality." God will not bless the Community in this enterprise, he warned, if the Community does not improve the condition of its workers.[20]

As the Bible communists pondered how things could be bettered, it occurred to them that their situation as employers presented an opportunity to benefit others. "We want a spirit of liberality toward our workmen," a Community member averred, "and not the spirit of the world which grinds them down and seeks to get all it can from them for the least money." The result was a generous personnel policy that featured good wages, decent working conditions, and, in the Trap Shop, an eight-hour day. The Community offered a wide range of education and transportation benefits. The Bible communists feasted their employees with strawberries and feted them with music in the Mansion House. By 1873, employees were also provided with shelter: some twenty-four units of housing including tenant homes and boardinghouses. The Perfectionists were, in their time, exceptionally good employers, labor-relations scholar Esther Lowenthal concluded.[21]

What did the workers think of their employers? There was, apparently, no union to articulate their views, and their actions received only occasional notice in the Community's reportage. What Perfectionist writers tended to record was the expression of gratitude. A young employee given a "workbox," for example, "was so delighted with it that she could not sleep, Christmas night." Or, the girls of the silk shop presented the manager, Charles Cragin, with a silver and glass fruit dish as a token of their friendship and respect. Accepting on behalf of the Oneida Community, Cragin said he hoped it indicated the Perfectionists "have succeeded in gaining your goodwill and esteem." Visitor Charles Nordhoff found that Oneida's hired people "like their employers. These pay good wages, and treat their servants kindly; looking after their physical and intellectual well-being, building houses for such of them as have families and need to be near at hand, and in many ways showing interest in their welfare."[22]

The ethnic tensions referred to above must have subsided—perhaps they did work themselves out—to judge by the fact that the Community continued to hire both "Irish" and "coloreds." As regards the latter, at least eight African Americans were employed by the Community in 1875.[23]

Tensions and Distractions

While the Bible communists employed outsiders mainly in the factory, other outsiders were put to work in nonindustrial capacities as well. By about 1865, for example, the day-to-day work of horticulture and farming was performed by employees.[24] This effectively put an end to horticultural bees formerly performed by men and women working outside together. Further, bees to process fruit ended, at least temporarily, in 1868 when the fruit business was discontinued. The problem was that horticulture and canning involved a double deadline—one for harvest, the other—in the absence of effective refrigeration—for preserving and processing the harvest. Unfortunately, the demand for labor to get all this done occurred at the same time of year workers were most needed in the trap-making business.[25] Competing with traps for workers, horticulture lost.

Another effect of outside labor was to drive a wedge between men and women at Oneida. Perfectionist men supervised outside male employees in the trap shop and field. Perfectionist women supervised female employees in the silk works.[26] With the sexes increasingly separated during the day, gender division within the Community became sharpened.

And while bees in later years might include men and women, they did not conform to the old horticultural ideal. When, for example, the canning business was started up again after four years, it was as a carefully planned-out commercial enterprise funded to the tune of $9,000—by far the biggest expense in the 1872 budget. The money was allocated for developing a fruit-processing facility staffed by hired help. That was accomplished by taking over and reconfiguring the farmers' dairy barn (the Ark, thereafter christened the "Arcade"). The money also paid for a state-of-the art fruit-preserving complex. Its centerpiece, named the "Keep," was a massive "Fisher's Patent Refrigerator," the construction of which was overseen by Mr. J. Hyde Fisher himself—brought all the way from Chicago to get that done.[27] This

was a real business, no longer motivated by the spiritual benefits of bringing male and female Perfectionists together. The new enterprise had plenty
of bees, but they were mostly emergency efforts in which Bible communists and employees worked together in the Fruit House feverishly canning
the fruit before it spoiled.[28] Although these activities resembled earlier bees,
they were not occasions encouraging the Bible communists to mingle outside. Perfectionists looked back on the pre-employee, horticultural bees
with nostalgic fondness. "Those were the days," one of them wrote in 1873,
"when much of our irksome work was performed by 'bees,' which were
well attended by men, women and children. . . . Ah! those were happy days."
"I have heard old members say regretfully," Pierrepont Noyes echoed, "'those
were our happiest years.'"[29]

In effect, the relations of production were altered. A workplace oriented
to wage labor, they realized, had the effect of devaluing mingling, spirituality, and practical gender equality. Why, in view of the major ideological and
social implications of the shift, was it allowed to happen? Why, if they did
not like it, did they accept the new order? The Perfectionists were aware of
change, and occasionally they took steps to resist it. Alarmed about the disappearance of bees in 1864, George Cragin exhorted the Community "not to
abandon this old ordinance of doing work in that way." When a "grand bee"
was summoned two years later to pick raspberries, it was proudly noted,
"78 persons were counted in the field, and 266 qts. were picked. The family
voted last evening to pick the raspberries themselves, without the assistance
of hired help. The bees are a good ordinance, stimulative of unity of heart
and resurrection influx."[30] One central member, the financially knowledgeable Amasa Carr, apparently left the Community in late 1865 after voicing
opposition to incurring debt from building the Willow Place factory and,
perhaps, to the hiring of outsiders.[31]

But for the most part, the Oneida Community was distracted and diverted
from attention to the problem. As the system of wage labor was being initiated, Community members were beset by internal problems so serious as to
prevent them from taking much notice of anything else. When these were
over, the Bible communists were assured that the salient industrial problem
was not employees but debt, a difficulty that Noyes and his twenty-six-year-
old son, Theodore, would correct.

During the winter of 1863–64, the Community was prostrated by an
epidemic of diphtheria infecting 112 and killing 5. The illness challenged
the Community's notion of sickness as a symptom of weak faith and forced
the Perfectionists to turn to the outside world for medical help. In the end,

they salvaged the substance of their religious convictions by concluding that the only effective cure was mutual criticism. "Being no better at night, but rather worse, I sent for a committee," one of them testified. "Their criticism immediately threw me into a profuse sweat, till I felt as though I had been in a bath; and before the committee left the room, my head-ache, back-ache, and fever were all gone. The criticism had an edge to it, and literally separated me from the spirit of disease that was upon me."[32] Noyes vigorously advocated the therapeutic value of mutual criticism throughout the crisis. On one occasion, he offered to demonstrate its effectiveness by submitting to criticism himself in public view. The problem with this was that Noyes, occupying the pinnacle position in the system of ascending fellowship, did not regard himself as subject to evaluation originating from below. The solution he hit upon, apparently, was to criticize himself in front of a presumably silent audience.[33]

Then, during much of 1864, the "Mills War" monopolized Community attention. William Mills, about the same age as Noyes, had joined in 1857. Seceding shortly after, he demanded the return of his money with interest, and the Community complied. Somehow he obtained readmittance on a probationary basis about 1859. Noyes came to detest Mills, calling him "the meanest human parasite we have ever encountered"—"a nuisance and a stench" who endlessly importuned the females for sex (unsuccessfully, they said) "by boring, goading and forcing."[34] Community member Theodore Pitt (who will reappear in the future as a spiritualist) gave voice to the fear that Mills was a sorcerer in league with evil spirits: "He voluntarily confessed, or we might say boasted, that he had some spiritual connection with certain accidents and deaths which occurred while he was among us, and the subjects of which were persons who had incurred his displeasure. A full examination of his character and operations convinced us that there was a basis of truth in his confessions. One of the persons who died, a very intelligent woman, testified her firm belief and consciousness that the oppressing power of his spirit was killing her. This man had in early life, according to his own account, deliberately sold himself to the devil."[35]

For months, Noyes wrote obsessively about Mills and his threats to sue the Community, actions which reminded the Bible communists that they had no mechanism for compelling obedience. Social control evidently was so weak that the Community could not even pressure individuals to change if they were unwilling to do so. Mills did not pose the only problem of this sort. A young, mentally disturbed man named Charles Guiteau was behaving badly at the same time. Guiteau would soon leave the Community under his own steam and, in 1881, assassinate President Garfield. Mills, meanwhile, in what must have been an action of supreme frustration, "was carefully set out of doors."[36] "I heard sudden angry shouts and a struggle," six-year-old Jessie Kinsley remembered years later. "Then from the window came into view the sight of a man thrown by other men into a snow drift—violently thrown, without excuses. I saw the man emerge, pick up the things that had been thrown out with him, and walk away sending back loud, angry words and burning glances, shaking his fist as he shouted. That was the last act, I believe, of 'The Mills War.'"[37] Mills was the only person forcibly expelled from Oneida, and even this ejection could only be effected with a substantial cash settlement for the miscreant.[38]

The Mills War caused the Community as a whole to tighten up admission policies and to rethink the nature of legal protection for the organization. Since the beginning, it had been understood that all members ceded all property to the associative whole. If the individual seceded, his or her property would be returned. "This practice however," it was explained in the Community's first annual report, "stands on the ground, not of obligation but of expediency and liberality; and the time and manner of refunding must be trusted to the discretion of the Association. While a person remains a member, his subsistence and education in the Association are held to be just equivalents for his labor; and no accounts are kept between him and the Association, and no claim of wage accrues to him in case of subsequent withdrawal." This arrangement, it was now clear, did not afford adequate protection from suits for back wages. Nor did it discourage the efforts of former members more inclined toward blackmail and extortion. To better protect the organization, the Bible communists now constituted the Oneida Community into a legal entity owned by four individuals: John Noyes, Erastus Hamilton, William Woolworth, and Otis Kellogg. "It was understood at all times that this arrangement was merely one of convenience," according to Holton Noyes. Every Bible communist, he believed, had equal ownership in all property.[39]

Just as the Perfectionists were emerging from illness and threats from malcontents, they were urged to ramp up their religious enthusiasm. We must make business our religion, Noyes proclaimed.[40] Doing business in the Pentecostal way, he elaborated, meant selling as low as possible, paying cash in full when buying and demanding the same terms when selling, and liquidating everything not in immediate use.[41] Noyes's exhortation to sell everything off came out of a financial analysis focused on short-term debt and immediate cash flow. The result was a program that raised the intensity of religious feeling without affecting the speed with which the wage-earning system entered every pore of Community life.

Noyes began writing about Community finances in 1865 to express concern with a drop in trap sales and a rise in debt, the money chiefly being owed as a result of the building program. To correct the imbalance, Noyes proposed, first, that the manufacturing sector should be enlarged, a suggestion that would lead to establishing the thread industry the following year. Second, he urged the Community to borrow money. "If any of our readers know or can find men or corporations that will lend us money on the terms indicated, i. e., on good notes at 6 per cent; or secondly on bond and mortgage at 6 per cent; or thirdly, on good notes at 7 per cent; they will confer a favor by sending us immediate information."[42] Noyes continued to worry about debt the year after. When payment came due on the trap-factory property and there appeared to be a cash shortage, he instigated a draconian liquidation of everything from pocket watches to land. These measures apparently solved the proximate problem of debt by the end of 1866.[43] However, the financial tocsin sounded even more loudly in late 1867 when the annual cost of employee wages was discovered to be about $40,000.[44] Noyes viewed this as a great crisis, which his oldest son, Theodore, was fitted to solve if granted broad economic powers.

The Community had begun sending young men to college in 1865 so it would have its own professionals to consult in the event of further diphtheria epidemics or Mills Wars. Eventually, about a dozen were sent, mostly to Yale's Sheffield Scientific School, to become medical doctors, lawyers, or engineers. Theodore, among the first to matriculate, received a medical degree in 1867. Since John Noyes was not residing in the Community (he lived in New York City and Wallingford for three and a half years between 1864 and 1868), it made sense to have an educated person at the helm in Oneida. Theodore, at the time, was regarded as the leader of the rising generation.[45] Accordingly, Noyes urged the Community to accept Theodore as financial officer, and they did so. When Theodore was asked to enfold "some of the workings of his mind on the financial question," he indicated that he would look at the books to see what was going on in the businesses.[46] With or without policy, Theodore liquidated horticulture and bag making, thus delivering a death blow to spiritually beneficial industries in which men and women customarily worked closely together.

The Bible communists peeked into a different world when they asked outsiders to build Community buildings. They entered that world—a realm of wage labor—when they arranged to have outsiders manufacture their products. Now the Perfectionists were locked into circumstances requiring them to generate money to pay others to get work done. Dependence on employees put an end to the old horticultural practices and their attendant ideals of gender equality. However, wage earning and factory production also ushered in financial prosperity and material plenty, which posed a new challenge. Could Perfectionists enjoy wealth? Could one feel any pride in an abundance of worldly things?

Abounding

The answer was—yes. As the new economic order took shape around the Bible communists, they accepted it because they enjoyed its benefits. People in the Oneida Community, it has seemed to many, *were* happy. Over time, hundreds found Community life to be immensely gratifying.[47] Sentiments to that effect were chiefly articulated during the Community's later years when the labor of employees brought prosperity. While doubtlessly sincere, the happiness they expressed had a deliberate feel to it. In words and pictures, the Perfectionists look a little theatrical as they show things off and explain—to themselves as much as to others—how good Community living is.

Heaven, it will be recalled, had come to Putney but never to Oneida. With the passage of time, its arrival seemed increasingly remote. "The object of the Community," they announced ten years after its founding, "is to live a true life—manifest Christ in the world—realize an answer to his prayer that all his followers might be one—develop a beginning of the reign of the Kingdom of Heaven, among men." "The sole end and aim of the Oneida Community," they explained several years further on, "is to make a happy home by reconciling man and woman to each other, and by reconciling both to God."[48] Furthermore, it was Oneida's business to present, to the world and most especially to visitors observing the Community firsthand, "a working model of Communism, and leave its effect on others to the silent action of truth and the Providence of God."[49] Such goals were enunciated with reference to having an audience.

Their new residence and its surroundings bore wonderful testimony to a happy home and successful communism. Images of these were recorded by outside photographers beginning in 1863 and, later, by one of their own— D. Edson Smith. In many of these images, one can see the Perfectionists becoming performance artists as they strike poses setting off their architecture and lifestyle to good advantage (see figure 13).

The Oneida Community marketed the prints as illustrations of Perfectionist life and "how Communism renders labor attractive."[50] They also sold them as souvenir keepsakes to some of their many thousands of visitors. "We acknowledge that selfishness must be rooted out before men and

Figure 13. Bible communists distribute themselves in front (east side) of the Mansion House, 1871.

women will be fit to enjoy our style of Communism, and it may take a long time to do it," it was explained in the *Circular*. "We mean to help all we can by showing the way."[51] Trying to project casualness, the Perfectionists showed the way in these pictures.

Earlier, visitors had been tolerated. Now that successful Bible communism demanded an appreciative audience, the public was urged to come. Accordingly, the Oneida Community set about inculcating the "hospitality spirit" and developing central New York's first tourist industry. The Oneidans created a reception room near the front door for visitors awaiting guided tours. They prepared handbills advertising musical entertainments in the family hall and a menu of meals available to hungry tourists. Enthusiasts of Perfectionist food could even take home an official Oneida Community cookbook.[52] Other promotional literature included guidebooks, which, after conducting visitors through the Mansion House, invited them to climb the North Tower to view "a landscape of unspeakable beauty."

"At our feet, the lawn with its neatly-trimmed paths, the flower gardens with their brilliant colors, and the rustic seats and arbors, half concealed in shaded nooks, entice the eye with their quiet loveliness. Beyond are the orchards and vineyards, then the emerald meadows and winding stream, and in the distance, the gently rounded hills which bound the sides of the valley."[53] After directing tourists' attention to "the best farm and grazing lands in the State," the guide literature then marched visitors briskly through barn and factory areas.[54]

Visitation to the Oneida Community increased with time, the new Mansion House apparently being an important draw. An estimated fifteen hundred to two thousand visitors dropped by on July 4, 1863. Over the next five years, the Community welcomed some forty-five thousand guests. Many more came when a railroad was constructed across the Community's land in 1868.[55] In exchange for a free right-of-way, the Midland Railroad built a depot about one hundred yards from the Mansion House. One train on a single day disgorged thirteen hundred visitors to pour through the Mansion House and over its grounds. The Oneida Community entertained more visitors than any other utopian community in America, probably more than all the others put together.[56]

Tourists wanted to see the exotic Perfectionists and enjoy their scenic domain, of course, but the chief point of curiosity continued to be sex. Visitors who purchased Oneida Community handbooks could learn that complex marriage had a religious basis. The manuals stated that love choices for the young should be under the guidance of older people; no two people should become exclusively attached to one another; and no one should be forced into having sex.[57] Nevertheless, enough lascivious curiosity remained to keep the Perfectionists busy correcting rumors about sleeping partners being chosen by lot and everyone spending the night together in a giant circular bed.[58]

Bible communists frequently were asked about the place of women in communal life. What the handbooks said on this topic was that the women had it, relatively, very good. "The sexes freely mingle in many departments of industry, and women enjoy many privileges denied them in ordinary society," it was explained in the 1867 handbook. "They are at least relieved from household drudgery, and from the curse of excessive and undesired propagation, and allowed a fair chance with their brothers in education and labor."[59] The subject was tackled in the next edition in a statement titled "A Woman's Definition of Woman's Position in the Community":

Communism gives woman, without a claim from her, the place which every true woman most desires, as the free and honored companion of man. Communism emancipates her from the slavery and corroding

cares of a mere wife and mother; stimulates her to seek the improvement of mind and heart that will make her worthy [of] a higher place
than ordinary society can ever give her. . . . Gradually, as by natural
growth, the Community women have risen to a position where, in
labor, in mind, and in heart, they have all and more than all that is
claimed or can be claimed by the women who are so loudly asserting
their rights. And through it all they have not ceased to love and honor
the truth that "the man is the head of the woman," and that woman's
highest, God-given right is to be "the glory of man."[60]

As if feeling pressed on that point, the Perfectionist handbooks drew attention
to the larger picture. The Oneida Community, in fact, advocated a stance on
social equality and justice that would seem progressive in any age. "Do you
believe in the equality of men and women?" a fictional visitor asks. "No," a
generalized Perfectionist answers, "but we don't believe even in the equality
of men; but we do believe that every man, woman and child should be sur-
rounded with circumstances favoring the best development of heart, mind
and body, and that no one should be excluded on account of age, sex, race,
or color, from engaging in any occupation for which he or she is adapted by
nature or culture."[61]

As they showed things off, they also cultivated a positive attitude toward
enjoying the things money could buy. Back in the day when they made their
own traps, when silk thread was undreamed of, "and fruit-preserving hardly
known any where in the world; when the O.C. was indulging in the pastoral
fancy of making our living by raising fruit and vegetables," as one of them
wistfully recalled—back in those days, selflessness and harmony seemed
easy. Now the problem, as Erastus Hamilton put it, was that "prosperity
puts this power of harmony to a greater test than adversity."[62]

If taking pleasure in prosperity was something that had to be learned,
Noyes was the man to teach it. "It is a blessing to the universe that God
himself is happy, and utterly refuses to suffer," he observed. Noyes had
always thought God wanted the same for people and invited them to share
in the sensory pleasures of his creation.[63] "We must never forget that God
is married to matter. He made the world and caused the earth to bring
forth all manner of things, and pronounced them 'very good.' . . . He has not
set the fashion of despising the things that are made to eat and drink. . . .
God made our bodies to rejoice and be happy in his creation; and he will
never be satisfied until the marriage he projected at the beginning has been
consummated—until his glorious bounties have been truly appreciated."[64]
While Noyes believed it a virtue to be free of covetous attachments of any

sort, he also looked forward to a state in which the Bible communists "would be free to use the luxuries of the world, if they come to hand." From the beginning, he alerted his followers, as Parker put it, "to the future, to the possibility of an ideal community home." As creature comforts increased, Noyes recommended that the Oneida Community learn how to abound.[65]

The Bible communists abounded as never before by delighting in intellectual pursuits. In their new digs, they had the opportunity to expand their library and, incidentally, make it a showplace of the house—a light-filled spot with notable carpentry. They equipped it with close to four thousand volumes spanning the range—as they thought—of human knowledge. They subscribed to nearly a hundred journals and periodicals (see figure 14).[66]

The resource of written material fired them with ambition to become scholars. They had always been readers, of course, but now they became amateur academics and scientists. Noyes originated the trend in the mid-1860s when he began to study genetics. This effort would lead, in time, to the establishment of a Community eugenics program and to Noyes's 1872 treatise on the theory behind it—*Essay on Scientific Propagation.*[67] Noyes also initiated research into American communitarianism, which would become

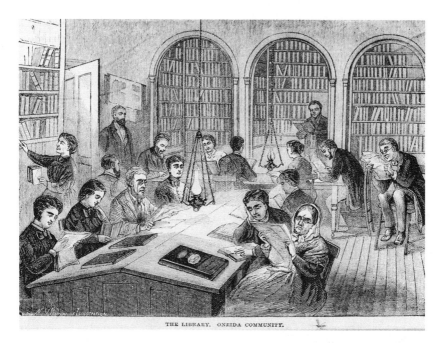

THE LIBRARY, ONEIDA COMMUNITY.

FIGURE 14.   The Oneida Community library, a drawing from life made into a woodcut published in *Leslie's Illustrated Newspaper*, 1870.

the 1870 book *American Socialisms*. This in turn encouraged fellow Perfectionist William Hinds to begin his research into utopias with the use of questionnaires. Indeed, of three surveys of American utopianism published in the 1870s (the third being Charles Nordhoff's *The Communistic Societies of the United States*), no fewer than two were written by Oneida Community members. The books remain important to scholars today, and Noyes's is still highly regarded. The historical impulse demonstrated by these works would lead the Oneidans, in 1876, to refocus their weekly newspaper with the title the *American Socialist*.

Others launched themselves into research projects such as a twelve-part history of the Oneida Indians, which drew on information mostly gathered from books in the Community library. Those less interested in historical research turned their attention to becoming naturalists. Henry Seymour and Alfred Barron, for example, penned lyrical essays about enjoying nature. Others threw themselves into recording the weather, witnessing astronomical phenomena, and in viewing one-celled organisms seen through the lens of a microscope. They delighted in the Victorian exercise of collecting and classifying the natural world—bugs, rocks, stuffed animals. The biggest collection of all was a museum showcase for visitors. This cabinet of curiosities was assembled from family keepsakes (many exotics from relatives traveling the world as sailors on clipper and whaling ships) and items gathered by their agents and friends in the outside world. Constructed of black walnut in 1868, the cabinet is still a high point in tours of the Mansion House today.[68]

Some Perfectionists invented gadgets supposed to cut down on work. Jonathan Burt's corn-cutting machine, for example, could separate corn from the cob "as fast as a man can place ears in the frame and work the treadle, say at the rate of twenty per minute, thus saving the labor of five or six hands."[69] Mechanical devices of this sort washed clothes, cut bread, sliced string beans, peeled potatoes, cleaned fish, and addressed packages. Possibly the lazy Susan was created in the Oneida Community. The best inventions were extolled as embodying Community ways and values. Wondering what kind of shoe best met the needs of a Perfectionist lady, for example, the women (as one of them reported) arrived at a new form of footwear: "Fashion, we resolved, should not say any longer. We would not have high heels, and we would not have high-laced boots. We could not spare the time to tie up balmorals, and we were convinced that they weaken and cramp the ankles. We held meetings (chattering women's meetings), the shoe-maker sent in his models; they were passed from hand to hand and discussed; a consulting committee was appointed, &c., &c. One pattern after another was introduced and tried, but we fixed at last upon . . . 'The Final Shoe.'"[70]

Community pride in inventiveness focused, rather strangely, on two simple contraptions invented by John Leonard in 1868. His mop wringer and potato washer are described in Community writings as benefiting the Oneida Community and affirming its worth. Not only did these labor-saving inventions result from the Community's system of job rotation; they demonstrated the wisdom of placing men in the realm of women. They rendered menial chores less onerous and ameliorated the drudgery of women's work. The mop wringer and potato washer exemplified Bible communist success.[71]

One of the signs of the unity and flexibility of the Community, a Perfectionist observed, "is seen in the hearty readiness with which new and revolutionary manners are adopted at the suggestion of the scientific and spiritual."[72] Fairly careful research would be conducted into a new gadget or technology, and the results would be presented for public scrutiny. The merits of different courses of action were then debated with enthusiasm in the evening meeting. For example, what cutting-edge features should a new wing added to the Mansion House in 1869–1870 possess? First, there would be central steam heating. Because of the scale of economy that came from sharing everything, they could afford a heating system otherwise available only to the very rich. Second, there would be "earth closets"—toilets flushed with soil and ashes. Consulting the scientific literature of the day, they concluded that earth closets—as opposed to water closets—could convert "night soil" to fertilizer. That, in turn, would solve the problem of passing one's waste on to those living downstream. Third, there would be a mansard roof. At the risk of seeming to favor the fashionable, the Perfectionists chose the mansard form of roof for a purely utilitarian reason. It provided more usable space in the top story than did the low-gabled roof of the Italian Villa style.[73]

Planning and taking the measure of things were virtues of the Community way of life, but there were other benefits as well. One, the *Daily Journal* bragged, was adaptability. "S.W.N. is this morning engaged cutting a direct path from the main entry of the New House to the office door of the Store, intersecting the oval green in front of the portico. A kind of contest has been going on in the minds of a good many between the taste that preferred to keep the oval intact and the necessity that demanded the path; but it may be assumed as a safe principle that beauty and utility are never really antagonistic. At some future time the paths and grass plots may be entirely re-arranged in conformity with new requirements and new ideas."[74] It made

Perfectionists happy to think that, in the natural order of Bible communism, all would work out for the best.

With prosperity came leisure. By one calculation, Perfectionists worked about six hours and fifty minutes of the day, leaving a fair amount of disposable time.[75] Women, relieved as they said from household drudgery, care, and vexation, surely had more free time.[76] Everyone, however, had ample opportunity to relax. A good way to enjoy one's leisure was to take up new recreational activities. After transforming the Mansion House grounds, for example, the corps of landscape gardeners moved west to create another pleasure ground in "Spring Grove," the woods near their water source.[77] For years, they expatiated on the pleasures of strolling through this beloved landscape until they hit on other bucolic pastimes to enjoy. They picnicked at the Cascades to the south and vacationed at Joppa, their summer resort on Oneida Lake to the north. They staged innumerable theatrical and musical performances.

A craze for sports swept the Community in the 1860s, beginning with baseball. Highly competitive and limited, at first, to male participation, the game earned the reputation of being disharmonious. Baseball's popularity waned with the introduction of croquet in 1866.[78] Croquet, a game that men and women could play together, quickly became the Community's sport of choice and inspiration for Perfectionist philosophizing. After one croquet match, Noyes announced "that he had got a new view of the subject of competition." If God is on both sides in every fight, he reasoned, competition is legitimate and good. "By loyally recognizing God in the game, and that he controls the result and gives the victory to whom he pleases, we may enter it heartily and exercise our utmost skill and power to win."[79] Soon after, Noyes's sentiment was supplanted by that of another writer, probably Harriet Skinner:

One secret of the popularity of [croquet] evidently is its adaptation to both sexes. Then the question arises, how can the men best preserve this social and civilizing feature—the partnership of the women? First, I should answer, let the gentleness and moderation of the women, modify the tendency to excess and competition in the men. The violent way in which many of the men croquet their opponent's balls, seems very directly calculated to spoil the attractiveness of the game, especially for the women. . . . The toning down of the eagerness and excess of the masculine element, would, in the humble opinion of one at least, add very much to the attractiveness of the game, and serve very much to perpetuate it, as a pleasant and improving pastime.[80]

Thus, the Community redefined a competitive sport as an occasion for men and women to enjoy each other's company.

Twilight of Mingling

While men and women mingled more in sports, they mingled less in real life. The operation of the employee-factory system tended to separate males and females during the working day and to encourage the formation of feminine task groups. Women in the Oneida Community had the opportunity seldom found the outside world of living in close association with other women.[81] As a communitarian venture, Oneida had always offered an unusual density of female interactions with the potential to become organized and to accomplish major tasks. Late in time and as a consequence of increasing gender separation, that seems to have happened.

An impressive example of a task-specific women's activity was a large-scale quilting project. "For the last month the feminine part of the O. C. has been busily engaged in a unitary plan," it was announced in 1873. "They resolved themselves into an impromptu school of design"—for quilt making.[82] About one hundred completed blocks were assembled into two quilts, which together were the product of a largely spontaneous group effort independent of the committees and departments running many aspects of Community life. Almost every girl and woman in the Oneida Community took part in this cooperative endeavor for two months. One of the resulting works, the "Best Quilt," documented a wide range of jobs being performed by Community women, including tasks of a nondomestic nature largely unavailable to women in the outside world.

The women also were organizing themselves to accomplish long-term, economically productive tasks such as silk skeining—the preparation of threads used in hand sewing as opposed to machine sewing. Whereas the manufacture of "machine twist" was a factory operation performed by hired help, the production of hand-sewing threads was done in the Mansion House by the Community women themselves. To skein silk, a person sat in front of a silk reel, a wooden stand with a crossbar about forty inches above the floor (see figure 15).

Starting with large skeins of coarse silk, the skeiner skillfully sorted, bunched, pressed, and tied the material up into small hanks ready for sale. Hand-sewing threads were prominently advertised and sold in stores throughout the country.[83]

Silk skeining made a significant contribution to the Community's economy, something that went far toward attaining a goal of the Associationist

FIGURE 15.   A woman skeining silk in her Mansion House room, about 1885.

movement: economic security for women. A Fourierist commune, it was thought, would overcome the economic exploitation of feminine domestic labor by freeing women from dependence on men. An argument for women's monetary independence followed logically. Equal pay for women was advocated at the Northampton Association. At the Brook Farm Association or Phalanx in 1844, Marianne Dwight declared feminine autonomy required that women have their own income by producing a marketable product. Toward that end, she organized a women's sewing group whose goal was "nothing less than the elevation of woman to independence."[84] Outside the Oneida Community, however, activity of this sort never amounted to anything more than gesture.

As an economically productive activity, the home thread industry brought a strong sense of pride. "It gives us women," Candace Bushnell explained, "a chance for a few hours in the day, more or less, to taste of the pleasures of *production*."

> This is a pleasure that most women are debarred from. The wives, daughters and sisters of men in good circumstances, are forbidden by fashion to do any thing with their hands, beyond the lighter chores of housekeeping and making some of their own and their children's clothes. There is *work* enough to be sure in this narrow field, as many a wearied, worn-out woman of fashion will say; but it is almost always monotonous, dispiriting work—a treadmill, never ending, still beginning. . . . It is a weariness to the flesh and spirit both, to drag on from year to year, as many women do, with no occupation but to study the fashions; dress and undress their children, curl their hair and keep the parlors in order. Women become first-rate consumers—trained and confined as most of them are by custom to that profession—but it is a miserable, life-absorbing profession, taken alone. The Bible says, "It is more blessed to give than to receive." It is more blessed to be producers than consumers.[85]

In this manner, Oneida Community women found something to enjoy even in the separation of the sexes.

The Noyes who returned to Oneida in late 1854 was determined to make more money by making more traps. He encouraged mechanization, urged that the trap-making machinery be operated by employees in a factory, and promoted a second factory industry of hired labor to produce thread for sewing machines. Traps and thread ushered the Community into the industrial age and brought material prosperity. They also made the commune dependent on outside workers and transformed communal life.

The new order, among other things, fostered an interest in financial profit antithetical to earlier concerns with spirituality. Bible communists were aware that their commune was changing, but their attention was focused on internal problems, including an outbreak of diphtheria and a disruption caused by an irrefragable troublemaker. They were also sidetracked by the economic analyses of Noyes and his elder son, Theodore, which focused attention on the subject of short-term debt.

Many Perfectionists found the more materialistic climate they had created distasteful. But an economy based on wage earners and factories ushered in prosperity. That proved to be tolerable, partly because Noyes taught that it was right to enjoy a higher standard of living. The Perfectionists threw themselves into exemplifying the good life by posing in photos and showing the Mansion House off. Community members happily pursued science, invention, and elaborating their architecture. They also put their leisure time to good use in landscaping and playing sports. However, because employees and the factory setting separated the sexes during the day, projects of exclusively feminine composition developed, including a new business devoted to manufacturing thread for hand sewing.

CHAPTER 8

Breakup

Oneida's concluding years were concerned with eugenics, an audacious attempt to breed a spiritually superior race of human beings. What the Oneida Community called "stirpiculture" was the largest program of its kind yet attempted, and it may have been the only controlled experiment in human breeding the world has ever seen.[1]

Stirpiculture, however, encouraged individualistic impulses that undermined Community stability. At the same time, an increasingly tendentious Noyes insisted that his son, Dr. Theodore Noyes, succeed him as Community leader. It was a grave mistake, which dispelled faith in Noyes's judgment.[2] Doubt progressed quickly to discontent and factionalism, which tore the commune apart.

Stirpiculture

Throughout Oneida Community times, scientific or selective breeding was discussed frequently by everyone from farmers developing specialized herds of milk cows to scientists publishing treatises on evolution. Noyes, also, was impressed by evidence for biological plasticity and had long supposed that the Community could produce sanctified offspring. He had first raised the idea of improving humankind by controlling human breeding in *Bible Argument* of 1848. Returning to the subject in the mid-1860s, Noyes reiterated the importance of science for human reproduction. "If the farmer achieves with perfect certainty the elevation of his flocks and herds to a certain standard of form and size, beauty and disposition, by observing the fixed laws of propagation," he wondered, "why should not something be done systematically for man in the same way?" Human improvement was described as developing "a new variation of the genus *homo*, in the direction of spiritual perfection, as distinct as any of the steps in the ascent from brutes to man." At this time he coined the word "stirpiculture," from Latin *stirpes* for race (also: root, stock, strain) to designate "the science of improving mankind by attention to the law of propagation."[3]

Late in the 1860s, the Oneida Community decided to make the attempt, as they so often did, to translate Noyes's views on breeding into reality. Feeling prosperous enough to raise children, the Perfectionists completed a new wing of the Mansion House to receive the intended offspring in 1870. Evidently they were in complete agreement to initiate the reproductive program and had no shortage of participants willing to carry it out. Some ninety young men and women enthusiastically stepped forward as soldiers in the cause of scientific propagation, according to a study of the program by two of its products, Hilda Herrick Noyes and George Wallingford Noyes. The older folk had agreed to engage in group sex for heavenly reasons. These younger Perfectionists agreed to reproduce as "living sacrifices" to God, to Noyes, and to true communism.[4]

Noyes and a committee of his senior advisers determined who would mate, although, for a time, decision making was vested in a stirpicultural committee composed of six men and six women. The standards for breeding selection, according to the two Noyes researchers, were "first the spiritual, second the intellectual, third the moral, and fourth the physical departments of human nature."[5] Selection, according to John Noyes, would also take into account the good of the parents, as well as "the effect on the social relation of the parties and on the organism of society around them."[6] The basic procedure was that couples wishing to become parents would submit applications for reproduction to the governing agency. Most requests were approved (forty-two of fifty-one applications during one "typical period of about fifteen months"). "If an application were disapproved," Noyes and Noyes explained, "the Committee would always interest itself in an attempt to find a combination agreeable to those concerned which it would approve."[7] Couples who had babies by accident or without authorization were not punished, and in fact their offspring were treated the same as those formally approved.[8] During the decade of stirpiculture (1869–1879), some fifty-eight children (called stirpicults) were born to forty-one mothers (median age thirty years) and forty fathers (median age forty-one).

Theologically, the stirpicultural program was a Plan B—a fallback action initiated in lieu of bringing the resurrection state into earthly reality. "We should give up insisting that God should convert the world immediately," John Noyes averred in 1856, "and have instead a far-reaching purpose to save the world by combining regeneration with generation." "We had better set the world to work in that direction," he added, "for it is useless to seek for the millennium in any other." Eugenics was tacit acknowledgment that heaven was not coming soon.[9]

Sociologically, stirpiculture seemed to offer a means to improve the human condition. A crisis is upon us, Noyes declared at the beginning and end of his 1872 *Essay on Scientific Propagation*. Humankind is degenerating; yet modern life demands a higher level of human capability than ever before. The human race has a duty to improve itself, especially since science now provides the needed knowledge. And "what ought to be done can be done."[10] Stirpiculture, then, was a utopian reform measure to make the world a better place.

The benefits of controlled breeding were, in any event, scientific fact, according to Noyes, who now presented himself to a reading public as a scientific savant. The chief "law" of scientific propagation he inferred from the animal-breeding literature of his day was that one should select the quality in question, then intensify it through generations of inbreeding. Breed from the best, then breed in and in, was his maxim. Since the idea of humans "breeding in and in" trespassed on the emotionally fraught subject of incest, Noyes tried to anticipate possible objections. One answer offered in the pages of the *Circular* was that human consanguinity is difficult to define. Such little evidence as existed indicated that the mating of close relatives is not necessarily bad and may in fact be quite good. Noyes cited an article claiming that continuous interbreeding of cousins in rural France resulted in beautiful women. Finally, he purported to demonstrate that the Jewish people of the Old Testament became a perfect race by inbreeding.[11]

Nineteenth-century notions of incest, according to historian Brian Connolly, moved increasingly away from biblical reference toward biology and, specifically, to reproductive considerations. Mating close relatives, it was generally thought, was good for animals but bad for humans. That human incest resulted in degeneration seemed to be a scientific conclusion, as S. M. Bemiss argued in "Report on the Influences of Consanguinity upon Offspring," published in the *Transactions of the American Medical Association* in 1858. Hence, Noyes's suggestion that reproductive rules were the same for both humans and animals was a legitimate contribution to scientific discourse. That was recognized as such by the publication of his ideas in a prestigious New York periodical, the *Modern Thinker*, in August 1870.[12]

At about the same moment, a major publisher in Philadelphia issued the results of Noyes's communitarian research in the book *History of America Socialisms*. Up to this point, Noyes's output in print had been limited to the releases of his own organization. His writings, that is to say, were essentially self-published in the eyes of the world and not subject to the critical standards of the outside world. Now Noyes found himself showcased on the national stage as a historian and as a scientist. The immense gratification such recognition brought him could only have strengthened an already considerable sense of self-worth. For just as he had accepted divine appointment as his due years before, now he found it easy to suppose he was genetically fitted—even chosen—to improve humankind.

Noyes's study of animal breeding had convinced him that males are more important than females in a program of selective breeding, because males contribute more offspring. Some males, furthermore, are much more important than others. After reading Galton's *Hereditary Genius* in early 1870, Noyes was confirmed in the suspicion that eminent men throughout history have been the result of superior "strains of blood."[13] Noyes's interest in Galton's "great man" concept gave rise, in his writings, to an emphasis on the male contribution to breeding and to the especial importance of males with "good blood." It gave rise as well to the conviction that his own eminence owed much to the superiority of his own stock. The Noyes bloodline, it followed, was deserving of special encouragement by selectively breeding carriers of Noyes blood. That led Noyes to propose to his niece and lover, Tirzah Miller, that he should have a child with her. "I told him," Miller related, "I should like that. He said he believed it to be his duty, and he had considerable curiosity to see what kind of a child we should produce. He said to combine with me would be intensifying the Noyes blood more than anything he could do. He was just waking up to a full sense of his duty, which is to pursue stirpiculture in the consanguineous line."[14]

Noyes's Perfectionism had become genetic, a state of sanctification carried in the blood. One consequence was that Noyes genetic material was patriarchally emphasized in the stirpicultural program. Noyes did not have a child by Miller, but he did have nine children by other women and was, by far, the most prolific sire in the Community. His son Theodore ranked second in the father category with three offspring.[15]

Disaffection

With age, Noyes seemed to become more argumentative and overbearing.[16] Based on belief in his own sanctified blood, for example, Noyes moved to elevate his family to a position of aristocracy within the commune by having his son installed as its leader. As imperiously as any absolute monarch, Noyes informed the Community that Theodore was now in charge:

> In this last stage of my labor I find myself in front of the last problem of Community-building, which is the problem of successor-ship; how to carry a Community through the change from one generation to another. . . . The Community did not form itself by getting together and choosing a president. I was the president from the beginning, called not by vote of the members but by the will of God, and as such I formed the Community. . . . There has never been a time when I did not claim the prerogative of criticism and final decision over the whole Community and over every member of it: and there has never been a time when the Community as a whole did not concede me that prerogative. . . . On these grounds I claim that I have a certain right to dispose of the government of the Community. . . . I therefore designate Theodore R. Noyes as my successor.[17]

Named as the Community's economic adviser back n 1868, Theodore, usually called Dr. Noyes, operated in that capacity until dismissed for despotic behavior. When Theodore announced he did not believe in God, Noyes senior suggested he should look into spiritualism, with the hope that he would become convinced of life after death. There followed a period of dabbling with the supernatural in the Mansion House. "I attended several seances in the 'dark room' in the North Garrret [sic] where we sat around a table, and people *shook*," Jessie Kinsley remembered, "but I was not a medium."[18] The good doctor emerged from these sessions believing in spirits (see figure 16) and in the ability of Community member Ann Hobart (also called Bailey), to communicate with those spirits.

Now, responding to a direct command, the Perfectionists named Dr. Noyes as head of the Community. The younger Noyes assumed the mantle of leadership in May 1877 and—in company with his consort, Hobart—instituted a harsh reign. Claiming that all aspects of Community life needed to be monitored more closely, the new regime required Community members to submit written reports accounting for all activities. With regard to sex, Theodore thought the Community had fallen into bad habits. Years before, he explained, "there was a regulation so that those in control knew what was going on. That was practically the case when the Community first went into complex marriage. Father and others associated with him knew pretty much all that was going on." Now the "great regulator" of sexual pleasure would be "walking in the light," meaning that Theodore would exercise strong hierarchical oversight.[19]

FIGURE 16. Theodore Noyes captured in a "spirit photograph," about 1875. "The other evening," it was noted in the *Oneida Circular,* "our photographer entertained us by explaining the various ways in which spirit photographs can be made." While photographer D. Edson Smith conceded the possibility of photographing spirits, his talk was about darkroom tricks and special effects.

These actions provoked outrage, forcing the removal of Dr. Noyes in January 1878 and the reinstallation of John Humphrey Noyes. The younger man's credibility was shattered, but at the same time the claim of divine inspiration advanced by the older was now revealed to be hollow. This was the series of events chiefly responsible for the demise of the Oneida Community.[20] "And then," Jessie Kinsley said, "doubt grew in the minds of *many*, regarding Mr. Noyes's ability to long be a leader. Doubt grew of his impartiality toward his son. There were doubts of J. H. N.'s 'inspiration.' Later, in the hearts of some, came doubt of the goodness of his intentions and of his acts."[21]

There were other sources of discontent, especially among younger people. Members of the rising generation had grown up in the Community and, unlike their parents, had never had to make a conscious decision to join. Such folk were accustomed to a high standard of living and to rubbing elbows with outsiders, the "world's people." Among young men, particularly those with college educations, there was widespread skepticism over Noyes's divine commission and over the very existence of the divine.[22] Some openly espoused agnosticism or even atheism.

For both men and women, stirpiculture contributed to discord by promoting individualistic tendencies long suppressed by Bible communism. Bringing couples into extended relationships encouraged a revival of exclusive conjugal love. "The young people as a class, and some of the older ones," Community member Frank Wayland-Smith observed in early 1879, "are free to speak of their preference for a more limited sexual fellowship than Mr. Noyes has always advocated. The more bold and ultra of them coolly declare in favor of a monogamic relation. They say one man is enough for one woman, one woman for one man."[23]

The real work of stirpiculture, of course, fell on the women as mothers. Being counted on as breeders, however, ran counter to the Community ideal of voluntary assent. This was a situation portended in Noyes's description of eugenics as far back as 1848. "We believe that good sense and benevolence will *very soon* sanction and enforce the rule that women shall bear children only when they choose," Noyes wrote in *Bible Argument*. "They have the principal burdens of breeding to bear, and they, rather than men, should have their choice of time and circumstances, *at least till science takes charge of the business* [emphasis added]."[24] Now that science apparently had taken charge, women may have perceived stirpicultural sex as an exacting and perhaps distasteful duty, particularly, one would guess, with Noyes. Noyes's desire to reproduce his bloodline and his increasing age must have lessened his attractiveness in the eyes of younger women, who now began to doubt the rightness of sex with him. Alice Ackley reported that when Noyes engaged in sex with her, he "quite disregarded the rules," presumably meaning he ejaculated. Ackley, according to Tirzah Miller, became "very much disaffected" with him, and even Miller, ever loyal to Noyes, dared to entertain this disturbing thought: "Oh! Is he a crazy enthusiast, who is just experimenting on human beings?" Not surprisingly, there seems to have been dissatisfaction among the women with the sexual roles in which they had been cast.[25] As doubt arose about the permanence of the commune, female misgivings ripened into fear. Following dismissal from the presidency, Theodore Noyes exited the commune, leaving behind three children by different women. He "claims that it is not his fault, but the fault of the system," Tirzah Miller confided to her diary. "The outlook for the future looks very dark for the women, if men can desert their children with so little compunction."[26]

That many young women were alienated from fundamental tenets of Bible communism is indicated by their espousal of outside standards of glamour far more openly than previously. In the past, the "dress spirit"—aspiring to be beautiful with stylish clothing and personal adornment—had drawn criticism but had always been overcome. "I am proud of our women, young and old. I see that in will and principle, and to a good extent in practice and feeling, they have conquered the fashions of the world in themselves," Noyes observed in 1865, "and are substantially free from hostage to the spirit of dress and ornament, and special love."[27] But when the dress spirit staged a comeback in the Community's latter days, it proved to be stronger than ever. At least one young girl growing up in the Community admired the fashion of the outside world and hated the frumpy appearance of Oneida women.[28] If Corinna Ackley's attitude had any currency, it was a sentiment undermining communism and eroding the ethos of selflessness. A telling incident in this regard is Ackley's only reported conversation with John Noyes: "I always tiptoed past his room, but one day, I remember, he saw me and asked if I wouldn't like to come in, that he had something pretty to show me. Then he took me on his knee, opened up a desk drawer and there, on a bed of cotton wool, were all the women's brooches. I had never seen so much jewelry before. They were dazzling, beautiful, but I didn't dare ask why they were there. Later I learned they had been temporarily banned to crucify the women's vanity and were later returned when their owners had conquered the 'Dress Spirit.'"[29] By late summer of 1879, a number of young women openly began to dress in "world's clothing" and to don "horsehair" attachments simulating long hair.[30]

Closely allied with the dress spirit went the possession of glamorous things stored in diminutive chests of drawers called miniature bureaus. Apparently unique to the Oneida Community, these objects date to the late 1870s when, it was said, almost every Community woman had one. As relics of the Community's final years, miniature bureaus became, as Edmund Wilson put it, "the first small triumph in a more general conquest of possessions."[31] The presence of this furniture attests to an increasing sense of private acquisition, and especially of individually owned jewelry and other items of feminine display fashionable in the outside world.

There was, then, dissatisfaction brewing in the Oneida Community from the imposition of the Noyes aristocracy composed of the aging and increasingly inflexible father and the agnostic and autocratic son. There was a drift toward secularism and monogamous marriage among the young. Among the young women, there was a desire for fashion and freedom. Disaffection crystallized into dissent, and, in the late 1870s, a party opposed to Noyes and his policies came into existence.

Dissolution

The disloyalists were called Townerites after one of their leaders, James Towner, a lawyer who had joined the Community in 1874. At least equally prominent in the faction was William Hinds, who had been with Noyes since Putney. The Townerite position called for representative government lodged in a president freely chosen by all Community members. The Townerites asked that social life be returned to the "old principles of the Community," a situation in which "every member is to be absolutely free from the undesired sexual familiarity, approach, and control of every other person."[32] Disagreements between Townerites and those loyal to Noyes ("Noyesites") became bitter and rancorous during the final years, the expression of enmity becoming a feature of Community life for the first time. "There were scenes in the Evening Meetings," Jessie Kinsley recollected. "The disaffected began to sit in the gallery and from there hurl words upon the loyalists. Open scorn, hatred and rebellion were shown in *many* places."[33] Fierce dissension gave rise to the fear that the Community would break up at precisely the moment the Community was threatened from without.

As the Perfectionists fell to arguing among themselves, a local academic, Professor John Mears of nearby Hamilton College, launched a moral crusade of ministers who viewed the commune as an affront to family values. Oneida, Mears raged, was a "corrupt concubinage," a "moral defilement," and a "utopia of obscenities" founded on "a system of organized fanaticism and lust."[34] Although newspapers gleefully lampooned the excesses of Mears's language and the foolishness of his posturing, the Community took the threat seriously. The 1870s were the high point of Victorian prudery and intolerance toward anything out of the ordinary in matters of the family, marriage, and sex. Anthony Comstock's fierce campaigns against immorality had just produced the first federal legislation against pornography, laws that made sale of Community literature mentioning birth control a crime. Comstock did not attack the Oneida Community directly, but he did prosecute Ezra Heywood and Edward Bliss Foote—popular writers on sexual matters who had been influenced by Noyes and the Oneida Community. Also at this time, the United States was attempting to break up Mormon polygamy, and the Perfectionists thought they would be the government's next target.[35] Times had changed. With the zeitgeist against them, the Perfectionists worried that the world would set upon them at any moment.

The clergymen's crusade made Noyes personally uneasy. After reading in the newspaper about plans for his impending arrest, he tiptoed out of the Mansion House on the night of June 22, 1879, never to return. The story of his arrest, it turned out, was untrue. Nor was the charge on which he was to be arrested ever clear. Noyes believed, however, that the Townerite faction was providing outsiders with information that would strengthen a legal case against him.[36] He may have feared prosecution for statutory rape stemming from his initiation of young girls into the Community's social life. Community historian Maren Carden pointed out that a possible basis for such a charge already had been documented by an outside medical doctor who examined Community women in 1877. When published some years later, the report stated that Community female sexual activity commenced after menstruation at an average age of fifteen. The ages given for twenty-nine females at first sex ranged between nineteen and, in one instance, ten years. In reality, however, a charge relating to underage sex could never have been maintained in court because the age of consent—that is, the age at which a man could have sexual intercourse with a girl without committing statutory rape—was ten years old in New York State.[37]

Carden and other Community historians have suggested that the Townerites were jealous of Noyes's "first husband" prerogative and wanted themselves to perform the office of *droit du seigneur*.[38] This hypothesis apparently rests on an inconclusive argument that occurred in 1880 over whether Townerites were gathering evidence for outsiders.[39] The idea also derives from a letter Dr. Theodore Noyes wrote in 1892 to a student of anthropology who was researching stirpiculture. "I cannot free my mind of an impression which was present all through the struggle, and without which it is difficult to account for all the facts, and the bitterness of the contest, and that is, that the control of the young women was pictured in the inner recesses of the minds of all persons of intelligence, as a matter not of committees and Councils, but of individuals and men—in short a prize to be contended for."[40]

The motivation Theodore imputed to others made sense in the context of his larger characterization of the Community. Oneida, Dr. Noyes revealed, was a sexual jungle in which libidinous older men competed to have intercourse with attractive younger women. "The government of the Community was by complex marriage," Theodore stated flatly. Since sex was the source of political power, John Humphrey Noyes was able to rule the primal horde by controlling sexual access to women.[41] The extreme expression of this interpretation is that the Community was autocratically governed by Noyes and his inner circle, who required all proposals for sex to be submitted to them for approval.[42] The thesis of tight sexual control, however, should be weighed in the scales of other, more contemporary evidence. It should be approached cautiously, because Theodore was a biased and compromised source. It was he who was accused of this sort of thing, and the effect of his argument was to shift blame onto his deceased father. As a single source of idiosyncratic information, Dr. Noyes's document should be treated as all such documents should be treated: skeptically.

Initially stunned by Noyes's departure, the factionalized Community found enough common cause over the next year and a half to agree to abandon the practices the world found objectionable. On Noyes's recommendation and out of deference to public sentiment, they put an end to complex marriage on August 28, 1879. Many who had been lovers bid a fond sexual farewell to one another for the term of their remaining earthly lives.[43] Soon after, most of the younger people bonded monogamously in the world's fashion of husband and wife. Thirty-seven marriages were performed. Men, in general, married the mothers of their Community children. That, of course, was not always possible, and about a dozen women with children remained single. For many, it was a time "of heartache and pain that came like a bitter wind." "I do not understand how the misery was borne," Jessie Kinsley reflected. She herself followed Noyes's advice to marry Myron Kinsley. Myron, in entering into the union, gave up the mother of his stirpicultural child and a lover with whom he was emotionally intimate. Both the other women became reconciled to the situation and assured the new couple of their continuing goodwill. The couple also had to learn to get along with two men who had hoped to marry Jessie. "Community *training told*," she emphasized, and the former rivals remained good friends to both Jessie and Myron.[44]

A year after doing away with complex marriage, the Perfectionists agreed to disband as a commune and to reorganize themselves into a joint-stock-holding business to be called the Oneida Community Ltd. It would be a legal corporation keeping the Community's lucrative trap and thread businesses intact, but equitably dividing common property into the form of stocks and dividends to be owned by Community members and their descendants. The corporation would care for the young, elderly, and disabled. It would give employment to all Community members desiring it, while guaranteeing a lifetime of support for those who did not. It would maintain the Mansion House as residence at a low rate of rent for those desiring to live there. The agreement of August 1880 to reorganize in 1881 was unanimous.

Where, in their bitterest period, did they find the goodwill to agree on such profound and complicated issues? In part, they may have been influenced by a pledge, signed by all, not to seek individual enrichment by lodging a court suit against the Oneida Community. Back in 1875, lawyer James Towner drew up a document affirming that none of them would ever "bring any action, either at law or in equity, or other process or proceeding whatsoever against said Community or its branches, or against the agents or property-holders thereof, or any person or corporation, for wages or other compensation for service, nor for the recovery of any property by us . . . nor make any claim or demand there—for, of any kind or nature whatsoever."[45] Whatever the force of law in such an agreement, force of habit strongly inclined them to harmony. Community discipline for unselfishness was, as Jessie Kinsley remarked, strongly ingrained.

Another source of concord was making music and comedy together. On or about the day Noyes walked out of the Mansion House, a traveling theatrical troupe performed the operetta *H.M.S. Pinafore*, the hit of the London stage. That show, staged in the Family Hall, gave the Perfectionists "unalloyed pleasure," and they resolved to mount their own production. They worked throughout the latter half of 1879 to bring it together and, in early 1880, performed it several times. *Pinafore*, it was reported, "wears well and always draws a full house of admiring listeners. All drop their 'whys and wherefores' and come and hear it. It promotes love and fellowship in our family circle."[46] The tuneful and witty musical was the Community's most ambitious theatrical production, and those who were then children remembered it vividly for a lifetime.

The fundamental rules for dividing Community property were that one-half of the value of property brought into the Community would be returned to the contributing individuals in shares of stock. The remainder of the capital stock would be divided among all Community members in proportion to the time they had been in the commune. These terms were accepted by the Community on September 15 by a vote of 199 to 1.[47] The lone dissenter was Sewell Newhouse, who believed he was entitled to a larger share than allotted because of his greater contribution—the Newhouse trap.

The opposing view was that Newhouse had been bankrupt when he joined, and the Community had paid off the indigent's debts. The Community, they averred further, made Newhouse, and not the other way around. Angrily, Newhouse moved back to Oneida Castle, a short distance away. After sulking for a few years, however, Newhouse quietly accepted the share that had been set aside for him.[48] "It must certainly be conceded that the peaceable accomplishing of this division was in itself an astonishing thing," stirpicult Holton Noyes observed wonderingly. Not a single lawsuit was ever instituted against the agreement to incorporate.[49]

During its last decade, the Community embarked on a eugenics program called stirpiculture to produce a spiritually elevated group of people who would benefit humankind. Feeling prosperous enough to raise children as responsible parents, the Bible communists built a new wing of the house for their intended offspring, then turned successfully to the business of reproduction. Stirpiculture, however, encouraged selfishness, which caused internal problems. Such difficulties were greatly exacerbated by Noyes becoming increasingly autocratic and more obviously fallible. His worst mistake was demanding that his eldest son, an agnostic unskilled in leadership, be appointed Community leader. The failed interregnum of Dr. Theodore Noyes revealed that the judgment of the elder Noyes was deeply flawed.

Opposition from without also contributed to the breakup. The 1870s were the heyday of Victorian domestic values in which unconventional sexual arrangements were widely regarded as intolerable. In the end, the Community voluntarily gave up complex marriage and common ownership. By vote, the Community transformed itself into a company, the Oneida Community Ltd., on January 1, 1881. The new entity was to continue operation of the industries of the Oneida Community in order to provide its stockholders, former members of the Community, with an income.

CHAPTER 9

A Silverware Company

The self-imposed exile of John Noyes culminated in residence at Niagara Falls. There, from an aerie called the Stone Cottage on the Canadian side, he gazed out on a silverware factory of the Oneida Community Ltd. getting under way on the American side. Noyes exerted considerable influence on the new company's policies—apparently with beneficial effect—until his death in 1886. Thereafter, the company sank rapidly under the weight of mismanagement.

Oneida's fortunes were revived in the late 1890s by one of John Noyes's stirpicultural offspring, Pierrepont B. Noyes. Recruiting his peers from the old children's department, the younger Noyes infused them with enthusiasm to resuscitate the Oneida Community's value of selfless commitment to the whole in the running of an industrial company. The youthful executives then restructured Oneida Community Ltd. around high-end silverware by increasing product quality, improving its look, and promoting it with innovative advertising.

Post-Community Adjustments

When the Oneida Community ended, the Bible communists had to begin life over again stripped of almost every comfortable certainty formerly taken for granted. Initially they struggled to understand individual ownership as something inhering in things. Among themselves they developed an exaggerated respect for private property, making them reluctant to lend anything. "When they borrowed a pin," Pierrepont Noyes remembered, "they felt duty bound to return it." New circumstances, not surprisingly, were unsettling. "The terror of that first plunge into individualism," the younger Noyes added, "left most of our people with an economy complex which persisted as long as they lived."[1] Uneasiness with noncommunist ownership, of course, was only one aspect of a new reality frightening in other ways.

With utopian sanctuary behind them, the Oneidans faced a fearful arena of ambition and selfishness around them, one that seemed implacably hostile to Bible communism. Increasingly, those living in the Mansion House sensed that what lay beyond their grounds was a threatening presence, coiling and drawing its energies together to strike them down. As the first year of joint-stock life drew to a close, the idea of attack from the outside became palpable with the discovery that someone was setting fire to Community buildings. A feeling of impending disaster gripped the Mansion House as weeks passed in fear of an unknown assailant. "My memory asserts that November, 1881, was a dismal succession of dark, rainy days, low-hanging clouds and thunderstorms," Pierrepont Noyes recalled. "This picture may be only a reflection of the gloom in my soul." On the night of November 18, the horse barn across the road went up in flames. "It was a spectacular blaze, a huge barn filled to the roof with hay and all on fire at once. I was not allowed to go nearer than the North Lawn. From there, with other boys, I watched the roof fall in, a terrifying roar, and then a great column of fiery sparks rushing far up into the darkness. . . . Between the crashes we talked of the poor horses and were sickened by the thought of their agonies." The world and the future "smelled of destruction—of charred wood and burnt flesh" when the eleven-year-old boy went to sleep that night.[2]

The arsonist turned out to be James Vail, a Perfectionist who seceded shortly before the breakup. Harboring a grudge against his former home, he sought revenge against it. For the Community, the fire "cleared the atmosphere of Oneida as a thunderstorm at the end of a rainy spell sometimes clears up the weather," wrote the younger Noyes. His impression was that "of a busy Community, whose members, emerging from the nervousness caused by our fire scare, had, through some kind of reverse suggestion, shaken off much of the questioning timidity which marked the first months of the new social order."[3] Now the former Bible communists were ready to get on with it.

For most, that meant continuing to live in the Mansion House. For others, it meant embarking on new lives elsewhere. Three groups who left the

Mansion House in the early 1880s headed for California or to Niagara Falls, to either the American or Canadian side. John Noyes, who earlier had departed for Canada, ended up on the Canadian side, where in 1880 the Community purchased a house for him. The Stone Cottage, as it was called, was large enough to accommodate a reconstituted association of Perfectionists wishing to rejoin their longtime leader. This circle included Noyes's wife, Harriet "Mother" Noyes; his sister, Harriet Skinner; the master gardener, Henry Seymour; and a coterie of faithful Bible communists including Theodore Pitt and Erastus Hamilton.[4]

Noyes had chosen the Niagara location with the expectation that it would be near an important branch of the Oneida company: a silverware factory. In 1877, the Community had begun manufacturing spoon blanks at Wallingford, some of which were supplied to the nearby Meriden Britannia Company. The early flatware consisted mostly of steel spoons that were unplated or tin washed. By 1878, forks had been added to the line, and some of the tableware was plated with silver.[5] The "spoon business" was regarded as promising. In 1881, the enterprise was relocated to Niagara Falls, New York, to escape malaria, which had become rife at Wallingford, and to benefit from greater waterpower there. The location also had the advantage of being close to John Noyes, whose home on the Canadian side looked directly across the Niagara River to the factory's new location on the American side.[6] A number of former Perfectionists came from Oneida to run the flatware facility. The first was Myron Kinsley, the company's cutlery superintendent responsible for moving both Noyes and the flatware west.

Next to leave was a large contingent of Townerites departing for California after the shareholders' election in January 1882. That vote established six company directors loyal to John Noyes, as opposed to two belonging to the Townerite faction. Feeling frozen out of power, James Towner emigrated with about forty of his adherents to Santa Ana, California. There they did well. Towner chaired the committee that organized Orange County, then served as that county's first superior court judge.[7]

Although he held no position in the Oneida Community Ltd., John Noyes played an important role in company affairs. Indeed, with the greater part of the old Townerite opposition gone, his authority may have been recognized more strongly than ever. "The officers and most of the directors of the company were of his selection, and any important move, whether business or social, always awaited his sanction," Pierrepont Noyes wrote. "Sometimes he summoned to the Stone Cottage at Niagara, for consultation, one or another of his representatives on the board of directors. Even men of the opposing party were occasionally invited to visit him." So strong were the habits of a lifetime, the younger Noyes added, that all who were invited went gladly.[8] The first two company presidents, Erastus Hamilton and George Campbell, were regarded as poorly equipped to handle business affairs but unwavering in their loyalty to Noyes. Fortunately, company affairs ran smoothly enough with Noyes back at the helm, and his governance resulted in what his son called "a reasonable prosperity—and 6 per cent dividends."[9]

In Kenwood, the newly minted name for the Mansion House neighborhood, and in Sherrill, the term now used for the vicinity of the trap factory, life continued during the 1880s and 1890s much as it had in Community days. Fabricating silk thread, canning fruits and vegetables, and manufacturing traps—all these businesses operated as before. Traps continued to be the biggest moneymaker. In 1886 the company launched Victor, a line of traps cheaper and lighter than the Newhouses. This was not the first attempt to do so. The Oneida Community, hard-pressed by competitors imitating their traps, tried to tap into a cheaper market with a product line named Hawley and Norton (begun 1874). Those devices pleased neither buyers nor makers, but the Victor line was better. Victors soon accounted for the majority of Oneida sales and would dominate the trap market for many years to come.

The year Victors were begun at Oneida witnessed the introduction of knives to the Niagara Falls line of cutlery. There, with modest success, the factory was turning out flatware that was lightly plated with silver.[10] Of at least equal importance to silverware was an industry of chain making. The Oneida Community had been fabricating chains for their traps since about 1857. An activity women and children could do, putting chains together was valued as a home industry. And, in fact, a new wing of the Mansion House, the "New House" built in 1878 to accommodate Perfectionists leaving the Wallingford branch, became the scene of chain making on a limited scale during the 1880s. However, when the spoon business had begun at Wallingford, it was discovered that the resulting scrap was perfect for cutting out chain links. Hence, the spoon and chain businesses became closely associated, and the major part of the chain industry moved to Niagara Falls along with the flatware. In that setting, chains grew into a substantial business, along with the addition of halters, dog chains, cow ties, and other products (see figure 17).[11]

When John Noyes died, in 1886, his body immediately was brought back to Oneida for interment. Today, many find his plot difficult to locate because it is marked by a simple tombstone indistinguishable from the egalitarian markers of the Community members buried nearby.

FIGURE 17.   Oneida Community Ltd. buildings at Niagara Falls, about 1905.

With his passing, control of the company fell to a group of men who had taken up the religion of spiritualism. The spiritualists said they were in daily conference with John Noyes, who, deceased, was directing them in the administration of the business. It made a certain psychological sense. "Having been spiritually shepherded all their lives, those old members were unhappy without a spiritual leader," Pierrepont Noyes observed. Spiritualism became, he thought, "an enthusiasm whose contagion spread through the membership of the new Company."[12] Initially, the spiritualists were led by Theodore Pitt, a former Community member who, in Pierrepont Noyes's estimation, "had soft-pedaled his Spiritualistic leanings in order to keep his 'place by throne.'" Subsequently, spiritualism came to be identified with John Lord, previously a Perfectionist salesman of silk thread who was elected to the presidency in early 1889. In addition to perpetuating the business incompetence of his predecessors, Lord ushered in a period of acrimony and peculation that carried the company to the brink of disaster. Lord, for one, was deeply involved in real estate speculation, which in a short time would bankrupt him.[13]

The production of traps, the company's chief moneymaker, dropped precipitously during the early 1890s. This was partly due to managerial problems at the departmental level. Under the spiritualists, the longtime head of the hardware department, Frank Wayland-Smith, left. He was replaced in 1892 by a team of two—George E. Cragin and Orrin Wright—who proved to be ineffective administrators.[14]

Pierrepont Noyes

Young Pierrepont Noyes, a son (born 1870) of John Noyes, appeared on the company's board of directors in 1894. This occurred almost accidentally as a result of his foster father, Abram Burt, being able to pass along *his* set of proxy votes. Pierrepont Noyes was one of a minority of four voters power-less to alter the decisions of the spiritualist majority holding five votes. But, as a director, he gained access to company records and was able to investigate the state of affairs in the various departments at Sherrill and Niagara Falls. What he discovered was widespread profiteering and corruption draining the company. Coupled with the knowledge that Oneida Community Ltd. stock was selling at a price far below par, Noyes became thoroughly alarmed about the company's future.[15]

The brash twenty-three-year-old determined to unseat the spiritualists in the stockholders' election of early 1895. A successful outcome would require shareholders who had been Noyesites and anti-Noyesites a short time before to find common cause against the new spiritualist faction. An event of deep symbolic resonance helped to make this possible. In 1894, Pierrepont Noyes married Corinna Ackley—daughter of two of the most vocal Townerites. The event was celebrated as a laying to rest of old sentiments lingering from the Community breakup.[16]

The young Noyes conducted a vigorous campaign, personally visiting or corresponding with every holder of Oneida stock. On the night of the elec-tion, both parties went to bed thinking they had lost. As Noyes lay awake reviewing the votes, however, he suddenly recalled "that a block of stock which had not been voted at all was figured by us as entirely negative, while it should have been reckoned one half in our favor." Those votes—sixteen out of twenty-four thousand—were indeed the winning margin. For the younger Noyes, the "new Oneida Community Ltd." was born at that moment.[17]

The first decision of the new anti-spiritualist majority was to elect Dr. Theodore Noyes as president, a contemplative man now mellowed with age. Dr. Noyes instituted a policy of charity toward the defeated and encour-aged inclusiveness to heal the wounds of political factionalism. Dr. Noyes also strongly backed his half brother, Pierrepont, nearly thirty years his junior, a man in whom he discerned the qualities for leadership he himself lacked. Pierrepont had always been recognized by his stirpicultural peers as their natural leader. His contemporary and half brother, Holton Noyes, observed of this man that he was never sick and seldom tired:

> He had the very happy faculty of throwing aside his cares and entering
> joyfully into recreations in his hours of relaxation. Temperamentally,

he was a glowing optimist, always expecting the best and never discouraged by setbacks. He considered them purely temporary, promptly forgot them and turned his attention to the future. He enjoyed fighting but was never quarrelsome, and he had the rare faculty of fighting relentlessly but never holding a grudge against his adversary. He appreciated the good in his associates and promptly forgot the bad. . . . Malice and envy had no place in his make-up.

Commercially, he was a genius. A wonderful salesman and manager himself, he had that enthusiasm which is contagious. His associates lived upon his vitality. He was a perfect negotiator, never losing sight of his own purpose and yet fairly recognizing the viewpoint of his adversary. Above all, he had vision and courage. His ambitions and energies were all for the Oneida Community, Ltd. and only incidentally for himself.[18]

Elected to effect change in 1895, Pierrepont Noyes (hereafter the "Noyes" referred to in the text) was put to the test to produce immediate results. With the approval of Dr. Noyes, the younger man was appointed superintendent of the Niagara Falls facility. After only a year of Noyes's aggressive salesmanship and attention to internal organization, the plant's profitability rose nearly 100 percent.[19] Thereafter, he often was asked to solve problems in other departments and to increase sales of all company products. He seemed to have a magic touch. After only three years, he was appointed to the position of general manager, a post created specifically for him in recognition of his interdepartmental labors contributing to company unity.

Thus began the watch of Pierrepont Noyes, a half century of shepherding the fortunes of Oneida. At the outset, he dreamed of reuniting his childhood companions and forging them into a team to, as he thought of it, cover his father's rear.[20] That meant ensuring a comfortable old age for John Noyes's followers and building a new Oneida on the foundations of the old. Oneida Community ideals that Pierrepont Noyes dusted off to carry into the future were doing "the greatest good to the greatest number, the renouncement of private ambitions and the most scrupulous honesty in all dealings."[21]

His biggest problem, initially, was traps. Though still the mainstay of Oneida, sales of that product had plummeted under the spiritualists. As general manager, Noyes was able to have Stephen Leonard, a childhood friend from Community days (born 1872), placed in charge of trap-making operations. Leonard, a college-educated mechanical engineer, boosted trap production to 1.5 million in his first year (1898) as superintendent of the hardware department. Within a decade, trap output rose to almost five million. Oneida was now the largest manufacturer of animal traps in the world. At least two of every three traps around the globe came from Sherrill.[22] The overall success of the company resulted from Leonard's factory modernization, expansion of manufacturing facilities beyond the old trap shop, and enlargement of the company's line of products. The Oneida Community Ltd., for example, moved into the market of wooden mouse traps by acquiring the Animal Trap Company of Lititz, Pennsylvania, in 1906. At Noyes's insistence, company salesmanship became more aggressive and wide-ranging.[23]

When English social commentator H. G. Wells visited Kenwood in 1906, he discovered in Pierrepont Noyes the perfect businessman: "I have heard much talk of the romance of business, chiefly from people I heartily despised, but in Mr. Noyes I found business indeed romantic. It had got hold of him, it possessed him like a passion. . . . I never met a man before so firmly gripped by the romantic constructive and adventurous element of business, so little concerned about personal riches or the accumulation of wealth. He illuminated much that had been dark to me in the American character. I think better of business by reason of him."[24] Wells also discerned that Noyes was driven not by an abstract love of business but by passionate attachment to the business of Oneida.

Noyes was able to enlist those about him in common service to what seemed a higher purpose. "Most men father their own ideas strongly, and often resist the ideas of others," Edith Kinsley mused. "Pierrepont, on the other hand, fathers the ideas of others and accords credit for creativeness more enthusiastically than he backs himself. . . . [He] is the father, brother and friend of every member in the group."[25] The effectiveness of his supervisory style reminded many of the charisma and magnetic power of his father. But whereas John Humphrey Noyes trafficked in divine truth, the younger man offered an irresistible brand of salesmanship and friendship.

Kenwood

At the outset, Noyes focused on recruiting his youthful peers and inspiring them with the idea that their generation, imbued with Oneida Community values, would now apply those precepts to the running of a modern business corporation. Community beliefs worth perpetuating were brotherhood, equality, and a record of human accord that, as Noyes put it, "idealists always hope for and theorists write books about."[26] Religion (no longer relevant to current circumstances) and communism (proved mistaken) would be dropped. As explained in a 1909 manifesto called "Basswood Philosophy,"

Noyes believed he and the younger men of Kenwood could create a new kind of industrial organization run by a team of semi-socialistic partners. Among themselves, there would be a "practical equality" of wealth and power. Although there had to be some hierarchy with real authority at the top, abuses and excesses would be held in check by the public opinion—the approval and confidence—of the Kenwood circle of stockholders. Further, those shareholders would naturally agree to limit any private accumulation of stocks.

Executive salaries would be held relatively low—just above the level of factory pay—to avoid sharp discrepancies between the incomes of administrators and assembly-line workers. In hard times, cutbacks in pay would start at the top and be proportionately greater higher up. Salaries among executives would be kept within narrow limits. That, and the relatively low pay, would encourage the executives to maintain a similar standard of living in Kenwood, the "land between the bridges" where no one was rich and no one was poor. The professional circle at Kenwood would always be open to talented outsiders—"joiners"—wishing to share the commitment felt by Community descendants. Such commitment was manifested in loyalty to the company and fidelity to one's peers.[27] Together, the boys of the Oneida Community Ltd. would pursue business as an athletic team whose members cooperated with one another and played by the same rules:

> Thou shalt not take offense at thy brother's words or actions no matter how great the provocation.
>
> Thou shalt not permit business differences to create in thee personal soreness.
>
> Thou shalt not be jealous of thy brother, nor envious.
>
> Strive to place thy loyalty to thy fellows above the reach of selfish interest or passion.
>
> Thou shalt not join cliques either to advance thyself or injure another.
>
> Thou shalt not resent criticism.
>
> Seek the causes for thy failures in thine own deficiencies rather than imagining unfriendliness in others. . . . Be humble as well as brotherly, for social equality is for us as necessary as official inequality.[28]

In the early years of the twentieth century, this group of young men worked well together and delighted in each other's company. They felt, as Noyes put it, "the romance of adventure and the rather delightful feeling we were adventurers."[29] They expressed their pleasure in joint enterprise by, for example, putting up a log cabin in conscious emulation of the old

Community work projects. That construction was described by an anonymous member of the group as "the product of 'bees' of the old-fashioned
sort. Anyone who helped erect the 'Mansion House' or the old 'Children's
Wing' or worked at clearing the swamp, back in the fifties, would, I am
sure, have been carried back to those early days had they joined the throng
of Cabin builders on any Sunday during the winters of 1905 and 1906.
The same energy and enthusiasm, the same enjoyment of labor, the same
sustained effort until the work was completed."[30] They all lived near one
another in newly built homes clustered around the Mansion House, now
called "The Big House" or just "The Big." During the first decades of the
twentieth century, company executives built, at personal expense, about
twenty new houses in Kenwood. Some were designed by Syracuse Arts-
and-Crafts architect Ward Wellington Ward. Many more were the works of
Kenwood architect Theodore Skinner—a stirpicult. Skinner, for example,
created a home for Pierrepont and Corinna Noyes in 1907 based on a pattern for a Tudor design Corinna saw in the *Ladies' Home Journal* and further
modified by Noyes's insistence on raised ceilings.[31]

Since golf had replaced croquet as the Oneida social game of choice, company officials recreated together on greens laid out in the former vegetable
beds and fruit orchards of the Oneida Community. "Golf has become an
integral part of business, that is, a happy combination of work and play,
shared responsibility and pleasure which promote and express brotherhood,
a brotherhood in interests more basically important than salaries or dividends," Edith Kinsley noted of life around her during the 1910s. "A man who
does not play as well as work is not one of The Gang." Such strongly developed male comradeship meant that life in Kenwood had strayed far from
the practical gender equality achieved by the Oneida Community. Golf and
business were the new religion of Kenwood, and both belonged to the men.
Where did that leave the women?

"Women are inferiors, dependents," Kinsley stated flatly. "The most
important function of woman is childbearing. The next, that she be a good
wife, sufficiently adequate to prevent her husband's attention from straying,
a conscientious and commonsense mother, and that she shall not be pos-
sessive and interfere with masculine preoccupations or with business and
fraternity." Within the family circle of Kenwood, "no man makes love to his
brother's wife," was the way Kinsley put it.[32] Divorce, also, was disapproved.
Excluded from business and golf, many Kenwood women focused, of necessity, on home life.

One of them, a child of Oneida Community parents, kept a diary in
the early 1920s indicating that her husband, another child of Community

FIGURE 18. The Oneida-Kenwood Women's Suffrage Group, 1917. Lotta Kinsley, in the front row, fifth from left, holds the captioned ball. Christine Allen is just above and to the right of Lotta Kinsley. Jessie Kinsley sits in the second row, third from right.

parents and a company executive, was seldom around. Lotta Kinsley's journal is largely an account of taking care of children (three of them) and keeping the domestic environment in order. The work exhausted her and often threatened, in her estimation, to overwhelm her. Yet she found some means to engage the world politically on her own idealistic terms, first on behalf of the women's suffrage movement, then as a candidate for the state senate representing Norman Thomas's Socialist Party of America. "I am glad to be working for a most worthy cause," she wrote of the latter experience. "What could be better than trying to bring about a better social order and to eliminate suffering from the world by striking at the base of economic disease?" She had no time to campaign, and when the election was over, she dropped by the Mansion House library "to look at the paper to see how much of a vote I polled. . . . I got about one thousand votes in the district. That was very fair for the socialist ticket. The Republicans won, of course, hands down" (see figure 18).[33]

The older people in Kenwood were not excluded from the new fellowship, and most seemed to approve it. Two who had been involved in the breakup, Dr. Theodore Noyes and William Hinds, for example, enthusiastically furthered the policies of the younger Noyes during their tenures as company president. "I rejoice to see you pressing forward with all the young people here toward an ideal—" Jessie Kinsley told her daughter, Edith, "an ideal not of commercialism, nor yet of communism, but with the creed of character-building, toleration and brotherly love." Yet Kinsley also harbored mixed emotions about the new order. "Having seen one dream of heaven on earth and realized its limitations, I do not imagine utopia established by socialism or any fundamental change brought about quickly."[34]

Community Plate

As of 1909, the company under Pierrepont Noyes could claim substantial prosperity in the form of steadily increasing profits, stock payments, and corporate worth since the 1895 ouster of the spiritualists. The shareholders were happy, but privately Noyes wondered whether the company had much of a future. "Men able to run a business profitably in the 'sixties or 'seventies, were just out of luck, struggling with the competition of the 'eighties and 'nineties," he observed, "when mass production was taking the place of the little factory on the mill stream."[35] An example familiar to him was a giant conglomerate of silver makers, the International Silver Corporation, formed in 1898 from a score of formerly independent firms into International Silver in the Meriden area of Connecticut.[36]

The worry was that the Oneida company would be unable to meet the industrial competition of the time. None of the firm's products inspired confidence in an expansive future. Silk thread, already the least profitable industry, promised little, because the raw material was exorbitantly expensive. The fruit business was losing money in competition with large, specialized corporations. Traps, traditionally Oneida's most profitable product, were thought to have limited growth potential. Those devices, furthermore, carried a public relations liability that came to the company's attention at this time. Read into the proceedings of a directors' meeting in 1900 was a letter from an elderly trapper who indicated that "although he had spent his lifetime using traps, he had become convinced that the use of traps should be discontinued as it violates in the most brutal and inhuman manner all laws for the prevention of cruelty to animals." The correspondent vowed that, henceforth, he would dedicate his life to eradicating these implements of suffering.[37]

Oneida's future, Noyes felt, depended on finding a product with an expandable market. The company would have to specialize in that product and promote it with something new at the time: a sustained advertising effort on a national level. The obvious candidate was silverware. As Niagara Falls superintendent, he was familiar with the product, and as salesman, he had demonstrated its substantial growth potential. By 1900, Noyes had formulated a complicated and risky plan to restructure the company around the manufacture of plated flatware. He, Leonard, and other young colleagues committed the company to developing a distinctive kind of silverware and establishing it in the public's mind.[38]

In 1895, the best-selling grade of silverware contained two ounces of silver per gross of teaspoons. Often marketed under the name Rogers, the product was made by Meriden Britannia and a number of other firms centered in the Meriden-Hartford-Waterbury area of Connecticut. Some makers of silverware also offered a higher grade of plated cutlery containing six ounces of silver. Considerably more expensive than the standard grade, "triple plate" silverware commanded a negligible share of the market. Whether standard or higher grade, the style of Connecticut silverware was hopelessly outmoded in Noyes's eyes. It was downright ugly, according to Grosvenor Allen, the stirpicult who became the Oneida Community Ltd.'s design specialist.[39]

Noyes's plan for the Oneida Community Ltd. was to manufacture "a line of silver-plated ware of a quality superior to anything ever before offered the American public, and in patterns more attractive than had hitherto been thought necessary for plated ware."[40] Even though some of the older directors were unenthusiastic about spending more on silverware, raising its quality was not controversial (see figure 19).

Former Perfectionists and their children took pride in their tradition that came to be called "OCQ"—Oneida Community quality. Traps, thread, and canned goods had always been the best money could buy. Cutlery, on the

FIGURE 19. Board of Directors of Oneida Community Ltd., 1907. Seated are (*left to right*) John Freeman, Martin Kinsley, William Hinds (president), Pierrepont Noyes (general manager), Harriet Allen Joslyn, and Henry Allen. Standing are George Wallingford Noyes, Stephen Leonard (hardware superintendent), Paul Herrick, Holton Noyes, and Grosvenor Allen.

other hand, had always been of secondary quality, and that made them a
little uncomfortable. According with company culture, upgrading was contextually correct. Further, the manufacture of high-end silverware posed no
major financial risk. The production expense of electroplating silver to the
base metal remained about the same whether one added two or six ounces.

In 1900, the Oneida Community Ltd. created a new plated ware containing about seven ounces of silver per gross of teaspoons—a higher silver content than anything else on the market.[41] It was called "Triple Plus," then
"Community Silver," and finally, about 1915, "Community Plate." Having
elevated the quality of the product, company officials now turned to the
problem of making it attractive. The first design for Community Plate was
thought up by Noyes himself in consultation with factory die makers in 1900.
Called "Avalon" and featuring rococo curlicues, it was followed quickly by
two floral designs commissioned by Grosvenor Allen: "Cereta" in 1901 and
"Flower-de-Luce" in 1903. Originating with Chicago sculptor Julia Bracken,
these styles could fairly be described as artistic. "You can see for yourself,"
Noyes would say, flourishing a competitor's spoon in a customer's face, "just
a lot of lumps and sausages thrown together by a diemaker! Now—look at
this! The work of an artist!"[42] Thereafter, the Oneida company laid claim to
the highest aesthetic standards in silverware design.

Getting people to agree that Oneida's silverware was real art, however,
required a quantum leap in advertising effectiveness. The company's first
advertising innovation was to depart from the existing convention of cram-
ming text into a small space. An Oneida magazine ad of 1903 enlarged the
presentational frame and made it visual with the picture of a middle-aged,
rather mannish-looking woman holding up an Oneida spoon (see figure 20).

"It's rotten, Noyes, rotten," the general manager was told. "What are you
doing—trying to advertise old women?" Silverware, the critic went on to
advise, should be made to look attractive in every possible way.[43] Oneida's
advertising manager, stirpicult Burton "Doc" Dunn, took the sentiment to
heart. His first effective ad campaign showcased the beauty of Oneida silverware by resting examples on a backdrop of quality lace. His second success
was to secure endorsements for Oneida flatware from high society hostesses.
Such ads often depicted the woman's dining room photographed by Baron
de Meyer, then at the height of his reputation.[44]

Most important, Dunn defined Oneida's target audience for silverware
as youthful and, in particular, female—the prospective brides most likely
to acquire flatware. Accordingly, Dunn hired a graphic artist adept at presenting young people enjoying themselves. Coles Phillips's first ad, in 1911,
depicted a seated man reading a newspaper as a pretty woman, perched on

A BEAUTIFUL OLD AGE IS ATTAINED BY

THE ONEIDA COMMUNITY
TRIPLE PLUS PLATE SILVER TABLE WARE
Superior in use to Sterling Silver, and in its old age will still be as bright and beautiful as the Solid Service.

The ONEIDA COMMUNITY QUALITY Silver-Plate Table Ware is durable, of elegant pattern and beautiful finish. It has the heaviest ornamentation, and in this respect is an almost equal counterpart of Sterling Silver. The famous AVALON pattern of the ONEIDA COMMUNITY is recognized as the most refined and chaste produced. The moderate price of the ONEIDA COMMUNITY Triple-Plate Plus enables it to take the place of the inferior plated ware, sold under fancy names, at fancy prices.

A Guarantee Bond good for 25 years with every piece of ONEIDA COMMUNITY Triple-Plate Plus Silver Table Ware.

Since 1848 "the ONEIDA COMMUNITY *quality*" has been recognized as the best. Their canned and preserved fruits, vegetables and jellies are recognized as this country's finest—their sewing and embroidering silk, the dealer will tell you, have no equal. Their Silver-Plate Table Ware has won the approval of the discriminating public.

Ask for the illustrated story about the ONEIDA COMMUNITY, Booklet F. It tells the story of their early struggles and their success in making a beautiful garden spot out of a dreary wilderness.

A Baby Silver-Plate Feeding Spoon of the famous ONEIDA COMMUNITY Triple-Plate Plus will be sent prepaid on receipt of fifty cents. A useful article and an elegant gift.

ONEIDA COMMUNITY Silver-Plate Table Ware can be found at most good dealers. If not at yours, write us, and the address of the nearest dealer will be sent.

ONEIDA COMMUNITY, Kenwood, N. Y.

FIGURE 20. Magazine ad for Oneida Community Ltd. silver-plated ware, 1903.

the armrest of the chair, tousles his hair. The copy Dunn supplied for this image began: "Are your pink ears listening, Betty?" (see figure 21).

"Never," Grosvenor Allen remembered, "have we had such a jump in sales." Some thirty years later, Allen, in a doctor's office, was asked his business. "I told him Community Plate made by the Oneida Community. His face was perfectly blank, but all of a sudden his secretary at the other end of

FREE OFFER

Any Community Silver customer can obtain *free* this Coles Phillips poster, with another in color. These posters contain no reading or advertising matter, and are printed on plate paper in a size suitable for framing.

Ask your silverware dealer to show you these pictures and to get them for you.

COLES PHILLIPS

"Are your pink ears listening, Betty?"
"Yes, indeed. Will they hear something nice?"
"Better than nice—it's true. Betty, are pearls any less lovely because they all have a grain of sand at the center?"
"No, but what of—?"
"Then how is table silver the worse for having a center of different metal?"
"Well, I somehow feel—"
"Pardon me, dear, but that's just it: you only '*feel*.' If you will stop to *reason* a little you will see that table silver is for a purpose. If it fits that purpose gracefully and completely, I'm for it. Let me read you this:

COMMUNITY SILVER

is built by overlaying solid silver upon a center of stronger, stiffer metal. Do not confuse it with ordinary 'plated' silver, for Community Silver is so specially thickened at the wearing points and toughened to withstand wear that in a long life-time you will never see or touch anything but the purest of silver. There are many attractive designs at your dealer's. The price is attractive too. For instance, six teaspoons, $2.00."

Guaranteed for <u>50</u> Years

LOUIS XVI DESIGN

ONEIDA COMMUNITY, Ltd., ONEIDA, N. Y.

FIGURE 21. Coles Phillips's first magazine ad for Community Silver, 1911.

the room piped up and said 'Are your pink ears listening, Betty?'"[45] Phillips had a talent for rendering sophisticated, youthful women that appealed to both men and women. The artist's trademark depiction was the "fadeaway girl," a fashionable lady rendered in colors blending into the background.

Many of Phillips's most notable fadeaway girls happily contemplated Oneida silverware. The pin-up girls of this artist had tremendous effect in the advertising world. As full-page ads in such national weekly magazines as *Saturday Evening Post*, *Ladies' Home Journal*, and *Good Housekeeping*, they sold a lot of Community Plate.[46]

Restructuring the company around quality silverware was a major risk, and Noyes and his associates knew that, even if successful, the new line would not be profitable for some years. In the meantime, traps would have to pay for everything, and to do that, traps would have to bring in more money.[47] That premise set into motion a series of moves and construction projects. To make room for greater silverware production at Niagara Falls, chains were moved to the trap works in Sherrill in 1901. There, chains were combined with traps in an expanded hardware department, which in turn needed more room. Some space became available by moving silk thread production out of the old trap shop into another new facility a mile away. More space for traps was created by erecting a large building for the hardware department in 1905.

In 1910, Noyes became president, as well as general manager, and trap production exceeded seven million—the all-time high. That same year, however, silverware also showed a substantial profit.[48] That was the point at which silverware was considered to be successfully established as the company's specialty. With victory declared for Community Plate, the old Oneida Community businesses were discontinued: chains in 1912, silk thread in 1913, canning in 1916. Traps held on a little longer. During World War I, however, their importance dwindled further as the company plated artillery shells with lead and made surgical scalpels for the military.[49] The Oneida firm sold off the trap business (both game and mouse) in 1925 to a group of former employees. Under the name "Animal Trap Company of America," the new company, in Lititz, Pennsylvania, continued to manufacture the traps of the Oneida Community and the Oneida Community Ltd. for many years.

Finally, in the interests of efficient concentration, silverware production was transferred from Niagara Falls to Sherrill. The long gamble on silverware formally ended with the opening of a new tableware factory, next to the Oneida Community's old trap and silk works, in April 1914. The new factory housed machinery brought from Niagara Falls along with the operators of that machinery—also brought from Niagara Falls. Offering to finance the relocation of its workers, the company chartered a train to bring them to Sherrill to look the place over. Most liked what they saw and moved there with their families. At the beginning of 1914, Sherrill's population was 89.

In 1915, it was 1,200. One year later, it was 3,750.[50] Present Sherrill owes its genesis to the loyal, enthusiastic employees originally from the "Falls." It was Noyes's hope that none of the employees would ever regret having made the move.[51]

After the breakup, some former Perfectionists relocated to Niagara Falls, the location of a small but promising silverware industry begun by the Oneida Community a few years before. Most, however, remained in the shadow of the Mansion House—a neighborhood now called Kenwood—and kept the trap and thread industries going in what was now called Sherrill.

John Noyes continued to direct the Oneida Community Ltd., at least informally. When he died in 1886, a spiritualist faction took over and nearly destroyed the company. That threat ended with a new slate of directors elected in 1895, including Noyes's stirpicultural son, Pierrepont. Immediately, the young man restored the silverware facility at Niagara Falls to financial viability, then moved to revitalize the entire company.

As this younger Noyes assumed effective control, he formulated a "Basswood Philosophy" redefining Oneida Community values of brotherhood and equality for a new generation. He motivated those around him to commit to an idealistic company vision and to build a new Oneida society imbued with the values of the older one. He also steered the company into carrying out a complicated and risky ten-year plan to specialize in silverware. The Oneida Community Ltd. boosted flatware quality and developed innovative advertising campaigns. When silverware became the company's most profitable item in 1910, older products such as traps and threads were discontinued. In 1914, the machines for making silverware were moved from Niagara Falls to Sherrill, along with the workers who ran them.

CHAPTER 10

Welfare Capitalism

During the early 1900s, the credo of group responsibility and selflessness derived from the Oneida Community was extended from the executives of Oneida Community Ltd. to the workforce. Officials of what was now a silverware company put into practice another set of ideals forged in Oneida Community times: all employees were entitled to good pay and good work conditions. All, furthermore, deserved to share in the company's profits and ownership. All contributing to Oneida should be able to own their own homes in an environment that enhanced the health and well-being of everyone. Company policy was to say nothing about this because of acute sensitivity to the paternalistic feeling of the enterprise. Nevertheless, the Oneida program of welfare capitalism was so signally effective that it secured the partnership of workers for at least a half century. When hard times dictated cutbacks, the commitment to share company benefits with everyone at Oneida always was reaffirmed.

During the second half of the twentieth century, what was now called Oneida Ltd. adapted so successfully to the production of stainless steel flatware that it became the largest silverware maker in the world—briefly, before collapsing just after 2000. That company, however, was no longer meaningfully linked to its past because it had ceased to be distinctive in its personnel policies, and its management values were greatly altered.

Bettering the Lot of Workers

Back in the late 1890s and just three years after Pierrepont Noyes became superintendent of the Niagara Falls plant, all the factories of the region had been closed by strikes aimed at unionizing the workforce. At heart, according to Holton Noyes, it was a struggle of principle between labor and capital over who would control the productive operation.[1] When the Oneida Community Ltd. facility was shut down, Noyes leaped onto a bench to address the assembled workers. "I believe that the labor unions have done an immense amount of good in this country," he remembered telling them. "If this Company planned to do no more for its people than the other manufacturers, I'd welcome a union into our plants. But fortunately, I have plans for the future of the Oneida Community, Ltd. and the prosperity of its working people which go far beyond anything the unions can do for them, and these plans cannot be carried out with a union shop. Therefore, I shall not admit a union, and I ask you all to stand with me."

More than a half century after this event, an elderly worker speaking to Noyes added this postscript: "I was a boy when you told us that day up in the buffing room that you would not have a union because you had better plans. You certainly have made good what you said."[2]

The company, at the time, successfully resisted unionization. Any lingering resentment from the incident was defused by accepting almost every striker back to work without rancor or reprisals. As for Noyes's plans for the workers, he was committed to paying good wages and vaguely thought of abolishing poverty among the employees. It seemed to him that such a thing might be accomplished cooperatively and without class conflict by practicing some form of welfare capitalism, the employer's assumption of responsibility for the welfare of the employees.[3]

Certainly welfare capitalism was advanced in the literature of the day. In, for example, the 1886 nonfiction bestseller, *Studies in Modern Socialism*, Thomas Edwin Brown suggested that captains of industry could address social inequality by voluntarily ensuring good pay and working conditions for the employees. The scheme would assure profit for the industrial owners and was highly paternalistic. Brown also insisted, however, that the workers should be directly involved in company affairs.[4]

The concept of benevolent paternalism was taken to a logical extreme in Edward Bellamy's science fiction novel *Looking Backward*. First published in 1888, it was perhaps the most popular utopian work ever written. Bellamy envisioned future society suddenly transformed, by general consent, into a state under the complete control of one central agency. "No man any more has any care for the morrow, either for himself or his children," it is explained in the book, "for the nation guarantees the nurture, education, and comfortable maintenance of every citizen from the cradle to the grave." No one in this future land could live off the toil of another. All competition and individual striving were submerged in the public interest overseen by a government that, on the one hand, supervised production and distribution of goods and, on the other, directed the lives of its people equably.[5]

In real life, the occasional industrialist attempted to integrate measures for benefiting workers into factory operations. A little east of Oneida, for example, was Dolgeville, recently named for its most prominent citizen, who owned a factory producing shoes and slippers of felt. Henry Dolge thought his workmen should receive higher wages, work shorter hours (nine, as opposed to ten), and enjoy, at company expense, a pension, life insurance, and disability assistance. Aiming to achieve partnership with employees, Dolge created an impressive array of recreational and social facilities for them and instituted profit sharing during the 1880s.[6]

Noyes would have been aware of Dolge, and he would have known, as well, of another voluntary venture into corporate welfare at Endicott, New York, south of Oneida. There, the nation's largest manufacturer of footwear— soon to be known as Endicott Johnson—was forging a reputation during the late 1890s for beneficence to workers. "The company pays larger proportionate wages than any other manufacturing concern in this region," one local observer enthused in 1900, "while privileges and kindnesses are freely extended to the employees by the superintendent and his assistant that generally are unheard of in large establishments. Indeed, this company never allows any of its faithful employees to suffer through want or distress, neither does it allow the property of any of its men to be sold under process of law. Between employer and employees there exists a bond of warm friendship, and the interests of master and servant are identical." Workers admired their boss, George F. Johnson, for his involvement in their affairs. However, while Johnson famously attended to workers in distress, the company developed no system of benefits pertaining to disability nor, prior to about 1915, any program of medical coverage. The company built houses in a new town for its workers (Endicott) but charged employees a substantial home cost of over $3,000. Company management contributed to local causes, but always and explicitly as acts of charity. During the years that the Oneida Community Ltd. would be creating its version of corporate welfare, Endicott Johnson's liberality toward workers remained distinctly personal and markedly paternalistic.[7]

Noyes absorbed sentiment for welfare capitalism from the world about him, remarking that his entire generation of young businessmen had embraced the idea of "group responsibility." Since Community upbringing strongly incul- cated concern for others, stirpiculture were already inclined toward corporate welfare. By 1900, he and other company officials were in favor of sharing fam- ily prosperity with all who worked for the company.[8] That was the year the company's board of directors appointed a committee to consider "ways and means of ameliorating the conditions and encouraging the progress of our work people."[9] Of four committee members launching Oneida's program in worker well-being, two were of the stirpicultural generation: Pierrepont Noyes and his half bother Holton Noyes. The others, Martin Kinsley and William Hinds, were of the Oneida Community's adult generation, and it was chiefly through them—especially Hinds—that some of the old socialistic intentions of the Oneida Community were preserved and brought to fruition in the early twentieth century.

Hinds, it will be recalled, had been a prominent Townerite opposing John Noyes's leadership in the final Community days. When the Community ended, Hinds served conscientiously on the company's board of directors from 1881 to his death in 1910. Like the elder Noyes, Hinds was an acknowl- edged scholar of socialism and communalism. He edited the Community's latter-day magazine-newspaper, the *American Socialist*. He wrote a book on the subject, *American Communities and Co-operative Colonies*, which still stands as an important source for the study of nineteenth-century communitari- anism.[10] Hinds continued to revise that work even during his later years as president of the Oneida Community Ltd. (1903–1910).

Hinds knew that the subject of worker relations had become increasingly important in the Oneida Community. "Are we not really indebted to our work- men," John Noyes asked in the summer of 1879. "I see as plain as can be that the Community is indebted to this constituency for its safety and exis- tence. . . . How can we establish the right kind of cooperation between us and our workmen, so as to identify their interests with ours beyond all possible danger of their falling into the ways of the strikers—into the enmity that exists in the world between capital and labor?" The solution proposed by the elder Noyes was that the Oneida Community share its profits with all employees. Remembering this, Hinds began pressing for a profit-sharing plan in 1900.[11]

Hinds also knew that John Noyes had once suggested the Oneida Com- munity make provision for a workers' village in which the employees owned their own homes.[12] As he looked into profit sharing, Hinds also made it company policy to encourage worker homeownership in pre- cisely the place (the area of present-day Noyes Park) that John Noyes had suggested. In 1900, according to Holton Noyes's company history, Hinds reported that an employee wanted to buy a particular house for $750 but did not have the money.

> Mr. Hinds proposed that the Company purchase the house and sell it to Mr. Candee on contract. . . . The Board decided not to go into this deal at that time but did agree that if Mr. Hinds cared to purchase the house personally and sell it to Mr. Candee as proposed, the Company would take the whole deal off his hands at the expiration of three years. Mr. Hinds, therefore, went ahead with it and the whole matter was carried through in this way. In the next few years Mr. Hinds made similar arrangements with certain other valuable employees, financing them from his own personal funds. . . . This general plan, with some modification, was generally adopted by the O. C. L. later on and has really been responsible for the building up of the City of Sherrill.[13]

Emerging from these actions was a feeling among the directors that the company should encourage private home ownership. In 1905, the Oneida Community Ltd. began to lay out streets on farmland north of today's Hamilton Avenue, sold lots to its employees below market value, then gave them cash bonuses to build houses.

As Hinds furthered profit sharing and worker housing, another company official nudged Oneida in the direction of more social services and welfare benefits for workers. Albert "Ab" Kinsley (born 1883), son of Oneida Community members Jessie and Myron Kinsley, was Pierrepont Noyes's most enthusiastic recruit to the vision of executive brotherhood among the younger generation. Kinsley went to work for the company at the age of seventeen and rose meteorically through the ranks: head of chain production in 1903, manager of traps and silverware in 1912, superintendent of all factories in 1913. In 1917, he became general manager.[14] To Noyes, the choice of Kinsley was especially satisfying "because of his ambition to make real my youthful dream of an honest-to-God 'sharing company' with no 'rich' and no 'poor.'"[15] No one doubted Kinsley's business ability, but what really distinguished him was a big heart and social conscience. "When the Niagara Falls factory made its move to Sherrill, it was Kinsley who was on hand to help the families get settled," according to the company biographer, Walter Edmonds. "He would back every suggestion for improvement of living or working conditions in Sherrill, no matter what it cost." In 1915, the Oneida Community Ltd. formed and funded, under Kinsley, a welfare department overseeing virtually every aspect of company activity touching the lives of workers and their families.[16]

As general manager, Kinsley raised factory pay so precipitously that it really amounted to profit sharing. Workers going off to World War I continued to receive their wages, less government pay, if they had dependents. If single, they were awarded half the money they would have received for factory work, again, less government pay. More important was a "High-Cost-of-Living" supplement for all employees: 25 percent of the base wage for every five-point rise in the weekly cost-of-living circular issued by the Bradstreet Company. This was a substantial sum that could amount to nearly half the base pay.[17] Kinsley also fashioned an extraordinary umbrella of welfare and recreational services for those employed by the Oneida Community Ltd. The Community Associated Clubs (CAC) was created by consolidating several worker-formed relief societies and athletic associations into one employee-run operation. The company provided a capacious space for the CAC in the former dairy barn of the Oneida Community. The company matched the fund formed from workers' dues (for each, ten dollars annually), then added life insurance, a program of disability support, and health benefits, including a visiting nursing service. A host of recreational facilities, including a bowling alley and a nearby lake, was then turned over to the CAC.[18]

The good intentions and socialist leanings of Noyes, Hinds, and Kinsley crystallized into a broad program of welfare capitalism in the early twentieth century. Company policy was that all employees deserved to be well paid and to work in good conditions. All were entitled to health insurance and pension benefits. As all employees were considered partners in the business of Oneida, stocks were made available to any worker inclined to share in company ownership. Further, all were entitled not only to the opportunity to own their own homes, but to reside near work in a community contributing to their well-being. The Oneida Community Ltd. established a model company town to achieve this outcome. In that town, the firm funded electrical, water, and sewage systems, as well as fire protection and garbage collection. The company paid for or contributed money toward building churches, a library, and recreational facilities.

"Better schools became a prime interest for all of us," Noyes remembered, and in 1906, the company was able to create a new district, which it supported generously. Between 1911 and 1918, the Oneida Community Ltd. donated lots for three schools and paid at least half the expense of erecting the buildings. The company doubled tax money raised for education and teachers' salaries and, for one dollar, made every teacher eligible for all the company's fringe benefits. Teachers also were offered free lodging in the Mansion House.[19]

To ensure the town would be politically independent, the company set aside village improvement money for presenting to the state legislature the case for recognizing Sherrill as a self-governing city. Five executives of the Oneida Community Ltd., dispatched to Albany to lobby for that outcome, were successful. In 1916, Sherrill received a state charter formally incorporating it as a municipality run by elected officials. Curiously, the incident is shrouded in some mystery, because those involved reported virtually nothing about it. Walter Edmonds, for example, the person commissioned to write the history of the company some three decades later, was told only that the city incorporation was accomplished "with the backing of the company, but with no interference."[20] Why were company sources so vague about Sherrill's founding?

Avoiding the Appearance of Evil

The answer is that the Oneida Community Ltd. was sensitive about public appearances. It was always concerned about how its conduct of business would seem in the eyes of others. The company funded, for example, the magazine *North American Trapper*, a publication containing trapping news as well as advertisements for Oneida traps. "At this time," Holton Noyes remarked, "there was a good deal of public agitation against the practice which had grown up of masquerading a 'house organ' as a bona fide trade magazine." Wishing to avoid the "appearance of evil," the company liquidated this property in 1912. For similar reasons, the company divested itself of the small retail store in existence since the time of the Oneida Community. "There was a great deal in the papers in those days," explained Holton Noyes, "about the manner in which corporations enslaved their employees and mulcted them of their wages through general stores, at which they were obliged to trade at high prices. Undoubtedly there was some foundation for such criticism of certain large and soulless corporations, but certainly nothing of the sort applied to the O. C. L. Nevertheless it was thought best to avoid the appearance of evil."[21]

The firm especially wished to avoid the appearance of evil in actions that could be interpreted as dominating or even patronizing its workers. Company policy was, in fact, to maintain a modest silence on all welfare efforts because of events that had recently taken place near Chicago. Pullman, Illinois, was the much-publicized archetype of planned worker communities in America of the Gilded Age. The year before Noyes became superintendent at Niagara Falls, a violent strike occurring there shattered the town and tarnished the philanthropic reputation of its founder.

George Pullman's wealth derived from a fantastic scheme to raise the buildings of Chicago, with jacks, a few feet above the floodplain. His pockets filled with money from this achievement, he turned to developing a railroad car devoted to sleeping. His success was such that the word "Pullman" went into English and other European languages as a synonym not only for the generic product (such as Kleenex or Xerox, for example) but as adverb and adjective signifying comfort and gracious living.

In 1872, Pullman was reading a book by the English novelist Charles Reade, a Dickensian writer who dealt with a wide range of social issues.[22] The book, *Put Yourself in His Place* (1870), was about an industrial town in which the oligarchical factory owner and the poverty-stricken workers blindly pursue their own interests with tragic consequences. Reade, coincidentally, was one of the Oneida Community's favorite novelists, and the Perfectionists particularly enjoyed this book.[23] A new edition of *Put Yourself in His Place* appeared in the Mansion House library at the time company directors were laying out their worker village.

As George Pullman read the book, he purportedly was transfixed by the opening passage describing the novel's setting:

> Industry so vast, working by steam on a limited space, has been fatal to beauty: Hillsborough, though built on one of the loveliest sites in England, is perhaps the most hideous town in creation. All ups and downs and back slums. Not one of its wriggling, broken-backed streets has handsome shops in an unbroken row. Houses seem to have battled in the air, and stuck wherever they tumbled down dead out of the mêlée. But worst of all, the city is pockmarked with public-houses and bristles with high round chimneys. These are not confined to a locality, but stuck all over the place like cloves in an orange. They defy the laws, and belch forth massy volumes of black smoke, that hang like acres of crape over the place, and veil the sun and the blue sky even in the brightest day.[24]

In emphasizing the ugliness of the workers' world, the passage expressed a widespread notion of the time: ugly environments make ugly people. Pullman supposedly drew from it the inspiration to design a beautiful community for his workers. Pullman bought a tract of land fourteen miles south of Chicago in what was then open prairie. He relocated the Pullman factory there, and next to it laid out the town for the factory's employees. Named Pullman, the worker community opened in 1880. Its houses, support businesses, and social centers were built at considerable expense to look good. The place was beautified, also at considerable expense, with shade trees and flowers, successively in bloom, everywhere. The idea was that the residents of Pullman, living as proper Americans, would now become proper Americans. Mostly Irish workers, these people would desist from being poor, miserable, and surly in their new surroundings. Pullman's company reserved the right to adjust its employment, production, and wage levels to market conditions. Rents for housing, however, were higher than in other places and did not fluctuate with the market. In the best of times, the workers had little choice, and there was smoldering resentment of what they experienced as an exploitative environment. Yet for many years the press and the academic community extolled Pullman as the solution to all social ills. Pullman was a famous place.

Cutting of wages and jobs in the early summer of 1894 led to a wild-cat strike in Pullman against the Pullman Company. The American Railway Union of Eugene Debs, over one hundred thousand strong, struck in sympathy. Invoking the Sherman Anti-Trust Act, the federal government sent in the army to ensure the unimpeded flow of mail across state lines. Hence, a law formulated to curb the excesses of the rich apparently was being employed against the poor. The result was widespread violence in the Chicago area in which American soldiers shot about sixty American workers. It was the largest strike that had ever occurred, and its suppression shocked the nation. Although laws protecting the rights of labor lay largely in the future, Congress sensed something should be done and rushed through a bill establishing a pro-labor holiday—the origin of our Labor Day. There was an extensive public postmortem into what had gone wrong. Everyone could see it had been a mistake to name the town Pullman. More importantly, a national commission concluded George Pullman's town had been un-American. By retaining ownership of the town and worker housing, Pullman behaved as a feudal baron toward his serfs.[25]

Over fifty years later, Noyes conveyed his memory of the Pullman strike to writer Walter Edmonds. In the ugly background of that bloody event, Edmonds recorded, "was the so-called 'model village,' which the Western company had erected, with plenty of fanfare, for its employees. The company said nothing about the rents and gas and water rates it charged, which were a quarter as high again as those of neighboring communities; but when the owner autocratically cut wages 20 and 25 per cent, he did nothing about lowering his rents, with the result that the company, through its 'model village,' was taking back from its employees nearly all the money it was paying them."[26] The moral Noyes drew for Edmonds concerned employer hypocrisy: "The general effect of most company welfare was to add a psychological fetter to the economic ones already binding the worker; and invariably the employers who did most to publicize their generosity were loudest in denouncing incidents which they described as the 'ingratitude' of their employees. Young Noyes, though his plans for a new kind of Oneida Community were then still in their first formative stage, made up his mind that he would never try to buy any man's gratitude."[27]

The larger lesson was that when the Oneida Community Ltd. founded its own version of Pullman, it should distance itself from that community in precisely the ways taught by the Pullman debacle. Individual residents, the Oneida company insisted, should build and own their own houses. Further, the workers' town should be self-governing and politically independent of the company. Company directors understood that the corporate reputation should not be tied to worker housing—that is, the Oneida Pullman-like venture would not be named Community or Noyes or Hinds. Finally, it seemed obvious that a company should avoid boasting about providing its workers with benefits.

Hence, spokespeople of the Oneida Community Ltd. said little about welfare and employee relations, beyond passing a quotable news item along to interested parties. "In 1915," according to sociologist Esther Lowenthal, "when the factories of most of the firm's competitors were closed by a strike, a trade-union organizer was sent to Sherrill by the silver workers. . . . A letter this organizer sent back to the strikers was read at a mass meeting and reported in the *Meriden Daily Journal* of November 3, from which I quote":

> I have investigated the Oneida Community Ltd. Silverware factory with the following results: I find this company is perfectly independent of any affiliation with any of the manufacturers' organizations, either in their own line or any other. They work their men short hours, give them good pay and treat them like human beings. Consequently there is the best of good will between the employer and the employee. . . . The employees seem to be perfectly satisfied with things as they are in the factory. Therefore, I do not believe that any successful organization could be formed among them. . . . In fact, the company makes a study of its employees in order to give them every opportunity of having good, clean amusements. . . .
>
> Those are a few of the reasons for the contentment of the employees of this company. I could go on and enumerate a great many more, but I believe enough has been said to convince you that this company is different from any company you have ever heard of in their treatment of their employees. It is not done for advertising purposes, as a great many of our corporations do, but is simply a business policy carried out by men who put the man and woman ahead of the dollar.[28]

Since the Oneida Community Ltd. also rarely mentioned unions, this quotation stands as a reminder that the company was always pro-worker and antiunion, precisely as Pierrepont Noyes indicated when he averted the strike at Niagara Falls. In general, the paternalistic tenor of corporate welfare reflected the employers' desire to avoid labor trouble by creating a loyal workforce. Indeed, some analysts see fear of class conflict as the real reason for welfare capitalism. "The emergence of corporate paternalism," according to Gerald Zahavi, echoing Holton Noyes's characterization of the Niagara strike, "was ultimately a product of conflict, at once a result of and a response to the struggle for control of the means and fruits of industrial production."[29] Defusing class hostility was one goal of Oneida management and yet another lesson that one could draw from study of the Pullman strike. Following that event, Eugene Debs, president of the American Railway Union, was imprisoned for defying a federal injunction against the strike. Debs, feeling victimized by capitalist oppression, cofounded the International Workers of the World shortly after. An avowedly proletarian union bent on overthrowing the employer class, the "Wobblies" scared industrialists everywhere, and they probably frightened corporate leader Noyes.

The heyday of welfare capitalism in America was the 1920s, when many of the largest corporations (Ford Motor Company, American Harvester, and Endicott Johnson, to name a few) voluntarily instituted measures for employee well-being. Such companies typically provided relatively good wages, promised decent working conditions, instituted profit sharing, offered medical and retirement programs, built homes, and furnished a range of athletic and recreational facilities for their workers.[30] The Oneida Community Ltd. was in the vanguard of this development and was arguably among the country's most successful examples of welfare capitalism. But because of Pullman, company officials referred diffidently to Sherrill or, better, spoke of it not at all. Their virtual silence on the subject helped to ensure that Sherrill would remain little known to scholars today. Nevertheless, the Sherrill of Pierrepont Noyes, of William Hinds, and of Albert Kinsley was long regarded locally as something like a second utopia, one that grew directly out of the values and people of the Oneida Community.

Through Hard Times and War

After appointing a new general manager to succeed him in 1917, Pierrepont Noyes left the company for three years of voluntary service to the government. Initially he worked in the wartime Fuel Administration in Washington. Subsequently, he accepted a posting as American representative on the

Rhineland Commission responsible for the postwar occupation of Germany.[31] Noyes had retained the company presidency, however, and returned to Oneida in time to see the war boom collapse in a business downturn of national proportions.

Although the panic of 1921 was a relatively mild depression, it caused substantial financial damage to the company. Managerial salaries were reduced, and, to avoid extensive layoffs, factory output was reduced by going to a four-day and then a three-day workweek.[32] Conditions seemed only to worsen, however. That summer, Edmonds related, Noyes called the workers together in general session to tell them the company was losing money and

> could not indefinitely go on paying them their present wages. Adding the High-Cost-of-Living bonus to their regular pay, he explained, had been a mistake, for it meant that in effect the company was sharing profits before they had been earned. Their jobs at Oneida depended on the financial soundness of the company just as much as his did. He had cut his own salary to $5,000, and all management salaries would be cut proportionately. What he wanted to know was whether the employees would agree to a thirty-three per cent cut in pay if the company promised to share profits with them after they had been earned.[33]

"This proposal," Lowenthal reported, "received the greatest hand clap in the history of the company."[34]

A casualty of the economic downturn was Albert Kinsley, who lost his position as general manager soon after. The company's recovery, however, was so rapid that the new contingent wage delivered $300,000 to employees in 1922 and $490,000 the next year. This form of profit sharing, devised by Kinsley (now promoted to a vice president), turned out to be a substantial transfer of money typically amounting to 20 percent of a worker's annual wages. Likewise, the company's commitment to employee welfare was undimmed. The social services budget, for example, begun at $37,000 in 1916, was $153,000 in 1923.[35]

In the atmosphere of renewed prosperity, the Oneida Community Ltd. constructed a new administration building, a stately edifice in the English Gothic style, which spoke to its Oneida Community heritage. Most of those running the firm were, of course, children of the Community who had grown up in a world dominated by their patents' architecture. In situating their administrative center near the Mansion House, company executives said, in effect: "We also live serious lives reflected in architecture, architecture complementing yours and worthy of yours" (see figure 22).

FIGURE 22. Aerial view of the administrative building (Oneida Community Ltd., 1926) and the Mansion House, about 1940.

The ties of young to old were also affirmed by depositing Oneida Community artifacts in the cornerstone of the 1926 structure. At the same time, the building bore material testimony to the company's progressive labor relations, as illustrated by the inclusion, in the same cornerstone, of the name of every employee and the constitution of the Community Associated Clubs.[36]

The executive who succeeded Kinsley was Miles "Dunc" Robertson—an outsider or "joiner"—who abandoned a budding legal career to work at Oneida Community Ltd. for seven dollars a week in 1913. Robertson was considered more of a hardheaded businessman than Kinsley, and certainly he looked it. In contrast to Kinsley's face, which tended toward curves, Robertson's was all sharp angles. But Robertson was a Kinsley recruit who shared with his mentor a strong idealistic commitment to Oneida. For Robertson, that meant emphasizing partnership between management and labor. The new general manager instituted frequent meetings with the factory foremen in which he briefed the workers on business, sales, advertising, prospects, and plans. Prior to issuing the annual shareholders' report, Robertson delivered a summary of the company's situation to all the company's employees that was said to be more complete than the formal financial statement.[37]

A measure of Oneida's success in silverware was afforded by the purchase, in early 1929, of Rogers (marketed as "Wm A Rogers" and "Simeon & Rogers")—the former standard of consumer preference back in the days Noyes dreamed of competing with them by creating a high-end plated ware. Before these properties could be modernized and integrated into the Oneida fold, Noyes warned investors in February 1930, "it is probable we shall find other sacrifices need to be made."[38] Indeed they would—the Great Depression had engulfed them.

"Those who did not live through it cannot now imagine it, and those who did can never forget it," was the concise testimony of Constance Robertson, wife of Miles Robertson and daughter of company president Noyes. Between 1929 and 1932, the company lost millions of dollars. For the management, those years "were made almost harder by the attitude of the employees as, piece by piece, the whole profit sharing plan, the wage standards, and in the end even the service wage [extra pay for seniority] had to be scrapped. The employees made it hard," as Edmonds expressed it, "because they made it easy. They accepted their own wage losses as if they, the management, and the company were all in the jam together."[39] In reply, Noyes promised that the company would, as soon as possible, return to sharing its prosperity with all who had made sacrifices for its survival.[40]

A short time later, writer Carl Carmer asked Noyes whether the communistic ideals of the Oneida Community had been jettisoned by the succeeding company. "Not exactly," was Noyes's answer:

We've had a liberal, perhaps I should say radical, tradition to uphold. The idea here has been to pay the bosses more than the employees—but only a little more. We have depressed top wages in order to raise those at the bottom. During the World War and immediately after, when the cost of living was increasing rapidly, we instituted a High Cost of Living wage. . . . [When the war boom ended,] we had to give up the idea, but we established instead a method of profit-sharing called the "contingent wage." We turned over to our employees each year half the earnings of the company after all obligations, including seven-percent dividends on common stock and surplus, had been fulfilled. One year the workers got almost a half-million dollars. We paid a service wage, too, giving automatic increases with increasing length of employment. But all that was wiped out by the depression.

Now we're starting all over again. We shall have profits to share with our workers and we will share them. Why shouldn't we? Before the depression, we had paid seven percent on our common stock for twenty-five years, besides several stock dividends which amounted in all to over three hundred percent. It pays to share profits, pays everybody.[41]

The company did indeed recover rapidly from the Depression, a feat many credited to Robertson's leadership. "We wouldn't have survived the Depression had it not been for Mr. Robertson, because the banks closed down on us among other things," his successor, Pierrepont Trowbridge ("Pete") Noyes stated. "But he was tough enough to show them. The banks believed in his toughness. They knew he could do it. . . . And Mr. Robertson had it going so well that in '33 we made money—and nobody else did." Shortly after and just as Noyes had assured Carmer, Oneida restored full wages with the service bonus. In 1936, the company reinstituted the profit-sharing contingent wage. Meanwhile, in 1935, the company shortened its name to Oneida Ltd.[42]

Recovery from the Depression was also helped by the creation of two of the most appealing styles of silverware ever marketed. "Coronation," initiated in 1936 on the occasion of Edward VIII's accession to the British throne, featured a wreath-like, three-dimensional design near the end of the handle. It was Oneida's all-time best seller and, very possibly, the last pattern actually made in Oneida, New York, about the year 2003. "Lady Hamilton," a pattern introduced in what was probably Oneida's worst year—1932—looked modern. But its simple curvilinear design felt more bourgeois than chic and seemed to embody some spirit of the time, which may have been why it endured on American tables for a quarter century. "Lady Hamilton" was named for Christine Hamilton Allen, a stirpicult married to head designer Grosvenor Allen. In real life, "Lady Hamilton" was a social activist prominent in the League of Women Voters. Through that organization, she became friends with Eleanor Roosevelt, wife of New York governor Franklin Delano Roosevelt. When FDR received the nomination for president of the United States in 1932, the couple flew from Albany to the Democratic Convention in Chicago, buzzing the Mansion House along the way.[43]

"I was enchanted by these people," writer Carl Carmer related of his visit to the Mansion House in 1935. "Most of them were big—I sensed the physical vitality in them; all of them were intelligent; and many of them were blessed with understanding sensitivity. Living in Kenwood, off the main lines of communication, traveling little, they yet succeeded in being sophisticated in the best sense of the word. They were people of taste, poised and articulate. All this they would seriously deny, satirically pointing out their own faults, belittling their virtues." They impressed Carmer as remarkably creative. Pierrepont Noyes, for example, was a novelist, as was his daughter. Advertising executive Burton Dunn was a sculptor. Edith Kinsley was a painter, and her mother, Community-born Jessie Kinsley, invented a new form of textile art: tapestries made not by weaving but by the folk technique of braiding rugs. One woman wrote poetry for the *Atlantic Monthly*. "And a sweet, white-haired lady who joked them all with charming aplomb said 'we creative artists of Kenwood' with just enough amused edge to get me to ask her the inevitable 'And what do *you* do?' so that she might reply, 'I write for *True Confessions*.'"[44]

A peculiarity of Kenwood behavior was the absence of gallantry displayed by the men. "After the Break-Up, when the eugenic and communist experiment was at an end, the value of extreme respectability was high," one of the women explained to Carmer. "The result of our desire to conform was that the pendulum swung as far as it could away from sex. There's no flirting at Kenwood. At our parties the men go off in a corner and talk shop or sport—the women amuse themselves as best they can. We have comradeship, intellectual companionship from our men, but not an admiring glance." Carmer also observed an extraordinary affection for children in Kenwood, derived, he thought, from the old regime of communal child-raising. Finally, Carmer visited a Sherrill diner to ask the proprietor about the workers' view of management. "'They like the joint,' said Fat, stomping over from the counter with the chili sauce. 'They know the bosses mean what they say. They've seen the bosses take pay cuts and share the grief and they know that when there's money they'll be gettin' some of it.'" Do the workers, Carmer wondered, know anything about life in the old Oneida Community? "They know enough to know that plenty went on up at The Mansion," was the reply. And, "t' tell the truth they're sort o' proud of it."[45]

With the advent of World War II, Oneida Ltd. was drafted into the nation's production effort. Forbidden by government order to produce consumer items, the company made military goods from 1942 through 1945. The wartime products of Oneida included surgical instruments, cutlery for the armed forces, casings for the M74 chemical (fire) bomb, and a variety of gun parts—bayonets for British and American rifles, sights for the Springfield rifle, and slide mechanisms for the M1 carbine. Sherrill factories turned out a bewildering variety of buckles and metal parts for safety harnesses and parachutes. The ingenious "quick release," a buckle permitting a paratrooper to disengage instantly from the harness, was designed and made by Oneida Ltd. For aircraft, there were fuel tanks, shackles that held bombs inside planes, and elevator controls for the navy's Helldiver plane. The single most important contribution to the war effort was a bearing essential to engines of the American Sherman tank. This silver-plated part also kept the major American and British bombers (B-17, B-24, Lancaster) and fighters (P-40, P-38, P-51, Spitfire, Hurricane) in the air. Oneida Ltd. turned out to be very good at making war matériel. The government bestowed an accolade for outstanding war production consisting of a flag emblazoned with the words "Army" and "Navy" and the letter "E." The latter, of course, stood for excellence, understood to mean quality of the highest order. Only 5 percent of the many thousands of companies engaged in the war production earned an "E," and of those elite companies, only 5 percent could match Oneida's four "E"s.[46]

Although Oneida made no silverware during the conflict, it continued to advertise it. Some wartime ads were especially memorable. "Back Home for Keeps," for example, was one of the most successful campaigns in American advertising history (see figure 23).

Created by artist Jon Whitcomb, this series of ads typically appeared on the reverse side of *Life* magazine's cover page. Each depicted a handsome, square-jawed serviceman embracing—in a very physical, full-torso hug—an attractive young woman being told (in the text) that her man had a war on his hands. When he came home, their romance would blossom into happy marriage with Oneida silverware, several patterns of which were thoughtfully illustrated below the image.[47]

BACK HOME FOR KEEPS

He's the man of your heart. He's the light of your life. He's all you want to live for . . . live *with*. And some day (fling out a rainbow!) some glad morning he'll be home. You'll hear his step on the stair. You'll move into the tight circle of his arms . . . *forever*.

Some day! Yes, it's for *that* day we of Community* are living, too. Thinking about it, while we *help to win the war*. Planning for it—planning brightly gleaming silverware for brides who never had a home, patterns as enduring as your postwar world together. Our craftsmen's hands keep their skill. Our designers' hearts hold fast their dream. We know—with you— *the day will come!*

Community
THE FINEST SILVERPLATE

Lady Hamilton Design

*TRADEMARK   COPYRIGHT 1944, ONEIDA, LTD.

BUY WAR BONDS!   SPEED THE DAY!

If its Community . . . its correct

FIGURE 23.   Magazine ad for Oneida Ltd. silver-plated ware by Jon Whitcomb, 1944.

The First Hundred Years

From the company's perspective, the war amounted to thorough institutional disruption of machinery, organization, and people. Nearly all the young men (about 28 percent of the employees), for example, were lost to the armed services, to be replaced by women—the first appreciable female presence in the factories. The end of the war brought another kind of disruption. "Factories had to be cleared of war equipment and material," Robertson reported in late 1945. "Peacetime machinery had to be brought back. Old employees had to be transferred back on the old jobs or trained for different ones. New employees had to be hired and training started. Actually over 1000 people [in a workforce of about 2,300] had to be trained to new jobs."[48] But, as had happened in the economic downturns of the 1920s and 1930s, Oneida's recovery was rapid, and with prosperity came the immediate reinstitution of programs benefiting workers. In 1946, the company's profit was modest ($340,000 paid in dividends to stockholders). But even so, more than that was paid to employee pensions ($433,000) and to the workers as profits shared ($415,000). In 1947, the profit bonus was more than doubled ($859,000) to workers who already had the highest take-home pay in the state. The company also paid out, in 1947, $60,000 to the school system, $35,000 to the City of Sherrill for street development, and $42,000 toward building a new hospital.[49]

Nineteen forty-seven was also the year of the "Burning," the destruction by Oneida Ltd. of much of the historical record pertaining to the Oneida Community. The largest collection of such archival material had been gathered together in the home of stirpicult and company executive George W. Noyes, who was using the papers in a documentary history of the Oneida Community. At the time of his death in 1941, the published volumes of this work consisted of one dealing with John Noyes's theological development (1923) and another recounting Noyes's years in Putney (1931). In addition, George Noyes had completed a manuscript about the early years of the Oneida Community, which Lawrence Foster later published as *Free Love in Utopia*.[50] Oneida Ltd. claimed legal ownership of this material by right of a documented chain of possession originating with the four "owners" of the Oneida Community named at the time of the Mills War, then traced through John Noyes at Niagara Falls, Dr. Theodore Noyes and George Noyes in Kenwood, and ultimately to Oneida Ltd. as heir, in unbroken succession, to the Oneida Community. The company's concern was that the sexual contents would tarnish Oneida's reputation.[51] Interviewing a participant in the affair in 1961, sociologist William Kephart was told: "I went through some of the stuff—old diaries and things—and a lot it was awfully personal. Names and specific happenings were mentioned—that kind of thing. Anyway, I reported these facts to the company, and it was decided that in view of the nature of the material, it should all be destroyed. So, one morning we got a truck—and believe me, there was so much stuff we needed a truck—loaded all the material on, and took it out to the dump and burned it. We felt that divulging the contents wouldn't have done ourselves or anybody else any good."

"While there is no doubt that the burned material would have shed much light on the sexual behavior of the Perfectionists," Kephart shrugged philosophically, "the action taken by the company is understandable. Oneida Ltd. is not in business to further the cause of sociological research."[52] It seems odd, however, that just a few years previously, Carmer had been given carte blanche to examine everything except the diaries. "You know there are still a few of the grandchildren who look on their parents' origins as not quite respectable," Pierrepont Noyes explained. "So we're delaying the publication of the diaries until the great-grandchildren are adults. By that time they'll be proud of their ancestors." Did the company president change his mind about keeping the diaries? Noyes's involvement with the Burning is puzzling, because he himself never concealed the nature of complex marriage.[53]

In any case, Noyes's attention was focused on a more positive assertion of continuity with the past: celebrating an Oneida century reckoned from Oneida Ltd.'s present in 1948 to the founding of the Oneida Community in 1848. The chief event of the centennial commemoration was a party for the people of Oneida Ltd. (see figure 24).

FIGURE 24. The company's centennial event in Noyes Park, 1948. General Manager Miles Robertson stands at the podium. Pierrepont Noyes, wearing a light-colored suit, sits to the right.

The crowd on that hot July day packed into Sherrill's Noyes Park to enjoy entertainment offered by Nana Woolford and her dachshunds; the Salton Sisters & Co. (acrobatic head-to-head balancing and tumbling, making their first appearance in this country); Paul Kohler, "Wizard of the Xylophone"; the sensational Rob Cimse Co. on the seventy-five-foot-high whirling motorcycle trapeze; and many others, including the Tommy Dorsey Orchestra. "There were upwards of 30,000 persons present who ate 38,000 hot dogs which, placed end-to-end would reach three miles," Constance Robertson enumerated. "They also consumed 30,000 rolls, 300 loaves of bread, 46 gallons of mustard, 46 gallons of relish, used 30,000 paper cups of ice cream and ice cream pies and drank 54,000 bottles of soft drinks."[54]

As part of the celebration, the company commissioned Walter Edmonds, author of *Drums along the Mohawk* and other works of regional historical fiction, to tell its story. Edmonds's volume, *The First Hundred Years* (1948), argued that the central feature of Oneida Ltd. was an "unusual friendliness and evident comfort and happiness of all those working together." This and the philosophy of sharing prosperity came from the Oneida Community and remained undimmed as organizational principles after a century.[55] What Noyes told the crowd that day was that Oneida Ltd. had grown twenty times in size and fifty times in production and sales over the past fifty years, a time elsewhere characterized by selfishness and self seeking. But at Oneida, growth had occurred without profiteering on the public or on Oneida workers. At Oneida, the ideal of sharing was kept bright and clear. That was the company's distinction and glory.[56]

Pierrepont Noyes was seventy-eight. In the decade remaining to him, he would write up his own company memoirs, *A Goodly Heritage*, dedicated to all who had worked to build the Oneida Community Ltd. on the foundations of the old Oneida Community. Only one interest "will remain with me for the rest of my life," he wrote at the end: the welfare, problems, disappointments, and rejoicings of Oneida Ltd.[57]

In the late 1920s, Esther Lowenthal observed that the Oneida Community Ltd. radiated a corporate goodwill that placed it in a class by itself.[58] But, she wondered, would it survive the generation of its creators? It scarcely did. Because of that, this story fades out with Noyes on the grandstand on that July day in 1948, gazing out at thousands of friends, family members, employees, and well-wishers. Few, perhaps, would agree with that assessment, because Oneida Ltd. continued for another half century, growing to become the world's largest maker of flatware and employing as many as five thousand people. It prospered, by any standard, for most of that time. By factory standards, it was an unusually happy place. Oneida, almost everyone said—even at the end—was a good place to work.

The year 1948, however, is not an entirely arbitrary place to close the story. That was the last year, for example, that Oneida Ltd. contributed to local schools. Public schools all over the country were being folded up in a movement to create larger, centralized districts. Sherrill schools, thereafter, made up a small portion of a district now including two neighboring towns, Vernon and Verona.[59] Then, too, the world had caught up to Oneida Ltd. in significant ways by about 1948. Since the New Deal, programs for home-buyer and retirement assistance were offered by the federal government. Pension plans, insurance, hospitalization, and maternity benefits, on the other hand, became, in Maren Carden's estimation, "only elaborations of the existing material benefits to be got by working in any good company."[60] Responsibilities once shouldered voluntarily by the company were now widely accepted and assumed by others. Oneida welfare capitalism was no longer unique.

Most importantly, company culture at the upper echelon changed after 1948. The old Oneida values were displaced—dismantled internally at the top—by a new corporate ethic. The Oneida that went into the later twentieth century was not the same as that created by Noyes, Hinds, Kinsley, and Robertson.

Stainless to Corporate Collapse

General Manager Miles Robertson succeeded Pierrepont Noyes as company president in 1950 and continued in that capacity for a decade. During his tenure, Oneida was sustained by a lucrative Defense Department contract to manufacture military hardware. Beginning in 1952, Oneida produced large numbers of compressor blades for air force jet engines.[61] "We will sorely miss the sales volume, hours of labor, and profits of this division in the year ahead," Robertson lamented at the beginning of 1958.

The crisis of Robertson's watch was the threat to silverware—flatware, that is, plated with silver—posed by non-silver-plated cutlery. "The ever-growing competition of lower quality, short profit, stainless steel knives, forks and spoons, with their positives of not tarnish, easy to keep clean, wear forever, etc. had appeal with those housewives who were searching for the practical," Robertson sniffed. "The art of gracious living, the desire to dine rather than to eat, has been temporarily we hope, overlooked by many hostesses. It is our problem to revitalize these desires."[62] Beyond the fact that Robertson found consumer taste disappointing, the economic difficulty was that cheap stainless cutlery made in Japan and Europe was being sold in America at prices Oneida could not match.

Yet, by the early 1960s, stainless steel not only displaced silver-plated ware as the company's chief product—it reestablished Oneida in the vanguard of flatware. The achievement of restructuring around stainless was attributed to innovations in manufacturing process, to aggressive sales efforts, and to increased advertising. It also owed something to mastery of a new styling aesthetic. The corner was turned, Oneidans felt, with the popular stainless patterns of "Paul Revere" (1958) and "Chateau" (1960), and with a 1960 ad campaign ("Look Again, It's Stainless!") regarded as unusually effective.[63] Supervised by Robertson, the changeover to stainless would prove to be Oneida's last major success in adapting to new technology, to new consumer tastes, and to international competition and cheaper labor abroad.

For a number of years, the ownership of Oneida stock had been allowed to become widely dispersed. In the early 1960s, a group of New York City investors assembled a significant block of stocks and came to the share-holders' meeting to gain admittance to the board of directors. They hoped, apparently, to effect change, to have Oneida be run like other American businesses.[64] Their presence provoked a dramatic showdown in which loyal Kenwoodians flocked into the Big Hall of the Mansion House to vote their stock against what seemed to them a foreign invasion. The local sharehold-ers were successful. A tree on the front lawn of the Mansion House called the "Proxy Oak" commemorates their victory, still remembered, vaguely, as a stand against outside takeover. At the time, however, some wondered about that. Carden, then a sociology student conducting doctoral research at the Mansion House, spoke with an old-timer, a Community descendant and retired company official, who had given everything—"talent, time, devotion, and capital"—to Oneida since 1901. That individual was struck by the fact that the party introducing outsiders actually was the home team. The incumbent board of directors proposed three non-Oneida people for the board, as opposed to the outsiders, who dared nominate only two. The elderly observer commented sadly "that he had been there when P. B. Noyes had turned the Oneida family into an idealistic corporate entity." Now, he feared, this election formally signified its end.[65]

Instead of attempting to buy stock back, to re-concentrate it in family hands, the company opened the gates to outside ownership. In November 1967, Oneida shares went public on the New York Stock Exchange. This "significant forward step in the planned growth of the Company" was done, according to President Pete Noyes, to give "more widespread recognition to the Company and its products, a broader market for its stock and a market that offers economy, convenience and efficiency of trading."[66] In preparation for the event, Pete Noyes redefined company philosophy in a statement called the "Oneida Ltd. Creed." It began: "With its GOODLY HERITAGE of more than one hundred successful years of existence, ONEIDA LTD. is dedicated to making the Corporation a continuously profitable venture, thus providing its owners with security and growth, and its members with an opportunity to earn a good living under fine working conditions. We believe that the business of the Corporation must be conducted in every respect so that the shareholders' investment will be safe and will earn an adequate return."[67]

Elsewhere in America, it may have been common for a corporation to acknowledge that making money was the primary aim of its business. Elsewhere, it may have been standard practice to privilege shareholders as the party to whom the firm was responsible. At Oneida, however, the affirmation of these sentiments as central tenets of purpose was entirely new. Pete Noyes's "Oneida Ltd. Creed" marked disjunction with the philosophy of his father and with the partnership with labor forged by his older brother-in-law, Dunc Robertson.

What most troubled people at the time was not departure from the old ways but the revelation that the old ways had been sent packing long before and nobody had been told. To have its stock listed on the New York Exchange, Oneida Ltd. was required to make public certain information never previously released. One fact emerging at this time was that salaries of high company officials were about comparable to those received by senior executives elsewhere, meaning that compensation had gone sky high by Oneida's standards. The proxy statement of 1966 revealed that top officials were making about $30,000 to $40,000 and that Pete Noyes's pay was $65,000. "Kenwood resounded with surprised exclamations," Carden reported, "as retired personnel and people working in lower levels of management realized that top management had abandoned tradition."[68]

As the years passed, money paid to the top executives spiraled upward faster and faster. Pete Noyes's salary, for example, had grown to $107,616 in 1976. Five years later, it was $271,316—and that was when he was no longer working. The salary of the active president that year was $279,054; three years later it was $311,442.[69] This corporate world did not believe in keeping pay low and roughly the same among those running the show. Further, the top executives increasingly received larger and larger benefit packages. In small print hidden in a footnote of the 1985 proxy statement, for example, a "Supplemental Retirement Plan" was baldly described as a "non-qualified, non-contributory and unfunded" program that committed the company to continue paying top executives 50 percent of their salaries throughout their retirement years.[70] The great lesson of 1921—money has to be made before it can be shared—had become: those on top should put a lien on future earnings to ensure payments to themselves in perpetuity. The corporate operating environment was now geared to personal remuneration for high-ranking executives who said they were answerable to distant shareholders. Those who ran the company scarcely knew anything else. Of five men who followed Pete Noyes in the top position (president or chief executive officer), none was a descendant. Only one lived in Kenwood and had some slight firsthand acquaintance with functioning Oneida idealism. As time widened the gulf with the past, corporate Oneida grew increasingly indifferent to the old ways.

By the 1980s, a number of Oneida Community descendants working at Oneida Ltd. came to believe they were no longer welcome in the company. Other descendants, about the same time, began to wonder about the future of the Mansion House in company hands. "During the post–World War II era," one of them wrote in 1984, "the Mansion House and the grounds and paraphernalia of the old Community should have been spun off from the modern industrial corporation. It is not too late, however, to do this now. The Mansion House is one of America's most important historic and cultural monuments, and it should be owned by a nonprofit foundation. Then it will not matter, as far as the clan and modern Perfectionism is concerned, what happens to the silver corporation."[71] In 1988, an association of concerned Oneida Community descendants effected the separation of the Mansion House from the company. Renamed the Oneida Community Mansion House, it is a not-for-profit museum still in existence at this writing.

Oneida Ltd. collapsed in 2004, victimized, officials explained, by the competition of cheap labor abroad and, in the wake of 9/11, the disappearance of airline demand for Oneida cutlery. At the last shareholders' meeting held in the Mansion House, the president announced sale or closure of Oneida plants, laying off of workers, ending health insurance benefits for worker retirees, freezing pensions for remaining workers, and eliminating stock dividends. When one stockholder questioned the judgment of top executives, he was told the management team was doing a superlative job. When Lang Hatcher, stockholder, former company executive, and grandson of Pierrepont Noyes, asked about the high pay for top executives and the wisdom of having recently bought a suite of outside firms, he was told: "We did it for the benefit of the company." A third stockholder received no answer when

he asked if management had it in them to apologize for destroying the company.[72] Soon after, the company went into Chapter 11 proceedings for bank-
ruptcy. What emerged was an entity still called "Oneida Ltd." but owned by
distant hedge-fund financiers and manufacturing nothing at all.

Consciously building on their heritage, the children of the Oneida Community envisioned a renewed community built on the old, a foundation
regarded as secular, industrial, and beneficent to hired help. Pierrepont
Noyes, with the help of former Community member William Hinds and
the younger Albert Kinsley, then enlarged the Oneida Community's idea of
family to embrace the entire workforce of the company. Everyone involved
in production, it was now assumed, was entitled to share the benefits of production. Capping their own salaries, company executives mandated that, in
hard times, everyone's pay would be cut but the cuts would start at the top
and be proportionately greater there. Those who ran the firm made certain
their employees were provided with generous pensions, health and welfare
benefits, a share of the profit, and a share of company ownership.

In 1914, the machines for making silverware were moved from Niagara
Falls to Sherrill, along with their operators. Silently and without fanfare, the
Oneida Community Ltd. built a workers' community, Sherrill, which was
politically independent of the company. For years, the Oneida firm contributed substantial amounts of money to Sherrill to ensure that a high standard of living obtained there. The company never publicized this liberality,
however, because those at the top were haunted by the specter of Pullman,
Illinois—a model workers' town that had gone wrong. Nevertheless, Sherrill
was long regarded locally as a second utopia, one that had sprung directly out
of the people and values of the first.

Worker benefits decreased during business downturns over the years.
Yet the company never wavered from its commitment to welfare capitalism, always reinstituting and expanding its partnership with labor. Oneida
had to retool for military production during World War II but did so quite
successfully.

Later company history includes an industrial achievement—the development of stainless steel to replace silver-plated ware as the company's major
product—and prosperity for some years. But after about 1950, Oneida Ltd.
was no longer the philosophical extension of the Oneida Community and
Oneida Community Ltd. When the Oneida of later years foundered, the
corporate mentality that failed with it had nothing obviously to do with generosity or selflessness.

Conclusion

Looking Backward

            People at the time believed that the post-Community company was a success because it enriched the store of human contentment. "Whatever the final destiny of the O.C.L. turns out to be," Holton Noyes mused, "its first fifty years have added to human happiness and prosperity . . . continuing, in a modified way, the communistic principles of the Oneida Community."[1] With some qualification, the academic scholar Maren Carden agreed. "Descendants of the original Community probably were happier in the new Oneida Community, Limited, than were their forebears in the original Community. Indeed, P. B. Noyes may well have achieved his objective of making them happier than people elsewhere."[2] If happiness can be accounted a company goal, the Oneida Community Ltd. was successful on its own terms.

    Much the same could be said of the Oneida Community and its members, who often expressed satisfaction with their existence. We have seen that the older folks looked fondly back on the Community's first phase, calling it their happiest period. For that matter, expressions of contentment with communal existence were enunciated more frequently later in time. "I am sure I was happy," Jessie Kinsley wrote years later. Constance Robertson recorded how her maternal grandmother, an anti-Noyesian at the time of breakup, "told me in her old age that there had never been such happiness as they knew in the old Community. I believe this was honest testimony. . . . They worked, they lived together, they loved one another and above all—or because of this—they were simply happy. They were gay; they played as well as prayed. They saw all of life as good and their own lives as especially fortunate. So—until the last days—they were happy."[3]

Later researchers would come to different judgments about the degree of personal satisfaction Bible communists derived from Community life. Spencer Klaw, for example, thought that if one could put up with some loss of personal freedom, the Oneida Community was well worth it. Noyes inspired his followers to embark on a thrilling voyage of spiritual and social discovery, which hundreds found richly gratifying. Klaw could not contemplate the end of the commune "without a stabbing pain of loss."[4] Carden, on the other hand, thought Community life must have been rather oppressive. She saw Oneida as a religious despotism in which people were motivated by faith to give up their selfhood. Coercion was applied in complex marriage, perhaps most of all by peer-group pressure that compelled people to give up emotionally satisfying relationships and to have sex with members of high standing.[5]

But happiness, whether affirmed by insiders or assigned by outsiders, is not necessarily the best gauge of utopian success. It may be more meaningful to wonder whether and how the commune, as a model society, impacted wider society. It has seemed to some that the Oneida Community made no imprint on the world.[6] How can such a thing be determined?

Ripples

An obvious starting point is to question Oneida's religious influence. Robert Fogarty concluded that Oneida Perfectionism was notable for being an original American invention. He stopped short, however, of specifying any lasting impact it may have had on the world.[7] It has to be conceded that as a religious cult, the Oneida Community's effect on its surroundings was minimal or nil. Most obviously, the Bible communists apparently failed to achieve the aims of bringing heaven to earth and hastening the return of Christ.

More generally, given the fact that the Oneida Community was founded on Noyesian theology, we should wonder about the wider impact of his religious teachings. Much of Noyes's appeal and persuasiveness is forever lost to us, of course, because it came out of a considerable personal magnetism. In the larger context of his time, his teachings, spun from personal "divine inspiration" and from personal reading of scripture, must have seemed excessively idiosyncratic. Mainstream America, after all, was asked to envision history as God making sequent covenants with different groups of people and with Christ putting in an extra appearance. The Victorian reading public was invited to imagine that heaven was a pleasure ground of blissful, communist sex. Such ideas probably did not comport with prevailing views and evidently did not appeal to the majority of the churchgoing public. Noyes's doctrines fared poorly in competition with mainstream Protestantism.[8]

In the historical perspective emphasized throughout this book, Noyes's doctrinal innovations were responses to proximate circumstances. Repelled by the libidinous reputation of the Perfectionists, for example, Noyes formulated a counter-theory of sexuality asserting that free love was heavenly and good. Confronted by a rival view of end times, Noyes lopped apocalypse cleanly off the millennium. Grief-stricken by the loss of his favorite lover, Noyes imagined an afterlife filed with sleepy souls awaiting activation to rise out of the sod. The point is that having been formulated in piecemeal fashion, individual innovations in doctrine needed to be clarified in relation to each other. Noyes, however, never synthesized his thinking, even when explaining the nature of Oneida Perfectionism to a mainstream reading audience.[9] While notably creative, Noyes's theology was fragmented, and in consequence Noyes as theologian was not influential. His religion left no mark.

Considered as a secular phenomenon, the effects of the Oneida Community are, again, elusive. Oneida presented, for example, an unusually clear instance of utopian success in overcoming the problem of the isolated household and revolutionizing the conditions of the domestic sphere. One would suppose that fellow socialists would have taken an interest in the demonstration. A few outsiders, it is true, were impressed by the efficiency of Oneida's communal kitchen and child-care system. Yet Dolores Hayden's study of material feminism during the late 1800s and early 1900s failed to identify any Oneidan influence on efforts to improve the lot of women by socializing domestic work and collectivizing child care. It is difficult to see that the outside world took much notice of Oneida's precedent.[10]

Or, one might look to the movement for women's rights for traces of the Bible communists' influence. Both, after all, were part of a larger dialogue about feminine roles in American life. Both had in common a number of progressive views on women's issues, including reproductive rights. Community life at Oneida spoke to matrimonial bondage, a central issue of the "Declaration of Sentiments," the document of the first Women's Rights conference at Seneca Falls in 1848. Oneida presented an obvious model (perhaps the only one) of an alternative to traditional marriage in a truly cooperative living situation.[11] Oneida, one would think, would surely have attracted the attention of women's rights advocates.

In fact, such people scarcely mentioned Oneida at all. When they did, it was to register disapproval. One prominent figure in the women's movement, Mrs. Joslyn Gage, supposedly said that Oneida Community women were "subject to the men in the sense that they are kept here in sexual bondage; and to enforce her thought in that regard, and claiming to speak from personal observation, [Mrs. Gage] said that a sadder and more forlorn set of women she had never seen anywhere." Backing off from issues that might detract from their cause, advocates for women's rights distanced themselves from the Perfectionists because of Oneida's unsavory reputation.[12] Indeed, Oneida's problem with most everyone was its ill repute. In the eyes of Victorian America, the Oneida Community was not something to hold up as a model to emulate. One can get a sense of how disreputable Oneida had become by the manner in which the controversial feminist Victoria Woodhull defiantly flung it into the faces of her critics:

If a hundred people living anywhere in this country can so organize themselves industrially as to make the doctrine of equal love for self and neighbor possible, then that hundred have solved the problem for all the rest of the world. Go ask Oneida if among the number there organized industrially, there are any who suffer for the common necessities of life? Ask of the detested Oneida Perfectionists if there are any children there who suffer for food or for raiment or shelter? Ask if there are any laborers there who have been discharged because their labor was no longer profitable to their employers—whose families or dependencies are in want or distress? Ask if there are any pinched-cheeked and hollow-eyed women there who are obliged to offer up their bodies as a living sacrifice to the lusts of man, to gain the few paltry dollars that are needed to satisfy the demands of the landlord, or the butcher and grocer; and ask a thousand other practical questions of everyday life, and from the replies let the Christians learn a lesson of brotherly love from those whom they despise.[13]

The bad reputation always came from sex. Since the days of spiritual wifery, the public had known Perfectionists as the most libidinous of the religious cults. The common perception was that Perfectionists reveled in sexual activity, their "vile bodies steeped to the lips in lust."[14] The scandalous appearance of Oneida women and the commune's open endorsement of free love did nothing to dispel a perception of licentiousness. Anyone who perused Bible Argument could see that this group rejected the institution of holy matrimony, condoned coitus outside monogamous marriage, and acknowledged female sexuality. Sex was interesting and drew visitors, but it was deeply objectionable to many. The 1870s were a prudish time in American history, notable for an emotionally charged debate about sexual morality in which the name "Oneida" became a code word in the public dialogue for free love.[15]

The Community did impact the world in one detectable fashion—through the printed word, especially through the essentially nonreligious writings of John Noyes. For example, an article by him published in a prestigious periodical made explicit a key point of "scientific propagation": breeding humans closely "in-and-in" was precisely how breeders of plants and animals developed desirable traits. The measure of the seriousness with which Noyes was taken is indicated by usage of his neologism "stirpiculture"—often in preference to Galton's "eugenics"—during the late nineteenth century. Noyes also reached the world as a historian as a result of his book *History of American Socialisms*. Issued by a Philadelphia printer, the work drew attention to the importance of the Associationist-Fourieristic varieties of communitarianism in American life. It is still read with profit.[16]

Noyes's most influential writings, however, were about sex. His thoughts on the subject entered the mainstream medical literature through the pages of Edward Bliss Foote's physiology bestseller, *Plain Home-Talk* of 1870. This work, favorably noting complex marriage and male continence among the Perfectionists, was closely followed by *Cupid's Yokes*, an 1876 pamphlet by sex radical Ezra Heywood that advocated the Oneida method of birth control. Both Foote and Heywood were arrested for breaking new federal pornography laws enforced by moral vigilante Anthony Comstock. Noyes's method of male self-control continued to attract attention in subsequent years. Published anonymously by sociologist Henry M. Parkhurst in 1882, *Diana* (subtitled *A Psycho-fyziological Essay on Sexual Relations for Married Men and Women*) explained a philosophy of love—"Dianaism"—based on male continence. Beginning in 1896, the Oneida way of love requiring males to abjure orgasm was popularized yet again by Dr. Alice B. Stockham as *Karezza: Ethics of Marriage*.[17]

"When the pill, the sexual revolution, and the women's liberation movement arrived in the 1960s," observes writer Peter von Ziegesar, "a good part of their DNA was derived from Oneida." Noyes's theories were absorbed into the hippie movement through the pages of *Kaliflower*, a San Francisco newsletter that acquainted the long-haired young with a legacy stretching back to the Oneida Perfectionists. And, as imbibed from Noyes's writings, the Oneida Community's marital system is recognized as the forerunner of today's polyamory movement.[18] As a theorist of sex, Noyes *did* impact the world. Perhaps he really was, as Kern phrased it, the father "of modern sexual attitudes and sensibilities."[19]

If I seem somewhat dubious about that last, it is not because I disparage Noyes's insights into sex. Rather, I am bemused to imagine that, in the end, Noyes may have cast an intellectual shadow longer than the commune he created. Perhaps that is not so surprising. It has always been difficult to identify how small, short-lived, and isolated groups can have much effect on the world.[20] Such communities, it was once thought, could remake the world. But today they seem to be, as Chris Jennings pointed out, little more than cautionary tales or castles in the air.[21] The definition of a utopia (and, in our case, its sequel) I like best is that of Rosabeth Kanter: utopias are society's dreams, good dreams that allow us to take the pulse of human idealism and potential.[22]

Noyes and His Disciples

Developing out of ardent revivalism about 1830, the new religion of Perfectionism proclaimed the reality, in this life, of personal sanctification. The newly regenerate were, theoretically, free from external authority. This gave rise to the thought that Perfectionists also were free of legalistic bonds. Into the mix was added the idea of spiritual affinity, a mystical bond of true love between a man and a women. When Perfectionists put these notions together near Syracuse, New York, in 1834, it seemed a natural thing to pair up in platonic male-female teams to demonstrate superiority over both law and flesh. Such unions led to sex, which led to scandal. In the minds of many, Perfectionism became synonymous with fornication.

Among the best educated of those espousing the new doctrine of "salvation from sin" was John Humphrey Noyes. He wielded considerable influence on the movement in its early days but backed away as the sect became increasingly controversial. His rejoinder to the ill repute of Perfectionism was to suggest that sex might better be thought natural and good. Since everything in heaven is common property, Noyes reasoned, and since everyone there loves one another fully and selflessly, then heavenly men and women must be loving each other in every way, including sexually. Ideally, then, each person is a conjugal spouse to everyone of the other sex in the marital condition of complex marriage.

Noyes believed himself divinely appointed to prepare the world for the millennium—the widely held expectation that Christ would return to render judgment on humankind and then, with the righteous, rule over a combined heaven and earth for a thousand years. Noyes recruited a fellowship of believers to prepare the world for end times and to assist in bringing them about. At the beginning of 1848, he composed a planning document for his disciples explaining why they would found the Oneida Community. The tract, *Bible Argument*, linked complex marriage to the millennium by pointing out that unrestricted love is both the way of heaven and the earthly means to hasten Christ's return. It also asserted that the practice of heavenly love on earth would duplicate God's kingdom and, in so doing, help to establish it here. *Bible Argument* justified free love, espoused a lifestyle of common ownership (Bible communism), and called for associative action along Fourieristic lines. The latter would create a utopian environment in which men and women would reside in a unitary home, love one another, and work together. "Loving companionship in labor, and especially the mingling of the sexes, makes labor attractive."[23]

Noyes's followers were deeply religious people. In an age of intense theological questioning, Noyes offered them certainties and the hope of eternal existence. Those drawn to Noyes found meaning and inspiration in his teachings. These disciples—Perfectionists or Bible communists of Oneida—acknowledged Noyes as paramount because he was Christ's representative charged with ushering in the kingdom of heaven. Buying into Noyes entailed little in the way of onerous obligation. Noyes issued few direct commands, and his religion encouraged happiness. "The truth is, God made man to enjoy, not a part, but the *whole* of things," was the burden of his song.[24] Finally, Noyes's mesmerizing personality made his followers feel content in his presence because he seemed to radiate peace and well-being. As a result, Noyes's disciples wanted to please him. Trying to carry out his wishes, they did what they could to make his dreams become real.

Noyes took Perfectionism to its logical extreme in claiming that salvation from sin, once attained, was absolute and forever. Curiously, however, Oneida Community members were effectively exempted from actual perfection in this life. Noyes gave his followers to understand that salvation was progressive, an ongoing process that would take time. Beyond that, he never instructed them how—proximately, specifically—to attain the regenerate state. The result was that daily existence focused generally on progressive Perfectionism, on how to improve spiritually and morally. "Improvement is the motive power here," William Hinds said early on, and improvement required daily attention and effort. That is why Community life was experienced, as one member expressed it, as "a school for the discipline and refinement of character." The commune, said another, was "a brave and noble experiment, not only in religion but in the art of human association; a school of unselfishness, sacrifice and dedication whose equal I could not name."[25]

Living in the Oneida Community, always aspiring to be selfless and always aiming to be better, could be hard work.

A Pastoral Utopia

The first task of Noyes's group from Putney, Vermont, now united with Perfectionists from elsewhere, was to construct a home for themselves in upstate New York. This, the Mansion House, was America's first truly communal dwelling in which males and females were not compartmentalized into monogamous pairs or nuclear family units as custom prescribed. The Oneida Community members forged a sense of themselves as a group in the course of carrying out this works project.

An innovation emerging from that effort was the collectivization of childcare. Initially the raising of children was separated from parental supervision. Then, the children were segregated from the adult world with the construction, in early 1849, of a Children's House. Distinct residences for adults and youngsters meant the physical concentration of household labor and childcare. When this was performed cooperatively, the result was less work. The arrangement revolutionized the domestic sphere by lightening household drudgery regarded as feminine.

Noyes had proposed in *Bible Argument* that men and women should mingle in their daily pursuits. Such a thing was physically impossible for women so long as they wore the stays, crinolines, petticoats, and ground-dragging garments then considered fashionable. Another innovation that came out of the first construction project was the creation of a new costume for women, permitting them to work with men both indoors and out. The revolutionary Oneida short dress with pantalettes may have been the prototype for the "Bloomer costume" of the incipient women's rights movement.

Accomplishments on this order promoted communal pride, which the Perfectionists needed to confront a threat to their existence in 1852. This came in the form of legal action directed against one of the members for whipping a young woman. The lawsuit was prosecuted in the nearby court of Utica by a district attorney hostile to the existence of the Oneida Community. Although Noyes thought the commune should disband to avoid trouble, the Oneidans enlisted local sentiment and won a victory. The outcome strengthened their resolve and reinforced their sense of collective identity.

Noyes had departed from Oneida as soon as the Mansion House was completed. From a distance, he recommended courses of action, which the Bible communists in Oneida endeavored to operationalize. Early on, for example, Noyes proposed a doctrine of spiritual ranking with himself at the apex (ascending fellowship). At Oneida, they took the measure of the concept, then administered its logic to one another. In general, the Oneida Bible communists worked out the essentials of communal existence themselves. They developed effective social arrangements, including mutual criticism and the evening meeting. They promoted intellectual improvement. They crafted a system for labor in which committees assigned tasks on a rotating basis and working brought contentment. Oneidans laid the foundation for future economic developments by learning how to make metal animal traps. They established a diet of mostly vegetable foods and formulated a visitation policy tolerant of tourists. Oneida Perfectionists built Eden from the ground up.

During the early years, Community members also worked out the emotionally challenging terms of sexual communism, and did so well enough to establish a system of group marriage, perhaps the world's first, that worked. Sex at Oneida was supposed to be a pleasurable and spiritually fulfilling experience in which the partners recreated and drew nearer to God. It was to be an unselfish act in which the male suppressed ejaculation to relieve his partner's fear of pregnancy and to heighten her enjoyment. Women in the Oneida Community were freed from unwanted pregnancy and marital bondage—at least more so than in the outside world. Rather incredibly, Oneida sexual practices transformed what Aldous Huxley called "a wild, God-eclipsing passion into a civilized act of worship, a prime cause of crime and misery into a source of individual happiness, social solidarity and good behavior."[26] There were hierarchical regulations at work in the Community's sexual arrangements. Noyes and his inner circle monitored romantic couplings to discourage amative selfishness and head off socially disruptive affairs. The system of ascending fellowship encouraged the young to have sex with older partners. But strictures of control were softened and ameliorated by a deeply engrained notion of justice: sex in the Oneida Community required the consent of both partners. No compulsion, the Perfectionists claimed, was permitted in love.

By the early 1850s, the practice of men, women, and children working together outside became bound up with the Community's interest in tending fruit trees and berry bushes. Noyes never elaborated a real scheme for subsistence from garden produce, nor did he propose that such a lifestyle could elevate the standing of women. Nevertheless, that is what happened when a horticultural regime was developed in real life. Oneidans discovered that bringing men and women together in outdoor work was socially satisfying, spiritually enriching, and fun. It pleased them to realize they were advancing female standing in practical ways. Oneida, Klaw rightly suspected, was the most successful attempt ever made "to build a society in which men and women could live together as brothers and sisters, sharing with absolute equality the fruits of their common labor."[27] In effect and in Noyes's absence, the Oneida Community fashioned gender relations that were essentially egalitarian.

An Industrial Utopia

The most distinguished of many thousands of tourists to Oneida, as far as the Perfectionists were concerned, arrived from London in the summer of 1866. William Hepworth Dixon was a man of letters and editor of the *Athenaeum*—the most widely read literary magazine of the English-speaking world. Dixon came bearing the recommendation of Horace Greeley, editor of the *New York Tribune*, probably the most prestigious paper in the United States. These were irresistible bona fides to a group valuing literary attainment and journalistic acumen. Dixon was welcomed and given complete freedom to ask any question that came to mind. What Dixon reported of the Oneida Community was that it ran itself. Its members were God-fearing folk who recognized John Humphrey Noyes as God's representative and shepherd. At the same time, they governed themselves through faith and individual profession of faith ("confessing Christ"). Such was the principle of "grace," beyond which these people "made no rules, they chose no chiefs." It turned out, however, that social life also required "sympathy," which Dixon defined as public opinion and we would understand to be peer-group pressure. "Sympathy corrects the individual will, and reconciles nature with obedience, liberty with light. Thus, a brother may do anything he likes; but he is trained to do everything in sympathy with the general wish. If the public judgment is against him, he is wrong— that is to say, he is going away from the path of grace, and his only chance of happiness lies in going back to what is most agreeable to the common mind. The Family is supposed to be always wiser than the unit."[28] A theme of this book is that the Oneida Community was essentially self-governing, as Dixon observed it.

Architecture, the best-documented sphere of communal action, is also the clearest manifestation of collective decision making. Planning an enlarged home was one of the Perfectionists' favorite activities during the late 1850s, and together they developed a domestic environment that reflected their values and facilitated their lifestyle. Inside, the setting was comfortable. Outside, the architecture projected respectability and success while conveying harmony and peace. The Mansion House of 1862 was built in the Italian Villa style of America's premier architectural theoretician, A. J. Downing. More accurately, the Perfectionists' design of the building reflected their reading of Downing, just as their transformation of the surrounding grounds reflected their understanding of Downing's theories of landscape architecture. While it is true that the Bible communists said little about how they created their built works, their architectural accomplishments remain today as impressive testimony to collective will.

This is not to say that Noyes was unimportant. Later in time, however, his interests and consequent influence tended toward matters that seemed less overtly religious in character than they had earlier. For example, he presented himself to the wider world as a scholar of utopias in the book *History of American Socialisms* (1870), published in a respectable, non-Community venue. Another secular interest was eugenics, and in that realm Noyes gained some recognition as an authority on genetic science. Pursuing Noyes's interest in selective breeding, the Oneida Community instituted stirpiculture, possibly history's first eugenics program.

Noyes's most important secular influence on the Community was to prod it in the direction of industrial development. On returning to Oneida in late 1854, he touted animal traps as the economic underpinning of Oneida and encouraged mechanization in their production. As orders increased for the popular "Newhouse" devices, it seemed a good idea to build a new facility and staff it with paid outsiders. Bringing that to pass with customary effectiveness, Oneida's Bible communists became the premier trap manufacturers in the United States. Noyes then promoted a second factory industry of hired labor to produce thread for sewing machines. Traps and thread together ushered the Community into the industrial age.

Factory production made the commune dependent on paid workers, a relationship fundamentally at odds with Bible communism. To the Perfectionists, the state of "wage bondage" differed from actual slavery only in degree. Feeling guilty about being employers, the Perfectionists rationalized their industrial system as an opportunity to provide others with the means to make a good living. At the same time, they assumed responsibility for employee well-being and formulated labor policies unusually generous for the day.

Factory production and wage labor altered the fabric of communal life. Fostering an interest in financial profit, the new conditions discouraged spirituality and the mingling of men and women in cooperative work. On the other hand, the new order brought prosperity, as well as Noyes's assurance that it was right to enjoy a higher standard of living. The Bible communists of the industrial utopia devoted themselves to demonstrating the benefits of communism and Perfectionism by exemplifying the good life. They entertained throngs of visitors in their new, communally planned Mansion House. Happily they pursued science, invented labor-saving devices, landscaped their domain, played sports, and found many other ways to enjoy increased leisure time. This later period is voluminously documented in photos, newspaper coverage, and in many writings. As a result, the second half of the Oneida Community is better known than the first. The industrial phase is what most people understand as being the Oneida Community.

Industrial Continuity

The Oneida Community lasted over thirty years, far less than the communist Shaker society but far longer than any of the secular, socialist communes. Klaw considered Oneida as a striking success in its own time, "flourishing for more than a generation while other utopian communities quickly withered."[29] An important reason for longevity was factory production. Having a foundation in economic enterprise was hardly a unique feature among any of the communes of the age, of course, but Oneida stood out for its industrial focus. Associations such as Brook Farm and the North American Phalanx, for example, survived for a time by farming and by handicrafts, that is, making goods such as furniture and shoes. Oneida, in contrast, was the only one to develop a factory mode of production. Employing machines and outside workers, Oneida became the nation's largest maker of traps and one of its leading producers of sewing machine thread. Oneida was in the mainstream of American industrialization.

Industry, consequently, was stamped into Oneida's core during its final years. Industry was the aspect of the commune that most obviously survived the Community's breakup, because the succeeding company was formed around the existing industrial core. There was never any question that whatever continued after dissolution would be organized around manufacturing and commerce. It was essential for survival, and those born in the eugenics program of the 1870s took industry for granted. After the breakup, some former Perfectionists moved to Niagara Falls, the location of a small but promising silverware industry begun by the Community in 1877. Most, however, remained in the shadow of the Mansion House, in Kenwood, and continued the manufacture of traps and thread in nearby Sherrill.

The major figure in post-Community developments, Pierrepont Noyes, a stirpicultural son of John Noyes, initially concerned himself with company solvency and long-term profitability. Around 1900, the younger Noyes formulated a ten-year plan to restructure the company around silverware by upgrading its product and advertising its quality. When silverware became the company's most profitable item in 1910, traps and threads were discontinued. Thereafter, Oneida's reputation for high-end silverware and innovative advertising was firmly established. Pierrepont Noyes also fostered a new sense of family in and around the Mansion House. Reuniting his peers from the old children's department, he imparted to them the vision of renewing the company by reviving the Oneida Community's sense of brotherhood and unselfish commitment.

The industrial tradition that began in the Oneida Community continued well into the twentieth century. This is what an earlier generation of scholars knew and found most exemplary in the Oneida story. The Oneida Community—"most famous of all early American socialisms"—was remarkable for the perseverance of its economic success, in Whitney Cross's estimation. "Trap manufacturing brought prosperity and silver plate production continued it to modern times." No other socialist group in American history, he added, approached "in prosperity or in significance the adventure of the perfectionists in central New York."[30]

Idealistic Continuity

"It is abroad in the land that no longer can the old problems of capital and labor be ignored," declared the president of an upstate New York manufacturing firm in 1912. "No longer can the working class be bullied or bribed to lie still." This was Pierrepont Noyes delivering a speech at the annual meeting to shareholders and executives of Oneida Community Ltd. Nearly everyone present was a child or descendant of the Oneida Community. Now, dining together in the old family hall of the Oneida Community, the participants thought they were gathered to celebrate continuity with the old and success in the present. Building on the small cutlery business started by the Oneida Community, the Oneida Community Ltd. had created a high-end line of silverware just now beginning to turn a substantial profit. But Noyes was determined to lecture them on corporate responsibility. There would have to be a settlement emancipating workers from wage slavery, he stated flatly. Beyond making a living, each worker was entitled to accumulate property, to own his own home, and "to have leisure to enjoy that home and his family, and to develop himself." What lies ahead of us, Noyes stated, "is the opening up of a field for this most successful method of pursuing happiness—a broader field for dividing our lives and efforts with others. . . . A self-respecting course for us is to arrange our systems irrespective of what other manufacturers may do, so that the working man will get a bigger share of the product of his labor. . . . Before we are ten years older—before we are five years older—I believe we shall feel a little ashamed if each employee who is honest and efficient cannot own a home and enjoy that home." More than ever, he concluded, we are engaged "in doing something that is worth while for other people."[31]

In this fashion, Noyes reminded his listeners that their bonds to the past involved more than bloodline, more than manufactured product, and more than business success. The executives of the Oneida Community–derived industry must now embrace the essence of the Oneida Community's outlook: selfless concern for others. Now, however, the welfare of all encompassed more than the old Oneida Community family. "All" meant everyone in the company. Everyone involved in production was entitled to share the benefits of production, which included good pay, health-retirement benefits, and profit sharing. Thus was the Oneida Community's heritage to the future enlarged beyond industry to include idealism.

Following Noyes's address, the Oneida Community Ltd. embarked on an ambitious program of welfare capitalism. At its center was the creation of Sherrill as a workers' community independent of the company. At a time of little governmental interest in the laboring class, the company contributed substantially to Sherrill to underwrite its prosperity. To encourage private home ownership, for example, the company sold lots to its employees below market value and then gave them cash bonuses to build houses. The firm funded electrical, water, and sewage systems, fire protection and garbage collection, and facilities for public health and recreation. To encourage quality education, the Oneida Community Ltd. donated land for schools and contributed more than half the cost of erecting the buildings. The company assumed half the salary paid to each teacher from city tax money, then, for a dollar, made every teacher eligible for all company benefits. Teachers could live—free room and board—in the Mansion House. These actions remain largely unknown today because the Oneida Community Ltd. never publicized them. Nevertheless, as a corporate creation dedicated to the health and prosperity of employees and neighbors, Sherrill was one of America's greatest business successes.

The Oneida Community chapter of this history has been told before, almost always as the colorful tale of a Rasputin-like leader running a religious sex cult. But "the truth is," as they put it and "as all the world will one day see and acknowledge," the Perfectionists saw themselves as "social architects, with high moral and religious aims, whose experiments and discoveries they have sincerely believed would prove of value to mankind."[32] Early on, the Bible communists built what probably was America's first truly unitary home and, within it, instituted cooperative household arrangements. They invented a unique system of raising children with collectivized child care.

They instituted cooperative household arrangements while working out effective means of governance. They developed a system of group marriage with an unusual method of birth control that effectively freed women from unwanted pregnancy. They crafted a system in which committees assigned tasks and work brought satisfaction. They created a subsistence regime that fostered spirituality and resulted in practical gender equality.

In later years, the Oneida Community became a successful producer of traps and thread. Factory manufacture, the Bible communists found, entailed both material prosperity and dependence on hired labor. Finding themselves in the unaccustomed role of supervising employees from the outside world, the Bible communists formulated personnel policies that were the most liberal in the region.

The commune became, by vote, a company based on Oneida Community industry. Shortly thereafter, the Oneida Community Ltd. set traps and thread aside to concentrate on manufacturing high-quality silverware while simultaneously reaffirming the Oneida Community's generous disposition toward workers. Those at the top of the firm reinstituted the Community's notion of family but greatly expanded it to include everyone at Oneida. Capping their own salaries, Oneida's upper management made certain that employees were provided with pensions, health and welfare benefits, a share of the profit, and the opportunity to share in company ownership. Silently and without fanfare, the company built and supported a politically independent workers' community.

Together, then, the Oneida Community and the Oneida Community Ltd. comprise a continuous history of industrial enterprise. Notably, both Oneidas achieved financial prosperity while trying to better their worlds. In the utopian commune, neglecting the welfare of others was a cardinal sin. The company insisted that doing well required close attention to the well-being of its workers. A narrative of successful industry with enduring high-mindedness lends itself to meditation. The question Carden posed after studying Oneida was, what lies at the center of a fulfilled life? Jessie Kinsley could have replied that "a great example of unselfishness was set to the world for all time," one that the future will find out. Pierrepont Noyes would have answered: "We are learning to use the real recipe for happiness, which as everyone knows (and the older they grow the more they know it) consists in doing something for someone besides ourselves."[33] Oneida is most meaningful as a morality play, the story of people living their ideals in unbroken succession for a century.

NOTES

Introduction

1. Chris Jennings, *Paradise Now: The Story of American Utopianism* (New York: Random House, 2016), 301.

2. Others award the laurels for longevity in secular utopianism to the Icarians, a group of French communists dated from 1848 to 1895. It depends, of course, on how one defines continuity. For me, a history consisting of seven start-ups, two bitter community divisions, the loss of well over 95 percent of the membership, the formulation of at least four distinct constitutions, and a contemporaneous opinion that true Icaria ended about 1862—for me, as I say, the Icarians have a serious amount of discontinuity in their story. See Jennings, *Paradise Now*, 269–92; William Alfred Hinds, *American Communities and Co-operative Colonies*, 2nd rev., 3rd ed. (Chicago: Charles H. Kerr, 1908), 376 (true Icaria); and Charles Nordhoff, *The Communistic Societies of the United States: Harmony, Oneida, the Shakers, and Others* (New York: Harper & Brothers, 1875), 223–28.

3. How utopian success can be defined has long been a contentious issue in utopian studies (see, for example, Yaacov Oved, "Communal Movements in the Twentieth Century," in *Utopia: The Search for the Ideal Society*, ed. Roland Schaer, Gregory Clacys, and Lyman Tower Sargent [New York: New York Public Library and Oxford University Press, 2000]). One of the first to grapple with the problem was sociologist Rosabeth Kanter, who showcased Oneida as the benchmark of nineteenth-century utopian success. Kanter's criterion was simple and arbitrary: a utopia is successful if it lasts for twenty-five years. Oneida fulfilled that requirement, of course, and also retained strong communal overtones persisting into the late twentieth century. See Rosabeth Moss Kanter, *Commitment and Community: Communes and Utopias in Sociological Perspective* (Cambridge, MA: Harvard University Press, 1972), 245–46.

4. Ellen Wayland-Smith, *Oneida: From Free Love Utopia to the Well-Set Table—an American Story* (New York: Picador, 2016); Spencer Klaw, *Without Sin: The Life and Death of the Oneida Community* (New York: Allen Lane, Penguin, 1993).

5. Substantial (book length) publications on the Oneida Community by scholars include Maren Lockwood Carden, *Oneida: Utopian Community to Modern Corporation* (Syracuse, NY: Syracuse University Press, 1998); Richard DeMaria, *Communal Love at Oneida: A Perfectionist Vision of Authority, Property, and Sexual Order* (1969; New York: Edwin Mellen, 1978); two Oneida Community diaries edited and commentated by Robert S. Fogarty, which are *Special Love / Special Sex: An Oneida Community Diary* (Syracuse, NY: Syracuse University Press, 1994) and *Desire and Duty at Oneida: Tirzah Miller's Intimate Memoir* (Bloomington: University of Indiana Press, 2000); three works by Lawrence Foster: *Religion and Sexuality: The Shakers, the Mormons, and the Oneida Community* (1981; Urbana: University of Illinois Press, 1984), *Women, Family,*

and Utopia: Communal Experiments of the Shakers, the Oneida Community, and the Mormons (Syracuse, NY: Syracuse University Press, 1991), and (edited and commentated by) *Free Love in Utopia: John Humphrey Noyes and the Origin of the Oneida Community, Compiled by George Wallingford Noyes* (Urbana: University of Illinois Press, 2001); Louis J. Kern, *An Ordered Love: Sex Roles and Sexuality in Victorian Utopias: The Shakers, the Mormons, and the Oneida Community* (Chapel Hill: University of North Carolina Press, 1981); Ira L. Mandelker, *Religion, Society, and Utopia in Nineteenth-Century America* (Amherst: University of Massachusetts Press, 1984); and Robert David Thomas, *The Man Who Would Be Perfect: John Humphrey Noyes and the Utopian Impulse* (Philadelphia: University of Pennsylvania Press, 1977).

6. Foster, *Women, Family, and Utopia*, 77, 89.

7. Another factor contributing to the predominance of Noyes in the printed record could well be the loss of handwritten records by others in a burning of documents in 1947, an incident discussed in chapter 10.

8. *Daily Journal*, January 17, 1866.

9. William Hepworth Dixon, *New America*, 8th ed. (London: Hurst and Blackett, 1867), 2:229, 246; Nordhoff, *Communistic Societies*, 182–83.

10. *Circular*, September 18, 1864; Community Journal, August 30, 1864 (one memorial); *Circular*, October 19, 1868 (summer-house); *Circular*, October 24, 1861 (image of the Lord's Supper); Community Journal, July 16, 29–30, and August 21, 23, 1863.

11. Community Journal, October 3, 1863.

12. George E. Cragin, "Trap Making on Oneida Creek, Part 1," *Quadrangle* 6, no. 4 (April 1913): 1–2.

13. E. Wayland-Smith, *Oneida: From Free Love*, 87–88.

14. *American Socialist*, August 28 and September 4, 1878.

15. I estimate Noyes was gone from the Oneida Community (mostly in New York and Wallingford) some eight years and seven months during the first twenty years of the commune. He may well have been absent more than that because I count Noyes as present in Oneida when nothing was documented about his location. After 1868, Noyes's whereabouts are difficult to track with much specificity.

16. Hubbard Eastman, *Noyesism Unveiled: A History of the Sect Self-Styled Perfectionists* (Brattleboro, VT: the author, 1849), vii–viii; the *New York Observer* article quoted from Foster, *Free Love*, 146; Professor Mears quoted from Klaw, *Without Sin*, 243–44; Charles Boswell, "Uncle Johnny's Woman Farm," *Men: True Adventures*, April 1959.

17. Carden, *Oneida: Utopian Community*, 74, 87–88, 106–7, 111 (no individual held accountable), 210.

18. Robert S. Fogarty, "Oneida: A Utopian Search for Religious Security," *Labor History* 14, no. 2 (Spring 1973).

19. Klaw, *Without Sin*, 105, 115–16, 182; Wayland-Smith, *Oneida: From Free Love*, 69–70, 162–63.

20. Theodore Noyes's letter to McGee of April 15, 1892, is quoted extensively in Constance Noyes Robertson, *Oneida Community: The Breakup, 1876–1881* (Syracuse, NY: Syracuse University Press, 1972), 16–20; Fogarty, *Special Love / Special Sex*, 214–17; and Foster, *Free Love in Utopia*, xxii–xxiii. Since about 1981, Dr. Noyes's epistle (or a facsimile of it) has resided among the Theodore Noyes materials in the Oneida Community Collection, Special Collections Department of the Syracuse University Library.

21. Carden knew of this letter in the early 1960s (*Oneida: Utopian Community*, 87–88, 98–99). Other researchers evidently became aware of it later. I think one can chart the impact of Dr. Noyes's sentiments as it changes interpretations earlier expressed by the same writers at, for example, Robertson, *Breakup*, 15–17; Fogarty, *Special Love / Special Sex*, 216–17; and Foster, *Free Love in Utopia*, xxiii.

1. Perfectionism

1. John Humphrey Noyes, *Confessions of John H. Noyes, Part 1: Confession of Religious Experience, including a History of Modern Perfectionism* (Oneida Reserve, NY: Leonard & Co., Printers, 1849).

2. Paul E. Johnson, *A Shopkeeper's Millennium: Society and Revivals in Rochester, New York, 1815–1837*, 2nd ed. (1978; New York: Hill & Wang, 2004), 3 (declared themselves impotent); Charles G. Finney, *Memoirs of Rev. Charles G. Finney, Written by Himself* (1876; New York: Fleming H. Revell, 1908), 23 (no longer sin).

3. Finney, *Memoirs*, 134–35; Johnson, *Shopkeeper's Millennium*, 3–4 (Finney's ideas).

4. Michael Barkun, *Crucible of the Millennium: The Burned-Over District of New York in the 1840s* (Syracuse, NY: Syracuse University Press, 1986), 23; Finney, *Memoirs*, 300–301 (contemporary assessment); Whitney R. Cross, *The Burned-Over District: The Social and Intellectual History of Enthusiastic Religion in Western New York, 1800–1850* (Ithaca, NY: Cornell University Press, 1950), 155; Johnson, *Shopkeeper's Millennium*, 13–14.

5. Cross, *Burned-Over District*, 151–55, 177–81; Johnson, *Shopkeeper's Millennium*, 96–102.

6. George Wallingford Noyes, ed., *The Religious Experience of John Humphrey Noyes, Founder of the Oneida Community* (New York: Macmillan, 1923), 389–92.

7. Ibid., 187–88.

8. Robert S. Fogarty, ed., *Desire and Duty at Oneida: Tirzah Miller's Intimate Memoir* (Bloomington: University of Indiana Press, 2000), 41n7.

9. G. W. Noyes, *Religious Experience*, 96.

10. Cross, *Burned-Over District*, 239, 242. Perfectionism, Kern observes, "was a form of antinomianism, maintaining that for those who had achieved perfection (sanctification), both civil and ecclesiastical law had become superfluous": see Louis J. Kern, *An Ordered Love: Sex Roles and Sexuality in Victorian Utopias: The Shakers, the Mormons, and the Oneida Community* (Chapel Hill: University of North Carolina Press, 1981), 373n23.

11. *American Socialist*, July 14, 1879.

12. J. H. Noyes, *Confessions*, 18. G. W. Noyes, *Religious Experience*, 109, gives the passage in Romans as "If thou shalt confess with thy mouth the Lord Jesus, and shalt believe in thy heart that God hath raised him from the dead, thou shalt be saved. For with the heart man believeth unto righteousness; and with the mouth confession is made unto salvation." See also John Humphrey Noyes, *The Way of Holiness: A Series of Papers Formerly Published in "The Perfectionist," at New Haven* (Putney, VT: John H. Noyes and Co., 1839), 217, 225–26.

13. The interchange about committing sin is quoted from G. W. Noyes, *Religious Experience*, 119; "I do not pretend" is from J. H. Noyes, *Confessions*, 23; and see J. H. Noyes, *Confessions*, 18–19. "I have taken away their license to sin" is J. H. Noyes, *Confessions*, 27.

14. *American Socialist*, August 28, 1879 ("the testimony"); George Wallingford Noyes, ed., *John Humphrey Noyes: The Putney Community* (Oneida, NY: the author, 1931), 16 ("shone like an angel"); G. W. Noyes, *Religious Experience*, 216–17. Incidentally, Noyes probably was clean-shaven during the 1830s, as prevailing American fashion dictated.

15. Lawrence Foster, ed., *Free Love in Utopia: John Humphrey Noyes and the Origin of the Oneida Community, Compiled by George Wallingford Noyes* (Urbana: University of Illinois Press, 2001), 88.

16. G. W. Noyes, *Religious Experience*, 169.

17. William Hepworth Dixon, *Spiritual Wives*, 4th ed., vol. 2 (London: Hurst and Blackett, 1868), 26; Cross, *Burned-Over District*, 245; G. W. Noyes, *Religious Experience*, 192.

18. Worden, in William Hepworth Dixon, *Spiritual Wives*, 2nd ed. (Philadelphia: J. B. Lippincott, 1868), 286.

19. Dixon, *Spiritual Wives*, 2nd ed., 237–38.

20. Women frequently played prominent roles in the Finney revivals and other religious enthusiasms of the time. See Cross, *Burned-Over District*, 177–78, 237.

21. Dixon, *Spiritual Wives*, 4th ed., 2:12.

22. Ibid., 2:15.

23. Ibid., 2:15–16.

24. Mark Holloway, *Heavens on Earth: Utopian Communities in America, 1680–1880*, 2nd ed. (1951; New York: Dover, 1966), 53; Louis J. Kern, "Breaching the 'Wall of Partition between the Male and the Female': John Humphrey Noyes and Free Love," *Syracuse University Library Associates Courier* 28 (Fall 1993): 89n9; Emanuel Swedenborg, *A Compendium of the Theological and Spiritual Writings of Emanuel Swedenborg: Being a Systematic and Orderly Epitome of All His Religious Works* (Boston: Crosby and Nichols and Otis Clapp, 1854), 300; Joscelyn Godwin, *Upstate Cauldron: Eccentric Spiritual Movements in Early New York State* (Albany: SUNY Press, Excelsior Editions, 2015), 127–28.

25. Worden quoted in Dixon, *Spiritual Wives*, 2nd ed., 286; Lawrence Foster, *Religion and Sexuality: The Shakers, the Mormons, and the Oneida Community* (1981; Urbana: University of Illinois Press, 1984), 131.

26. Dixon, *Spiritual Wives*, 2nd ed., 63, 236.

27. Dixon, *Spiritual Wives*, 4th ed., 2:17; Dixon, *Spiritual Wives*, 2nd ed., 286.

28. Dixon, *Spiritual Wives*, 4th ed., 2:18.

29. Ibid., 2:6, 20–21, 23.

30. Robert Allerton Parker, *A Yankee Saint: John Humphrey Noyes and the Oneida Community* (New York: G. P. Putnam's Sons, 1935), 38; Dixon, *Spiritual Wives*, 4th ed., 2:27–39; G. W. Noyes, *Religious Experience*, 196–99.

31. "He could carry a virgin" is Noyes quoted in Dixon, *Spiritual Wives*, 2nd ed., 349; Dixon, *Spiritual Wives*, 4th ed., 2:40–41, 47–48; G. W. Noyes, *Religious Experience*, 200.

32. "Calm brotherly love" is from *Oneida Circular*, August 24, 1874; J. H. Noyes, *Confessions*, 20–21; G. W. Noyes, *John Humphrey Noyes*, 1; G. W. Noyes, *Religious Experience*, 113–14, 156, 353–54. See also John Humphrey Noyes, *Salvation from Sin: The End of Christian Faith* (Wallingford, CT: Oneida Community, 1866), 2.

33. Sound introductions to a vast Shaker literature are Edward Deming Andrews, *The People Called Shakers: A Search for the Perfect Society* (1953; New York: Dover, 1963), and Henri Desroche, *The American Shakers: From Neo-Christianity to Presocialism* (1955; Amherst: University of Massachusetts Press, 1971).

34. Noyes in Dixon, *Spiritual Wives*, 2nd ed., 349.

35. Worden in Dixon, *Spiritual Wives*, 2nd ed., 287.

36. G. W. Noyes, *Religious Experience*, 201–2.

37. Cross, *Burned-Over District*, 244.

38. Richard DeMaria, *Communal Love at Oneida: A Perfectionist Vision of Authority, Property, and Sexual Order* (New York: Edwin Mellen, 1978), 37–38, 120–21; Helen Lefkowitz Horowitz, *Rereading Sex: Battles over Sexual Knowledge and Suppression in Nineteenth-Century America* (New York: Alfred A. Knopf, 2002), 265; Joanne E. Passet, *Sex Radicals and the Quest for Women's Equality* (Urbana: University of Illinois Press, 2003), 68; Hal D. Sears, *The Sex Radicals: Free Love in High Victorian America* (Lawrence: Regents Press of Kansas, 1977), 8.

39. Noyes, in Dixon, *Spiritual Wives*, 2nd ed., 348; Anthony Wonderley, ed., *John Humphrey Noyes on Sexual Relations in the Oneida Community: Four Essential Texts* (Hamilton College Library, Clinton, NY: Richard S. Couper Press, 2012), 69.

40. J. H. Noyes, *Confessions*, 30–31.

41. Cross, *Burned-Over District*, 241–42, 247; Erik Achorn, "Mary Cragin: Perfectionist Saint," *New England Quarterly* 28 (December 1955): 494; G. W. Noyes, *Religious Experience*, 310.

42. *Oneida Circular*, August 24, 1874.

43. Swedenborg quoted in Gay Wilson Allen, *Waldo Emerson* (1981; New York: Penguin, 1982), 456; John Humphrey Noyes, "Swedenborgiana—No. 13, Amphibious Morality," *Circular*, February 3, 1866; G. W. Noyes, *John Humphrey Noyes*, 81–82.

44. Dixon, *Spiritual Wives*, 2nd ed., 265; John Humphrey Noyes, *Dixon and His Copyists: A Criticism*, 2nd ed. (Oneida, NY: Oneida Community, 1874), 31.

45. *Oneida Circular*, August 24, 1874; *Circular*, February 18, 1867.

2. Putney

1. John Humphrey Noyes, *Confessions of John H. Noyes, Part 1: Confession of Religious Experience, including a History of Modern Perfectionism* (Oneida Reserve, NY: Leonard & Co., Printers, 1849), 69–70.

2. "When you were in his presence" is from William M. Kephart, *Extraordinary Groups: The Sociology of Unconventional Life-Styles*, 2nd ed. (1978; New York: St. Martin's, 1982), 145; Pierrepont Burt Noyes, *My Father's House: An Oneida Boyhood* (New York: Farrar and Rinehart, 1937), 297–98; James B. Herrick, "In luminatuo lumen videmus," *Quadrangle* 1, no. 2 (May 1908): 11 ("atmosphere of good feeling").

3. Corinna Ackley Noyes, *The Days of My Youth* (1960; Hamilton College Library, Clinton, NY: Richard W. Couper Press, 2011), 119.

4. George Wallingford Noyes, ed., *John Humphrey Noyes: The Putney Community* (Oneida, NY: the author, 1931), 30. "Brooked no opposition" is the characterization of P. B. Noyes, *My Father's House*, 225.

5. For George W. Noyes see *Circular*, June 14, 1864 (meetings) and John B. Teeple, *The Oneida Family: Genealogy of a 19th Century Perfectionist Commune* (Oneida, NY: Oneida Community Historical Committee, Mansion House, 1985), 58. For the sisters see Robert Allerton Parker, *A Yankee Saint: John Humphrey Noyes and the Oneida Community* (New York: G. P. Putnam's Sons, 1935), 95; Jane K. Rich, ed., *A Lasting Spring: Jessie Catherine Kinsley, Daughter of the Oneida Community* (Syracuse, NY: Syracuse University Press, 1983), 31, 36; "Harriet Noyes Skinner," by J., *Quadrangle* 1, no. 8 (December 1908): 10–12; P. B. Noyes, *My Father's House*, 28, 31; "Community Eating," *Circular*, July 5, 1869; and Victoria Carver, ed., *Oneida Community Cooking, or A Dinner without Meat, by Harriet A. Skinner, Oneida, N.Y., 1873*, http://tontine255.wordpress.com, 2013.

6. G. W. Noyes, *John Humphrey Noyes*, 22.

7. Ibid., 17–19, 22; *Circular*, February 26 and March 5, 1866; Parker, *Yankee Saint*, 77–85.

8. William Alfred Hinds, *American Communities and Co-operative Colonies*, 2nd rev., 3rd ed. (Chicago: Charles H. Kerr, 1908), 165–66; Teeple, *Oneida Family*, 22–23, 55–58; G. W. Noyes, *John Humphrey Noyes*, 49 (central committee).

9. G. W. Noyes, *John Humphrey Noyes*, 23; Parker, *Yankee Saint*, 52, 64–65; H.A.N., "History of the Printing Business of O.C." (ca. 1875, Oneida Community Mansion House Archives), 43.

10. G. W. Noyes, *John Humphrey Noyes*, 54–55; Hinds, *American Communities*, 163.

11. *American Socialist*, August 28, 1879, 277; Parker, *Yankee Saint*, 97.

12. At one point in the early 1840s, for example, they cut back on food preparation for three formal meals a day to one meal a day. The sign announcing this change read "Health, Comfort, Economy and Woman's Rights." The notice went on to explain that having to cook so much was a duty that subjected females "almost universally to the worst of slavery" (Parker, *Yankee Saint*, 97).

13. *Circular*, February 12, 1853.

14. *American Socialist*, August 28, 1879, 277.

15. G. W. Noyes, *John Humphrey Noyes*, 49.

16. For John Noyes arranging marriages see Parker, *Yankee Saint*, 93–95; *American Socialist*, August 21, 1879, 269 ("continued to walk in all the commandments").

17. *American Socialist*, August 21, 1879, 269.

18. Anthony Wonderley, ed., *John Humphrey Noyes on Sexual Relations in the Oneida Community: Four Essential Texts* (Hamilton College Library, Clinton, NY: Richard S. Couper Press, 2012), 112–13.

19. Ibid., 103.

20. George Wallingford Noyes, ed., *The Religious Experience of John Humphrey Noyes, Founder of the Oneida Community* (New York: Macmillan, 1923), 408, 382.

21. Sin "was the great object" quoted from John Humphrey Noyes, *Salvation from Sin: The End of Christian Faith* (Wallingford, CT: Oneida Community, 1866), 20; John Humphrey Noyes, *The Berean: A Manual for the Help of Those Who Seek the Faith of the Primitive Church* (Putney, VT: Office of the Spiritual Magazine, 1847), 157.

22. Noyes, *Berean*, 169.

23. Ibid., 157, 236–42.

24. Alfred Barron and George Noyes Miller, eds., *Home-Talks by John Humphrey Noyes, Vol. 1* (Oneida: The Community, 1875), 154.

25. Whitney R. Cross, *The Burned-Over District: The Social and Intellectual History of Enthusiastic Religion in Western New York, 1800–1850* (Ithaca, NY: Cornell University Press, 1950), 149.

26. J. H. Noyes, *Berean*, 245.

27. G. W. Noyes, *Religious Experience*, 76.

28. Ibid., 73 ("the sunshine and rain of religious discipline"), 76–77.

29. Ibid., 85, 411.

30. J. H. Noyes, *Confessions*, 39.

31. G. W. Noyes, *Religious Experience*, 73.

32. Ibid., 308.

33. Cross, *Burned-Over District*, 200.

34. Wayne R. Judd, "William Miller: Disappointed Prophet," in *The Disappointed: Millerism and Millenarianism in the Nineteenth Century*, ed. Ronald L. Numbers and Jonathan M. Butler (Bloomington: Indiana University Press, 1987), 17–35.

35. David L. Rowe, *Thunder and Trumpets: Millerites and Dissenting Religion in Upstate New York, 1800–1850* (Chico, CA: Scholars Press, 1985); Michael Barkun, *Crucible of the Millennium: The Burned-Over District of New York in the 1840s* (Syracuse, NY: Syracuse University Press, 1986), 33, 138; Cross, *Burned-Over District*, 287–321.

36. Wonderley, *John Humphrey Noyes*, 60.

37. Barkun, *Crucible of the Millennium*, 65, 98; H.A.N., "History of the Printing Business of O.C.," 7; Michael Barkun, "'The Wind Sweeping over the Country': John Humphrey Noyes and the Rise of Millerism," in *The Disappointed: Millerism and Millenarianism in the Nineteenth Century*, ed. Ronald L. Numbers and Jonathan M. Butler, 153–56; William Hepworth Dixon, *Spiritual Wives*, 4th ed., vol. 2 (London: Hurst and Blackett, 1868), 41.

38. J. H. Noyes, *Berean*, 329, 397.

39. J. H. Noyes, *Confessions*, 39.

40. J. H. Noyes, *Berean*, 55.

41. G. W. Noyes, *John Humphrey Noyes*, 53–56.

42. Ibid., 69.

43. Hinds, *American Communities*, 167–74; G. W. Noyes, *John Humphrey Noyes*, 72.

44. The Ebenezers prospered economically and grew in number. To obtain more land, they relocated to the Midwest in an orderly removal (1855–1864), which resulted in the Amana Community of Iowa. For Ebenezer and Amana see Frank J. Lankes, *The Ebenezer Community of True Inspiration* (Gardenville, NY: the author, 1949), and Bertha M. H. Shambaugh, *Amana: The Community of True Inspiration* (Iowa City: State Historical Society of Iowa, 1908).

45. See Edward Deming Andrews, *The People Called Shakers: A Search for the Perfect Society* (1953; New York: Dover, 1963); and Henri Desroche, *The American Shakers: From Neo-Christianity to Presocialism* (1955; Amherst: University of Massachusetts Press, 1971) for introductory works to the Shaker literature. Lawrence Foster estimates maximum Shaker population to have been between four thousand and six thousand, in *Religion and Sexuality: The Shakers, the Mormons, and the Oneida Community* (1981; Urbana: University of Illinois Press, 1984), 23, and *Women, Family, and Utopia: Communal Experiments of the Shakers, the Oneida Community, and the Mormons* (Syracuse, NY: Syracuse University Press, 1991), 7.

46. J. H. Noyes, *Berean*, 434 ("an unauthorized and evil use").

47. Parker, *Yankee Saint*, 155–57; Arthur Bestor, *Backwoods Utopias: The Sectarian Origins and the Owenite Phase of Communitarian Socialism in America, 1663–1829*, 2nd enl. ed. (1950; Philadelphia: University of Pennsylvania Press, 1970), 44.

48. Bestor, *Backwoods Utopias*, 30–31, 36; Rosabeth Moss Kanter, *Commitment and Community: Communes and Utopias in Sociological Perspective* (Cambridge, MA: Harvard University Press, 1972), 221; John Humphrey Noyes, *History of American Socialisms* (Philadelphia: J. B. Lippincott, 1870), 669–70.

49. Bestor, *Backwoods Utopias*, 160–201; Edward K. Spann, *Brotherly Tomorrows: Movements for a Cooperative Society in America, 1820–1920* (New York: Columbia University Press, 1989), 29–49; Chris Jennings, *Paradise Now: The Story of American Utopianism* (New York: Random House, 2016), 79–148.

50. Gay Wilson Allen, *Waldo Emerson* (1981; New York: Penguin, 1982), 305, 346; Spann, *Brotherly Tomorrows*, 50–64; Jennings, *Paradise Now*, 192–202.

51. Jonathan Beecher, *Charles Fourier: The Visionary and His World* (Berkeley: University of California Press, 1986), 274–96; Carl J. Guarneri, *The Utopian Alternative: Fourierism in Nineteenth-Century America* (Ithaca, NY: Cornell University Press, 1991), 18–19, 122–34, 181–82; Spann, *Brotherly Tomorrows*, 77–78, 102–6.

52. Albert Brisbane, *Association: Or, a Concise Exposition of the Practical Part of Fourier's Social Science* (New York: Greeley and McElrath, 1843); Guarneri, *Utopian Alternative*, 32–34.

53. Carl J. Guarneri, "Reconstructing the Antebellum Communitarian Movement: Oneida and Fourierism," *Journal of the Early Republic* 16, no. 3 (Autumn 1996): 475, 480.

54. G. W. Noyes, *John Humphrey Noyes*, 55, 71.

55. "I am every day more persuaded" quoted ibid., 192–93; "Formal community of property" is from Spencer Klaw, *Without Sin: The Life and Death of the Oneida Community* (New York: Allen Lane, Penguin, 1993), 54; John Humphrey Noyes, "Association," *Spiritual Magazine* 1, no. 1 (March 15, 1846): 4–7.

56. Hinds, *American Communities*, 175–76

57. H.H.S., "A Community Transplanted, from Putney to Oneida, III," *American Socialist*, August 28, 1879; G. W. Noyes, *John Humphrey Noyes*, 101, 206 (mutual criticism, residential consolidation); Wonderley, *John Humphrey Noyes*, 113.

58. So said Noyes relating the change at Putney to sex, and so say chroniclers of the Oneida Community who repeat him; see, for example, Klaw, *Without Sin*, 58, and Ellen Wayland-Smith, *Oneida: From Free Love Utopia to the Well-Set Table—an American Story* (New York: Picador, 2016), 54–55. *Circular*, January 11, 1852 ("her only ambition").

59. G. W. Noyes, *John Humphrey Noyes*, 201–2; Parker, *Yankee Saint*, 121–24.

60. "Fire at Brook Farm," *Harbinger* 2, no. 14 (1846): 220–22.

61. J. H. Noyes, *History of American Socialisms*, 537, 107, 615.

62. Guarneri, "Reconstructing," 472, and *Utopian Alternative*, 280; Jennings, *Paradise Now*, 204–6.

63. "In 1846" is from J. H. Noyes, *History of American Socialisms*, 615–16; "Fire at Brook Farm"; *Circular*, April 23, 1863.

64. G. W. Noyes, *John Humphrey Noyes*, 235.

65. Ibid., 237–38.

66. Francis Wayland-Smith, "What Held the O. C. Together," photocopy of eleven handwritten pages "given to Historical Committee by P. B. Noyes 5 Feb. 49" (Oneida Community Mansion House Archives, ca. 1910), 1.

67. G. W. Noyes, *John Humphrey Noyes*, 236.

68. Ibid., 240–50, 282–91; H.H.S., "Community Transplanted," 277; Parker, *Yankee Saint*, 124–42.

69. Parker, *Yankee Saint*, 130–31; G. W. Noyes, *John Humphrey Noyes*, 258–63; Oneida Community, *First Annual Report of the Oneida Association: Exhibiting Its History, Principles, and Transactions to Jan. 1, 1849* (Oneida Reserve, NY: Oneida Association, 1849), 2–3.

70. Anthony Wonderley, *Oneida Iroquois Folklore, Myth, and History: New York Oral Narrative from the Notes of H. E. Allen and Others* (Syracuse, NY: Syracuse University Press, 2004), 19–24.

71. G. W. Noyes, *John Humphrey Noyes*, 388.

72. *Circular*, November 29, 1869.

73. *American Socialist*, October 2, 1879.

74. G. W. Noyes, *John Humphrey Noyes*, 368.

3. Oneida Birthed and Left Behind

1. Brian Connolly, *Domestic Intimacies: Incest and the Liberal Subject in Nineteenth-Century America* (Philadelphia: University of Pennsylvania Press, 2014), 123–32; John D. Davies, *Phrenology: Fad and Science—a 19th-Century Crusade* (New Haven, CT: Yale University Press, 1955). Phrenologist Orson Fowler is quoted from Helen Lefkowitz Horowitz, *Rereading Sex: Battles over Sexual Knowledge and Suppression in Nineteenth-Century America* (New York: Alfred A. Knopf, 2002), 330.

2. *Witness*, August 20, 1837.

3. *Circular*, March 13, 1856, and November 26, 1866.

4. Oneida Community, *First Annual Report of the Oneida Association: Exhibiting Its History, Principles, and Transactions to Jan. 1, 1849* (Oneida Reserve, NY: Oneida Association, 1849), 18–42; Anthony Wonderley, ed., *John Humphrey Noyes on Sexual Relations in the Oneida Community: Four Essential Texts* (Hamilton College Library, Clinton, NY: Richard S. Couper Press, 2012), 59–91.

5. Wonderley, *John Humphrey Noyes*, 68.

6. Ibid., 65. This, incidentally, is one of the very few passages in which Noyes may acknowledge or make reference to the existence of homosexuality. I would say the documentary record of Oneida is silent in this regard.

7. Wonderley, *John Humphrey Noyes*, 61 ("the intimate union"), 63 ("the love-relation").

8. Ibid., 70.

9. Oneida Community, *First Annual Report*, 11–12; Oneida Community, *Bible Communism: A Compilation from the Annual Reports of the Oneida Association and Its Branches* (Brooklyn, NY: Office of the Circular, 1853), 7.

10. Wonderley, *John Humphrey Noyes*, 71.

11. Ibid., 67–68.

12. Ibid., 69.

13. Ibid., 75.

14. Ibid., 73–78.

15. Ibid., 79.

16. Ibid., 80.

17. Ibid., 86.

18. Ibid., 87–88.

19. Ibid., 89.

20. *Circular*, March 18, 1854.

21. Wonderley, *John Humphrey Noyes*, 86.

22. *Circular*, February 27, 1862; Lawrence Foster, ed., *Free Love in Utopia: John Humphrey Noyes and the Origin of the Oneida Community, Compiled by George Wallingford Noyes* (Urbana: University of Illinois Press, 2001), 2.

23. *Spiritual Magazine*, August 11, 1849 ("attraction and zeal"); Harriet M. Worden, *Old Mansion House Memories, by One Brought Up in It* (Oneida, NY: Oneida Ltd., 1950), 5 (the first enterprise); Oneida Community, *First Annual Report*, 4 ("many valuable lessons").

24. Janet R. White, "Building Perfection: The Social and Physical Structures of the Oneida Community" (MA thesis, Cornell University, 1994), 50.

25. Funk and Wagnalls, *The Practical Standard Dictionary of the English Language* (New York: Funk and Wagnalls, 1927), 699.

26. On "mansion" see Carl J. Guarneri, *The Utopian Alternative: Fourierism in Nineteenth-Century America* (Ithaca, NY: Cornell University Press, 1991), 185, and John Humphrey Noyes, *History of American Socialisms* (Philadelphia: J. B. Lippincott, 1870), 392.

27. Wonderley, *John Humphrey Noyes*, 86.

28. *American Socialist*, August 28, 1879.

29. Guarneri, *Utopian Alternative*, 185; "Fire at Brook Farm," *Harbinger* 2, no. 14 (1846): 220–22.

30. Associationists typically began community life by distributing themselves in various ways among preexisting buildings. When work began on a unitary dwelling, the result was a barracks of a temporary nature designed to house nuclear families (Alphadelphia, Integral, and La Grange Phalanxes) or couples (Clermont Phalanx). One phalanstery that may antedate that of Brook Farm (and Oneida) was the communal dwelling at the Wisconsin Phalanx. However, the function of that building as a unitary residence was problematic. In fact, the question of whether it was simply a multifamily apartment dwelling proved to be a divisive one contributing to the community's dissolution. The phalanstery of the North American Phalanx postdated the Oneida Community's Mansion House. See Guarneri, *Utopian Alternative*, 184–85, 201; and J. H. Noyes, *History of American Socialisms*, 365, 383, 392–98, 431–39.

31. Corinna Ackley Noyes, *The Days of My Youth* (1960; Hamilton College Library, Clinton, NY: Richard W. Couper Press, 2011), 50; Pierrepont Burt Noyes, *My Father's House: An Oneida Boyhood* (New York: Farrar and Rinehart, 1937), 65–67; Jane K. Rich, ed., *A Lasting Spring: Jessie Catherine Kinsley, Daughter of the Oneida Community* (Syracuse, NY: Syracuse University Press, 1983), 14–15.

32. Oneida Community, *First Annual Report*, 6–7.

33. Oneida Community, *Second Annual Report of the Oneida Association: Exhibiting Its Progress to February 20, 1850* (Oneida Reserve, NY: Oneida Association, 1850), 4–5.

34. Albert Brisbane, *Association: Or, a Concise Exposition of the Practical Part of Fourier's Social Science* (New York: Greeley and McElrath, 1843), 64–71.

35. George Wallingford Noyes, ed., *John Humphrey Noyes: The Putney Community* (Oneida, NY: the author, 1931), 55; Robert Allerton Parker, *A Yankee Saint: John Humphrey Noyes and the Oneida Community* (New York: G. P. Putnam's Sons, 1935), 97.

36. Oneida Community, *First Annual Report*, 7

37. Charles Pellerin, *The Life of Charles Fourier*, trans. Francis George Shaw (New York: William H. Graham, 1848), 102.

38. Brisbane, *Association*, 23, 27.

39. Wonderley, *John Humphrey Noyes*, 89–90.

40. *Circular*, August 28, 1856 ("in the present mellow state"); Tirzah C. Herrick, "To the Editor of the Sunday World," *Quadrangle* 5, no. 11 (September–November 1912): 13–14.

41. Oneida Community, *Second Annual Report*, 11.

42. Skinner quoted from *American Socialist*, April 6, 1876; Carl J. Guarneri, "Reconstructing the Antebellum Communitarian Movement: Oneida and Fourierism," *Journal of the Early Republic* 16, no. 3 (1996): 476.

43. Foster, *Free Love*, 33.

44. Ibid., 31, 91; *Oneida Circular*, July 12, 1875.

45. Foster, *Free Love*, 32; "a more quiet place" quoted from Oneida Community, *Third Annual Report of the Oneida Association: Exhibiting Its Progress to February 20, 1851* (Oneida Reserve, NY: Oneida Association, 1851), 17.

46. *Circular*, April 3, 1856 ("seek for association"); Alfred Barron and George Noyes Miller, eds., *Home-Talks by John Humphrey Noyes, Vol. 1* (Oneida, NY: The Community, 1875), 203–9; Robert S. Fogarty, "Oneida: A Utopian Search for Religious Security," *Labor History* 14, no. 2 (Spring 1973): 227.

47. Noyes on Hamilton and George Noyes is quoted from *Community Journal*, November 10 and 22, 1863.

48. Foster, *Free Love*, 57–58; Constance Noyes Robertson, ed., *Oneida Community: An Autobiography, 1851–1876* (Syracuse, NY: Syracuse University Press, 1970), 311.

49. Foster, *Free Love*, 48, 51.

50. Ibid., 46.

51. Oneida Community, *Third Annual Report*, 18; Parker, *Yankee Saint*, 195–96.

52. *Circular*, April 4, 1852.

53. *Circular*, November 6, 1851.

54. *Circular*, November 6, 1851; Foster, *Free Love*, 115–17.

55. Whitney R. Cross, *The Burned-Over District: The Social and Intellectual History of Enthusiastic Religion in Western New York, 1800–1850* (Ithaca, NY: Cornell University Press, 1950), 345–49; Hubbard Eastman, *Noyesism Unveiled: A History of the Sect Self-Styled Perfectionists* (Brattleboro, VT: the author, 1849), 254; Hal D. Sears, *The Sex Radicals: Free Love in High Victorian America* (Lawrence: Regents Press of Kansas, 1977), 7–8.

56. John Humphrey Noyes, *Confessions of John H. Noyes, Part 1: Confession of Religious Experience, including a History of Modern Perfectionism* (Oneida Reserve, NY: Leonard & Co., Printers, 1849), 41–42.

57. *Circular*, March 4, 1854.

58. Foster, *Free Love*, 153.

59. Ibid., 157.

60. Ibid., 146–48.

61. Ibid., 165, 193.

62. *Daily Journal*, April 10, 1866.

63. Worden, *Old Mansion House Memories*, 73.

64. P. B. Noyes, *My Father's House*, 143.

65. *Oneida Circular*, April 3, 1871; Erik Achorn, "Mary Cragin: Perfectionist Saint," *New England Quarterly* 28, no. 4 (December 1955): 490–518. Mary Cragin also was credited with initiating ascending fellowship, a system of spiritual ranking, in *Circular*, May 12, 1859.

66. *Circular*, October 19, 1868. The Mr. Cragin of this passage was, in all probability, George E. Cragin—Mary's son, and the same who explained (see introduction) how the bonfire of Community fruit trees gave rise to the trap industry.

67. Maren Lockwood Carden, *Oneida: Utopian Community to Modern Corporation* (1969; Syracuse, NY: Syracuse University Press, 1998), 71.

68. *Circular*, November 16, 1851.

4. Creating a Community

1. John Humphrey Noyes, *History of American Socialisms* (Philadelphia: J. B. Lippincott, 1870), 614–45.

2. See, for example, H.A.N., "History of the Printing Business of O.C." (ca. 1875, Oneida Community Mansion House Archives); and H.H.S., "A Community Transplanted, from Putney to Oneida," in nine sequent issues of *American Socialist* from August 14 to October 9, 1879.

3. Lawrence Foster, ed., *Free Love in Utopia: John Humphrey Noyes and the Origin of the Oneida Community, Compiled by George Wallingford Noyes* (Urbana: University of Illinois Press, 2001), 171; George Wallingford Noyes, ed., *John Humphrey Noyes: The Putney Community* (Oneida, NY: the author, 1931), 386.

4. Foster, *Free Love*, 137, 28, 95.

5. Ibid., 96–97.

6. Ibid., 262. "People were more severe in those days," observed Oneida Community–born Stephen R. Leonard Jr., in "Recollections," photocopy of unpublished manuscript (Oneida Community Mansion House Archives, ca. 1951), 22.

7. "Sensitive and high-minded women" quoted from Robert Allerton Parker, *A Yankee Saint: John Humphrey Noyes and the Oneida Community* (New York: G. P. Putnam's Sons, 1935), 188; Foster, *Free Love*, 138.

8. Foster, *Free Love*, 142.

9. Ibid., 185.

10. Ibid., 176–77.

11. Ibid., 77–78, 172–75, 180–81, 188–91.

12. Ibid., 182.

13. Ibid., 185; *Circular*, July 11, 1852.

14. Foster, *Free Love*, 189.

15. *Circular*, November 7, 1870.

16. *Circular*, January 5, 1860.

17. "I beg of Oneida" is from Foster, *Free Love*, 136.

18. Oneida Community, *First Annual Report of the Oneida Association: Exhibiting Its History, Principles, and Transactions to Jan. 1, 1849* (Oneida Reserve, NY: Oneida Association, 1849), 2; Robert S. Fogarty, "Oneida: A Utopian Search for Religious Security," *Labor History* 14, no. 2 (Spring 1973): 206. "Intelligent but relatively untaught and uncritical farmers and artisans" is another good description of the first gathering at Oneida, by Maren Lockwood, "The Experimental Utopia in America," *Daedalus* 94, no. 2 (Spring 1965): 408.

19. *American Socialist*, February 28, 1878.

20. "I beg of Oneida" is from Foster, *Free Love*, 136; Oneida Association, "Family Register, Jan. 1, 1849–March 17, 1850," photocopied typescript (Oneida Community Mansion House Archives); Fogarty, "Oneida," 226; Lawrence Foster, *Women, Family, and Utopia: Communal Experiments of the Shakers, the Oneida Community, and the Mormons* (Syracuse, NY: Syracuse University Press, 1991), 88.

21. Joseph Ackley, photocopy of letter to Corinna Ackley, November 26, 1892 (Oneida Community Mansion House Archives).

22. *Daily Journal*, January 14 and 29, 1866.

23. *Circular*, June 10, 1872.

24. John Freeman quoted from *Daily Journal*, April 22, 1867.

25. Oneida Community, *Third Annual Report of the Oneida Association: Exhibiting Its Progress to February 20, 1851* (Oneida Reserve, NY: Oneida Association, 1851), 22.

26. *Daily Journal*, March 6, 1866.

27. Spencer Klaw, *Without Sin: The Life and Death of the Oneida Community* (New York: Allen Lane, Penguin, 1993), 108.

28. "Almost fanatical horror of forms" is from Charles Nordhoff, *The Communistic Societies of the United States: Harmony, Oneida, the Shakers, and Others* (New York: Harper & Brothers, 1875), 188.

29. John Humphrey Noyes, *The Way of Holiness: A Series of Papers Formerly Published in "The Perfectionist," at New Haven* (Putney, VT: John H. Noyes and Co., 1839), 217, 225–26.

30. Pierrepont Burt Noyes, *My Father's House: An Oneida Boyhood* (New York: Farrar and Rinehart, 1937), 29.

31. *Circular*, February 28, 1856.

32. Harriet M. Worden, *Old Mansion House Memories, by One Brought Up in It* (Oneida, NY: Oneida Ltd., 1950), 46–49.

33. "Every thing objectionable" is from Oneida Community, *First Annual Report*, 10; Francis Wayland-Smith, "What Held the O. C. Together," photocopy of eleven handwritten pages "given to Historical Committee by P. B. Noyes 5 Feb. 49" (Oneida Community Mansion House Archives, ca. 1910), 8.

34. Oneida Community, *Mutual Criticism*, introduction by Murray Levine and Barbara Benedict (1876; Syracuse, NY: Syracuse University Press, 1975), 45, 61; Community Journal, May 15, 1863, and March 24, 1864.

35. P. B. Noyes, *My Father's House*, 136.

36. Oneida Community, *Second Annual Report of the Oneida Association: Exhibiting Its Progress to February 20, 1850* (Oneida Reserve, NY: Oneida Association, 1850), 22–23.

37. *Circular*, September 12, 1852.

38. Oneida Community, *Hand-Book of the Oneida Community: Containing a Brief Sketch of Its Present Condition, Internal Economy, and Leading Principles, No. 2* (Oneida, NY: Oneida Community, 1871), 34–35; Nordhoff, *Communistic Societies*, 183.

39. Oneida Community, *Second Annual Report*, 17; "the last half hour" is from Jane K. Rich, ed., *A Lasting Spring: Jessie Catherine Kinsley, Daughter of the Oneida Community* (Syracuse, NY: Syracuse University Press, 1983), 33; Worden, *Old Mansion House Memories*, 12; Corinna Ackley Noyes, *The Days of My Youth* (1960; Hamilton College Library, Clinton, NY: Richard W. Couper Press, 2011), 59; Lockwood, "Experimental Utopia," 406.

40. *Circular*, April 3, 1856; Richard DeMaria, *Communal Love at Oneida: A Perfectionist Vision of Authority, Property, and Sexual Order* (New York: Edwin Mellen, 1978), 157–58.

41. P. B. Noyes, *My Father's House*, 133.

42. Oneida Community, *Third Annual Report*, 25.

43. Foster, *Free Love*, 133.

44. *Circular*, September 10, 1853; "this spirit" quoted from Oneida Community, *Third Annual Report*, 25.

45. Worden, *Old Mansion House Memories*, 54; *Circular*, February 26, 1853.

46. Worden, *Old Mansion House Memories*, 59.

47. *Circular*, April 4, 1861; *Oneida Circular*, January 8, 1872, and January 6, 1876.

48. *Circular*, February 28, 1856.

49. *Circular*, May 23, 1854.

50. *Circular*, February 22, 1855.

51. *Circular*, February 15, 1855.

52. *Circular*, October 9, 1856.

53. *Circular*, July 10, 1856.

54. *Circular*, April 26, 1855.

55. Worden, *Old Mansion House Memories*, 28–29.

56. George Wallingford Noyes, "Sixty Years Ago," *Quadrangle* 1, no. 11 (February 1909): 6.

57. Worden, *Old Mansion House Memories*, 32; *Circular*, August 30, 1855, and March 10, 1859.

58. "Those who eat swine's flesh" quoted from *Circular*, March 9, 1853; Foster, *Free Love*, 249–60.

59. *Circular*, January 28, 1854.

60. John Humphrey Noyes, *Confessions of John H. Noyes, Part 1: Confession of Religious Experience, including a History of Modern Perfectionism* (Oneida Reserve, NY: Leonard & Co., Printers, 1849), 6–7; Parker, *Yankee Saint*, 48–50; Anthony Wonderley, ed., *John Humphrey Noyes on Sexual Relations in the Oneida Community: Four Essential Texts* (Hamilton College Library, Clinton, NY: Richard S. Couper Press, 2012), 93–102.

61. Oneida Community, *Third Annual Report*, 27; reading *Uncle Tom's Cabin* cited from *Circular*, May 30, 1852, and April 20, 1853; for Gerrit Smith in Congress see *Circular*, November 24, 1852, December 22, 1853, and August 12, 1854; *Circular*, July 27, 1853.

62. For Icarians see *Circular*, June 29, 1853, and October 21, 1854; Hopedale at *Circular*, October 14, 1854, and Community Journal, June 4, 1863, and March 21, 1864; Raritan Bay is *Circular*, November 27, 1852.

63. Carr at *Circular*, November 23, 1854; Considerant's visit is *Circular*, April 13, 1853.

64. *Circular*, August 1, 4, and 11, 1852.

65. William Alfred Hinds, *American Communities and Co-operative Colonies*, 2nd rev., 3rd ed. (Chicago: Charles H. Kerr, 1908), 266–75; J. H. Noyes, *History of American Socialisms*, 449–511.

66. *Circular*, September 12, 1852; Foster, *Free Love*, 70–71; "The Oneida Community," *Transactions of the New York State Agricultural Society, 1866*, vol. 26 (1867): 794; George E. Cragin, "First Canning in the Community," *Quadrangle* 6, no. 9 (September 1913): 3–6; *Circular*, April 19, 1855; *Daily Journal*, October 24, 1866.

67. George E. Cragin, "The Hubbard Farm," *Quadrangle* 7, nos. 2–3 (February–March 1914): 11; *Oneida Circular*, June 12, 1871.

68. *Circular*, June 21, 1855 ("it is impossible"), and *Circular*, May 6, 1858.

69. Foster, *Free Love*, 67.

70. *Circular*, June 23, 1859.

71. "The atmospheric opinion of us" quoted from *Circular*, July 7, 1859; *Circular*, February 22, 1852; "claim the right to possess" is *Circular*, August 7, 1865.

5. Gender and Sex

1. Anthony Wonderley, ed., *John Humphrey Noyes on Sexual Relations in the Oneida Community: Four Essential Texts* (Hamilton College Library, Clinton, NY: Richard S. Couper Press, 2012), 88.

2. The Putney farm, according to Harriet Skinner (*American Socialist*, August 28, 1879), "supplied our table with milk and butter, vegetables and nice garden stuff, with apples, nuts, etc., and filled our barn with hay."

3. Jonathan Beecher, *Charles Fourier: The Visionary and His World* (Berkeley: University of California Press, 1986), 251, 286; Carl J. Guarneri, *The Utopian Alternative: Fourierism in Nineteenth-Century America* (Ithaca, NY: Cornell University Press, 1991), 122–34, 181–82.

4. Albert Brisbane, *Association: Or, a Concise Exposition of the Practical Part of Fourier's Social Science* (New York: Greeley and McElrath, 1843), 52.

5. Oneida Community, *Third Annual Report of the Oneida Association: Exhibiting Its Progress to February 20, 1851* (Oneida Reserve, NY: Oneida Association, 1851), 4–6.

6. *Circular*, December 20, 1853; November 3, 1859; and February 25, 1853.

7. *Circular*, August 29, 1852, and November 3, 1859.

8. See, for example, *Circular*, January 8, 1857.

9. Oneida Community, *Second Annual Report of the Oneida Association: Exhibiting Its Progress to February 20, 1850* (Oneida Reserve, NY: Oneida Association, 1850), 4; "may have been thought" is from *Circular*, September 5, 1852; *Circular*, March 18, 1854.

10. *Circular*, September 21, 1853; *Daily Journal*, July 30, 1866.

11. *Circular*, December 15, 1853; George E. Cragin (attributed), "First Canning in the Community," *Quadrangle* 6, no. 9 (September 1913): 3–6.

12. *Circular*, March 6, 1856; January 28, 1858; March 6, 1856; and January 11, 1869.

13. *Circular*, October 10, 1852.

14. "As horticulture supplants farming" is from *Circular*, March 18, 1854; "gardens and orchards are the chosen scenes" quoted from *Circular*, September 5, 1852.

15. Wonderley, *John Humphrey Noyes*, 97–102; "I vow" is from Lawrence Foster, ed., *Free Love in Utopia: John Humphrey Noyes and the Origin of the Oneida Community, Compiled by George Wallingford Noyes* (Urbana: University of Illinois Press, 2001), 212–13.

16. Oneida Community, *Bible Communism: A Compilation from the Annual Reports of the Oneida Association and Its Branches* (Brooklyn, NY: Office of the Circular, 1853), 16; *Circular*, January 13, 1859.

17. *Circular*, April 2, 1857.

18. Dolores Hayden, *The Grand Domestic Revolution: A History of Feminist Designs for American Homes, Neighborhoods, and Cities* (Cambridge, MA: MIT Press, 1981), 298–99; *Circular*, March 18, 1854; January 8, 1857; and May 20, 1858.

19. *Circular*, September 18, 1856.

20. Lawrence Foster, *Religion and Sexuality: The Shakers, the Mormons, and the Oneida Community* (1981; Urbana: University of Illinois Press, 1984), 105.

21. Carl J. Guarneri, "Reconstructing the Antebellum Communitarian Movement: Oneida and Fourierism," *Journal of the Early Republic* 16, no. 3 (1996): 482.

22. *Circular*, February 10, 1859. The argument that traditional household work was done mostly by women is developed by Marlyn Klee-Hartzell, "'Mingling the Sexes': The Gendered Organization of Work in the Oneida Community," *Syracuse University Library Associates Courier* 28, no. 2 (1993): 61–85.

23. *Oneida Circular*, March 9, 1874.

24. *Circular*, May 26, 1859.

25. *Circular*, May 5, 1859; Wonderley, *John Humphrey Noyes*, 90.

26. *Circular*, July 11, 1870.

27. John Humphrey Noyes, *The Berean: A Manual for the Help of Those Who Seek the Faith of the Primitive Church* (Putney, VT: Office of the Spiritual Magazine, 1847), 65, 71.

28. *American Socialist*, June 26, 1879.

29. Hubbard Eastman, *Noyesism Unveiled: A History of the Sect Self-Styled Perfectionists* (Brattleboro, VT: the author, 1849), 161.

30. Robert S. Fogarty, ed., *Desire and Duty at Oneida: Tirzah Miller's Intimate Memoir* (Bloomington: University of Indiana Press, 2000), 25–26; Helen Lefkowitz Horowitz, *Rereading Sex: Battles over Sexual Knowledge and Suppression in Nineteenth-Century America* (New York: Alfred A. Knopf, 2002), 333–34.

31. Wonderley, *John Humphrey Noyes*, 77; Louis J. Kern, *An Ordered Love: Sex Roles and Sexuality in Victorian Utopias: The Shakers, the Mormons, and the Oneida Community* (Chapel Hill: University of North Carolina Press, 1981), 225–26.

32. Fogarty, *Desire and Duty*, 60.

33. Wonderley, *John Humphrey Noyes*, 75, 79, 120 ("has an *immanent* value"); "is reabsorbed by the blood" is George N. Miller, *After the Sex Struck; or, Zugassent's Discovery* (Boston: Arena, 1895), 69.

34. Horowitz, *Rereading Sex*, 92–98.

35. Wonderley, *John Humphrey Noyes*, 78, 122.

36. Richard DeMaria, *Communal Love at Oneida: A Perfectionist Vision of Authority, Property, and Sexual Order* (New York: Edwin Mellen, 1978), 104.

37. Robert Allerton Parker, *A Yankee Saint: John Humphrey Noyes and the Oneida Community* (New York: G. P. Putnam's Sons, 1935), 184.

38. *Daily Journal*, September 5, 1866.

39. "A happy religion" according to Pierrepont Burt Noyes, *My Father's House: An Oneida Boyhood* (New York: Farrar and Rinehart, 1937), 138; "not on the side of asceticism" quoted from *Circular*, April 4, 1852; Wonderley, *John Humphrey Noyes*, 64–65.

40. Wonderley, *John Humphrey Noyes*, 79.

41. William T. La Moy, "Two Documents Detailing the Oneida Community's Practice of Complex Marriage," *New England Quarterly* 135, no. 1 (2012): 125, 132; Herrick quoted from Carl Carmer, *Listen for a Lonesome Drum: A York State Chronicle* (1936; Syracuse, NY: Syracuse University Press, 1995), 197; Stephen R. Leonard Jr., "Recollections," photocopy of unpublished manuscript (Oneida Community Mansion House Archives, ca. 1951), 1. The popular woman was Tirzah Miller as cited in Spencer Klaw, *Without Sin: The Life and Death of the Oneida Community* (New York: Allen Lane, Penguin, 1993), 176.

42. Wonderley, *John Humphrey Noyes*, 79; Allan Estlake (pseudonym of Abel Easton), *The Oneida Community: A Record of an Attempt to Carry Out the Principles of Christian Unselfishness and Scientific Improvement* (London: George Redway, 1900), 90; P. B. Noyes, *My Father's House*, 131.

43. Constance Noyes Robertson, ed., *Oneida Community: An Autobiography, 1851–1876* (Syracuse, NY: Syracuse University Press, 1970), 336; Foster, *Free Love*, 218.

44. *Circular*, May 26, 1859; Robertson, *Oneida Community: An Autobiography*, 336; DeMaria, *Communal Love at Oneida*, 192.

45. DeMaria, *Communal Love at Oneida*, 136–38, 109.

46. Foster, *Free Love*, 160.

47. Oneida Community, *Bible Communism*, 22; Robert S. Fogarty, "Oneida: A Utopian Search for Religious Security," *Labor History* 14, no. 2 (Spring 1973): 210.

48. Foster, *Free Love*, 231; Joseph Ackley, "Joseph Ackley: An Autobiography," *Quadrangle* 1, no. 8 (November 1908): 11; *Circular*, November 6, 1851; "prayer and supplication" is from Jane K. Rich, ed., *A Lasting Spring: Jessie Catherine Kinsley, Daughter of the Oneida Community* (Syracuse, NY: Syracuse University Press, 1983), 9.

49. Foster, *Free Love*, 26.

50. Foster, *Religion and Sexuality*, 107.

51. Foster, *Free Love*, 246–47.

52. Oneida Community, *Hand-Book of the Oneida Community: Containing a Brief Sketch of Its Present Condition, Internal Economy, and Leading Principles, No. 2* (Oneida, NY: Oneida Community, 1871), 52.

53. Foster, *Free Love*, 247.

54. Cragin is in La Moy, "Two Documents," 131; Fogarty, *Desire and Duty*, and *Special Love / Special Sex: An Oneida Community Diary* (Syracuse, NY: Syracuse University Press, 1994); the "proud fellow" is from Carmer, *Listen for a Lonesome Drum*, 192–93.

55. Community Journal, February 17, 1864; Taylor Stoehr, *Free Love in America: A Documentary History* (New York: AMS, 1979), 30.

56. "Persons shall not be obliged" quoted from Oneida Community, *Hand-Book of the Oneida Community; with a Sketch of the Founder, and an Outline of Its Constitution* (Wallingford, CT: Office of the Circular, Wallingford Community, 1867), 15; "a woman was entirely released" according to Estlake (Abel Easton), *Oneida Community*, 87; Cragin, in La Moy, "Two Documents," 125; DeMaria, *Communal Love at Oneida*, 139, 173; "Woman's Subjection" by S.M.R., *Oneida Circular*, March 2, 1876.

57. DeMaria, *Communal Love at Oneida*, 145–58.

58. Foster, *Free Love*, 238–39.

59. Ibid., 224.

60. Fogarty, *Special Love / Special Sex*, 215.

61. Parker, *Yankee Saint*, 258.

62. Rich, *Lasting Spring*, 41.

63. *Oneida Circular*, March 2, 1876.

64. Lawrence Foster, *Women, Family, and Utopia: Communal Experiments of the Shakers, the Oneida Community, and the Mormons* (Syracuse, NY: Syracuse University Press, 1991), 91.

65. Instances in the Community Journal of pleasure seeking are indicated at January 24, August 14, August 18, and October 19, 1863, and July 26, 1864. Special love is a problem mentioned at May 12, October 29, and December 16, 1863, and February 17 and August 13, 1864.

66. The survey is *Circular*, February 28, 1861.

67. Rich, *Lasting Spring*, 40.

6. Buildings, Landscapes, and Traps

1. Oneida Community, *Third Annual Report of the Oneida Association: Exhibiting Its Progress to February 20, 1851* (Oneida Reserve, NY: Oneida Association, 1851), 3; Oneida Community, *Second Annual Report of the Oneida Association: Exhibiting Its Progress to February 20, 1850* (Oneida Reserve, NY: Oneida Association, 1850), 4.

2. Anthony Wonderley, "Oneida Community Buildings, Grounds, and Landscape, 1848–1880," cultural landscape report (Oneida Community Mansion House Archives, 2012), 23.

3. Ibid., 21–24, 43–45.

4. Lawrence Foster, ed., *Free Love in Utopia: John Humphrey Noyes and the Origin of the Oneida Community, Compiled by George Wallingford Noyes* (Urbana: University of Illinois Press, 2001), 52; *Circular*, September 24, 1853.

5. "I confess" is quoted from *Circular*, May 23, 1854; "tastefully shaped" is from *Circular*, September 24, 1853.

6. Albert Brisbane, *Association; or, A Concise Exposition of the Practical Part of Fourier's Social Science* (New York: Greeley and McElrath, 1843), 56; A. J. Downing, *A Treatise on the Theory and Practice of Landscape Gardening, Adapted to North America with a View to the Improvement of Country Residences*, 6th ed. (1841; New York: A. O. Moore, 1859); Judith K. Major, *To Live in the New World: A. J. Downing and American Landscape Gardening* (Cambridge, MA: MIT Press, 1997), 10, 113–19.

7. Major, *To Live in the New World*, 152.

8. *Circular*, June 4, 1857 (Bradley); *Circular*, June 15, 1853 (Barron).

9. Foster, *Free Love*, 93–94, 291; Constance Noyes Robertson, *Oneida Community Profiles* (Syracuse, NY: Syracuse University Press, 1977), 65–105; Oneida Community, *Third Annual Report*, 17–18.

10. "The successful management" quoted from Harriet M. Worden, *Old Mansion House Memories, by One Brought Up in It* (Oneida, NY: Oneida Ltd., 1950), 77; Robert Allerton Parker, *A Yankee Saint: John Humphrey Noyes and the Oneida Community* (New York: G. P. Putnam's Sons, 1935), 202.

11. *Circular*, October 25, 1855.

12. Dolores Hayden, *Seven American Utopias: The Architecture of Communitarian Socialism, 1790–1975* (Cambridge, MA: MIT Press, 1976), 186–223.

13. *Circular*, July 2, 1857.

14. "We are convinced" is from *Circular*, November 6, 1856; "we expect" is *Circular*, October 9, 1856.

15. *Circular*, January 7, 1858.

16. A. J. Downing, *The Architecture of Country Houses* (1850; New York: Dover, 1969), 286, 317, 353; Hayden, *Seven American Utopias*, 207, 213; see also Downing, *Treatise on the Theory*, 329–30, 334–36.

17. *Circular*, September 28 and October 19, 1868.

18. *Circular*, March 3 and May 12, 1859; "When We Made Brick," *Quadrangle* 6, no. 12 (December 1913): 9–10; *Circular*, January 17 and August 29, 1861; Worden, *Old Mansion House Memories*, 105.

19. Hamilton quoted in John Humphrey Noyes, *History of American Socialisms* (Philadelphia: J. B. Lippincott, 1870), 511.

20. *Circular*, September 5, 1861.

21. Albert Bates, "Architectural Design and 'Complex Marriage' at Oneida," *Communities* 95 (Summer 1997): 43–46, 95; Heather M. Van Wormer, "The Ties That Bind: Ideology, Material Culture, and the Utopian Ideal," *Historical Archaeology* 40, no. 1 (2006): 37–56. The eight hundred visitors are reported at *Circular*, March 4, 1864.

22. Foster, *Free Love*, 247. Two architectural historians see the single bedrooms of the 1862 Mansion House as evidence for the regularization of complex marriage. See Hayden, *Seven American Utopias*, 202; and Janet R. White, "Building Perfection: The Social and Physical Structures of the Oneida Community" (MA thesis, Cornell University, 1994), 81.

23. Pierrepont Burt Noyes, *My Father's House: An Oneida Boyhood* (New York: Farrar and Rinehart, 1937), 39.

24. Anthony Wonderley, ed., *John Humphrey Noyes on Sexual Relations in the Oneida Community: Four Essential Texts* (Hamilton College Library, Clinton, NY: Richard S. Couper Press, 2012), 124.

25. *Circular*, January 3, 1861 ("casting out of a devil"); *Circular*, July 10, 1862.

26. Community Journal, August 7 and August 8 ("damned good luck"), 1863, and January 16, 1864; A.W.C., "The Community and the War," *Circular*, May 29, 1865.

27. Major, *To Live in the New World*, 154–55; Barron, in *Circular*, March 20, 1862.

28. *Circular*, April 10, 1862.

29. *Circular*, April 3, 1862.

30. *Circular*, March 20, 1862; Major, *To Live in the New World*, 155.

31. Major, *To Live in the New World*, 150–52; *Circular*, May 22, 1862.

32. *Circular*, September 11, 1862.

33. Community Journal, March 22, 1864.

34. *American Socialist*, May 15, 1879; Hayden, *Seven American Utopias*, 218–19.

35. Foster, *Free Love*, 48.

36. Stephen R. Leonard Jr., "Trap Book," photocopy of unpublished manuscript in three parts (Oneida Community Mansion House Archives, ca. 1950), vol. 1, 79–85.

37. *Circular*, November 8, 1869; *Oneida Circular*, January 4 and March 22, 1875.

38. Foster, *Free Love*, 45, 286.

39. George E. Cragin, "Trap Making on Oneida Creek, Part 1," *Quadrangle* 6, no. 4 (April 1913): 2.

40. Foster, *Free Love*, 199–201.

41. Oneida Community, *Bible Communism: A Compilation from the Annual Reports of the Oneida Association and Its Branches* (Brooklyn, NY: Office of the Circular, 1853), 15.

42. Parker, *Yankee Saint*, 202.

43. *Circular*, October 23, 1856; Parker, *Yankee Saint*, 208–9; Worden, *Old Mansion House Memories*, 56–62.

44. Anthony Wonderley, "The Most Utopian Industry: Making Oneida's Animal Traps, 1852–1925," *New York History* 91, no. 3 (Summer 2010): 175–95.

45. *Circular*, April 17, 1865.

46. *Circular*, March 21, 1861, and June 27, 1864; George E. Cragin, "Trap Making on Oneida Creek, Part 2," *Quadrangle* 6, no. 3 (May 1913): 4.

47. George E. Cragin, "Trap Making on Oneida Creek, Part 4," *Quadrangle* 6, no. 8 (August 1913): 1.

48. *Circular*, September 24, 1863.

49. Richard Gerstell, *The Steel Trap in North America* (Harrisburg, PA: Stackpole Books, 1985), 167.

50. *Circular*, March, 18, 1867. Traps aside, the Oneida Community objected strongly to animal cruelty. For example, a sign in a Community barn reminded "milkers and herders" not to strike the beasts and to remember that "gentle words and kind treatment are enjoined" (*Circular*, June 26, 1871).

51. John Humphrey Noyes, *Dixon and His Copyists: A Criticism*, 2nd ed. (Oneida, NY: Oneida Community, 1874), 23–24; Oneida Community, *Bible Communism*, 16; *Circular*, June 27, 1864.

7. Industrialization

1. *Circular*, May 27, 1858.

2. *Circular*, February 2, 1860; George E. Cragin, "Water Supply at Kenwood, 1848–1911," *Quadrangle* 6, no. 5 (May 1913): 11.

3. *Circular*, October 17, 1864 ("in every respect a model of convenience"); Anthony Wonderley, "Oneida Community Buildings, Grounds, and Landscape, 1848–1880," cultural landscape report (Oneida Community Mansion House Archives, 2012), 30 (Tontine).

4. Anthony Wonderley, "Watervliet Shakers through the Eyes of Oneida Perfectionists, 1863–1875," *American Communal Societies Quarterly* 3, no. 2 (April 2009): 51–64.

5. *American Socialist*, April 20, 1876.

6. *Circular*, April 17, 1865.

7. "The Community have decided" quoted from Community Journal, October 3, 1863; *Circular*, January 6, 1868.

8. *Circular*, September 24, 1863.

9. *Daily Journal*, February 19, 1866.

10. *Circular*, January 1, 1866.

11. *Circular*, December 8, 1866.

12. *Circular*, December 10 and December 17, 1866.

13. *Circular*, January 10 and March 21, 1870.

14. "Unrivalled" quoted in *American Socialist*, April 6, 1876; "to supply the demand" is from *Oneida Circular*, October 16, 1871; *Oneida Circular*, January 12 and October 26, 1874.

15. *Circular*, January 10, 1870.

16. *Oneida Circular*, September 23, 1872; Oneida Community, *Hand-Book of the Oneida Community* (Oneida, NY: Office of the Oneida Circular, 1875), 18.

17. *Circular*, June 20, 1854 ("stop hiring"), December 1, 1859 ("crushed down"), and January 6, 1868 (only nominally better). For "the old vicious hireling system" see *Daily Journal*, November 26, 1867. When they became employers, Bible communists wrote less about exploitative aspects of the workplace and more about workers' freedom to make decisions. "Many young women go into the factories from choice," a Community writer explained of the silk girls, "preferring to handle belts rather than brooms, and the music of gearing to the rattle of the piano" (*Circular*, December 17, 1866).

18. Oneida Community, *Hand-Book* of 1875, 18.

19. Community Journal, October 21, 1863.

20. Community Journal, November 6, 1863.

21. "We want a spirit of liberality" quoted from *Daily Journal*, November 1, 1867. *Daily Journal*, June 18, 1864; November 1, 1867; and December 18, 1867. For employee housing see *Circular*, June 25, 1863; *Oneida Circular*, August 25, 1873; *Hand-Book* of 1875, 18. Esther Lowenthal, "The Labor Policy of the Oneida Community Ltd.," *Journal of Political Economy* 35, no. 1 (1927): 115.

22. *Daily Journal*, December 28, 1867; *Circular*, October 5, 1868; Charles Nordhoff, *The Communistic Societies of the United States: Harmony, Oneida, the Shakers, and Others* (New York: Harper & Brothers, 1875), 169.

23. *Hand-book* of 1875, 25.

24. Leanne E. Brown, "By Their Fruits Shall Ye Know Them: The History of Canning by the Oneida Community and Oneida Community, Ltd." (MA thesis, State University of New York College at Oneonta and Cooperstown Graduate Program, 1998), 16; *Circular*, September 18, 1865, and January 21, 1867.

25. *Circular*, January 11, 1869.

26. Louis J. Kern, *An Ordered Love: Sex Roles and Sexuality in Victorian Utopias; The Shakers, the Mormons, and the Oneida Community* (Chapel Hill: University of North Carolina Press, 1981), 261–62.

27. *Oneida Circular*, February 12 and March 4, 1872.

28. Pierrepont Burt Noyes, *My Father's House: An Oneida Boyhood* (New York: Farrar and Rinehart, 1937), 123–24.

29. "Those were the days" quoted from *Oneida Circular*, June 9, 1873; for "I have heard old members say" see P. B. Noyes, *My Father's House*, 16.

30. Community Journal, May 10, 1864; *Daily Journal*, July 12, 1866.

31. Community Journal, January 28, March 3–9, and April 3, 1863; *Daily Journal*, January 29 and December 10, 1866, and January 16, 1867.

32. *Circular*, April 4, 1864.

33. Community Journal, December 17, 1863 (Noyes's self-criticism) and January 9, 1864.

34. *Circular*, November 14, 1864 ("the meanest human parasite we have ever encountered"); December 26, 1864 ("by boring, goading and forcing"); *Circular*, February 6, 1865 ("a nuisance and a stench").

35. *Circular*, November 17, 1870; see also January 16, 1865.

36. *Circular*, December 19, 1864.

37. Jane K. Rich, ed., *A Lasting Spring: Jessie Catherine Kinsley, Daughter of the Oneida Community* (Syracuse, NY: Syracuse University Press, 1983), 18.

38. *Circular*, February 27, 1865.

39. Oneida Community, *First Annual Report of the Oneida Association: Exhibiting Its History, Principles, and Transactions to Jan. 1, 1849* (Oneida Reserve, NY: Oneida Association, 1849), 16; Holton V. Noyes, "A History of the Oneida Community, Limited," photocopied typescript (Oneida Community Mansion House Archives, ca. 1930), 7–8.

40. *Daily Journal*, January 18 and February 27, 1866.

41. *Daily Journal*, March 26, 1866.

42. *Circular*, February 20, 1865.

43. *Daily Journal*, March 27–28, 1866; *Circular*, January 21, 1867.

44. *Daily Journal*, December 16, 1967.

45. *Circular*, May 1, 1865; Robert S. Fogarty, ed., *Desire and Duty at Oneida: Tirzah Miller's Intimate Memoir* (Bloomington: University of Indiana Press, 2000), 57; Constance Noyes Robertson, *Oneida Community: The Breakup, 1876–1881* (Syracuse, NY: Syracuse University Press, 1972), 23.

46. *Daily Journal*, March 25, 1868.

47. Robertson, *Breakup*, 1; Spencer Klaw, *Without Sin: The Life and Death of the Oneida Community* (New York: Allen Lane, Penguin, 1993), 6–7.

48. "The object of the Community" quoted from *Circular*, September 2, 1858; "the sole end and aim" is from *Oneida Circular*, November 4, 1872.

49. Oneida Community, *The Oneida Community: A Familiar Exposition of Its Ideas and Practical Life, in a Conversation with a Visitor* (Wallingford, CT: Office of the Circular, 1865), 19.

50. *Circular*, June 19, 1865.

51. *Oneida Circular*, August 31, 1874.

52. Community Journal, June 20, 1863 (hospitality spirit); Victoria Carver, ed., *Oneida Community Cooking, or A Dinner without Meat, by Harriet A. Skinner, Oneida, N.Y., 1873*, http://tontine255.wordpress.com, 2013.

53. Oneida Community, *Hand-Book of the Oneida Community: Containing a Brief Sketch of Its Present Condition, Internal Economy, and Leading Principles, No. 2* (Oneida, NY: Oneida Community, 1871), 10.

54. Robert Allerton Parker, *A Yankee Saint: John Humphrey Noyes and the Oneida Community* (New York: G. P. Putnam's Sons, 1935), 241.

55. *Circular*, July 9, 1863; Robert S. Fogarty, ed., *Special Love / Special Sex: An Oneida Community Diary* (Syracuse, NY: Syracuse University Press, 1994), 4; *Circular*, June 22, 1868, and January 11, 1869.

56. *American Socialist*, August 29, 1878; William Alfred Hinds, *American Communities and Co-operative Colonies*, 2nd rev., 3rd ed. (Chicago: Charles H. Kerr, 1908), 185.

57. Oneida Community, *Hand-Book* of 1871, 49–52; Oneida Community, *Hand-Book* of 1875, 38–40.

58. *Circular*, June 6, 1870; *Oneida Circular*, September 21, 1874.

59. Oneida Community, *Hand-Book of the Oneida Community; with a Sketch of the Founder, and an Outline of Its Constitution* (Wallingford, CT: Office of the Circular, Wallingford Community, 1867), 19–20.

60. Oneida Community, *Hand-Book* of 1871, 27.

61. Ibid., 29, and *Hand-Book* of 1875, 25–26.

62. *Oneida Circular*, March 8, 1875; Hamilton quoted in John Humphrey Noyes, *History of American Socialisms* (Philadelphia: J. B. Lippincott, 1870), 511.

63. Alfred Barron and George Noyes Miller, eds., *Home-Talks by John Humphrey Noyes, Vol. 1* (Oneida, NY: The Community, 1875), 263.

64. *Circular*, April 4, 1852.

65. "Would be free to use the luxuries" quoted from Lawrence Foster, ed., *Free Love in Utopia: John Humphrey Noyes and the Origin of the Oneida Community, Compiled by George Wallingford Noyes* (Urbana: University of Illinois Press, 2001), 259; Parker, *Yankee Saint*, 232.

66. *Circular*, March 21, 1870; *Oneida Circular*, June 22, 1874; *Hand-Book* of 1875, 7.

67. Anthony Wonderley, ed., *John Humphrey Noyes on Sexual Relations in the Oneida Community: Four Essential Texts* (Hamilton College Library, Clinton, NY: Richard S. Couper Press, 2012), 127–62.

68. *Circular*, November 29, 1869, to February 14, 1870 (Oneida Indians); *Daily Journal*, March 16, 1866, and *Oneida Circular*, July 26, 1874 (Seymour); Alfred Barron, *Foot Notes; or, Walking as a Fine Art* (Wallingford, CT: Wallingford Publishing Co., 1875); William B. Meyer, "The Perfectionists and the Weather: The Oneida Community's Quest for Meteorological Utopia," *Environmental History* 7, no. 4 (2002): 589–610; *Circular* August 9, 1869 (astronomy); *Circular*, May 4, 1868 (microscope research). For cabinet of curiosities see Corinna Ackley Noyes, *The Days of My Youth* (1960; Hamilton College Library, Clinton, NY: Richard W. Couper Press, 2011), 105, and P. B. Noyes, *My Father's House*, 121.

69. *Circular*, July 16, 1866.

70. *Circular*, January 11, 1869.

71. *Circular*, August 2 and September 13, 1869; *Oneida Circular*, March 24, 1873.

72. *Oneida Circular*, October 28, 1872.

73. *Circular*, February 14, 1870; earth closets are described in *Circular*, March 8, 1869, and Janet R. White, "Building Perfection: The Social and Physical Structures of the Oneida Community" (MA thesis, Cornell University, 1994), 65; *Circular*, February 22, 1869.

74. *Daily Journal*, July 9, 1866.

75. *Circular*, March 28, 1870.

76. Oneida Community, *Hand-Book* of 1871, 19; *Oneida Circular*, July 13, 1874. There was more leisure during the later years and less work, according to Francis Wayland-Smith, "What Held the O. C. Together," photocopy of eleven handwritten pages "given to Historical Committee by P. B. Noyes 5 Feb. 49" (Oneida Community

Mansion House Archives, ca. 1910), 9. One diary of the 1870s scarcely mentions work: Fogarty, *Desire and Duty*.

77. *Circular*, June 19, 1865.

78. *Oneida Circular*, July 15, 1872; *Daily Journal*, August 11, 1866; T. A. Murray, "1866: The Year of Croquet," *Oneida Community Journal* 28, no. 1 (March 2014): 12–14.

79. *Daily Journal*, August 17, 1866.

80. *Daily Journal*, September 12, 1866.

81. Klaw, *Without Sin*, 133.

82. *Oneida Circular*, March 24, 1873.

83. Anthony Wonderley, "How Women Worked in the Oneida Community during the 1870s," *Communal Studies* 30, no. 2 (2010): 65–85.

84. Helen Lefkowitz Horowitz, *Rereading Sex: Battles over Sexual Knowledge and Suppression in Nineteenth-Century America* (New York: Alfred A. Knopf, 2002), 268; Maren Lockwood, "The Experimental Utopia in America," *Daedalus* 94, no. 2 (Spring 1965): 409; Carl J. Guarneri, *The Utopian Alternative: Fourierism in Nineteenth-Century America* (Ithaca, NY: Cornell University Press, 1991), 210.

85. *Circular*, February 21, 1870.

8. Breakup

1. Spencer Klaw, *Without Sin: The Life and Death of the Oneida Community* (New York: Allen Lane, Penguin, 1993), 233; Constance Noyes Robertson, *Oneida Community: The Breakup, 1876–1881* (Syracuse, NY: Syracuse University Press, 1972), 17; Pierrepont Burt Noyes, *My Father's House: An Oneida Boyhood* (New York: Farrar and Rinehart, 1937), 9.

2. Robert S. Fogarty, ed., *Special Love / Special Sex: An Oneida Community Diary* (Syracuse, NY: Syracuse University Press, 1994), 27–28; William M. Kephart, *Extraordinary Groups: The Sociology of Unconventional Life-Styles*, 2nd ed. (1978; New York: St. Martin's, 1982), 139, 193; Robertson, *Breakup*, 17.

3. *Circular*, March 27, 1865.

4. Constance Noyes Robertson, ed., *Oneida Community: An Autobiography, 1851–1876* (Syracuse, NY: Syracuse University Press, 1970), 335; Robertson, *Breakup*, 17; the passage about serving as living sacrifices is in Hilda Herrick Noyes and George Wallingford Noyes, "The Oneida Community Experiment in Stirpiculture," *Eugenics, Genetics and the Family* 1 (1923): 375–76.

5. H. H. Noyes and G. W. Noyes, "Oneida Community Experiment," 377.

6. *Circular*, March 22, 1869.

7. H. H. Noyes and G. W. Noyes, "Oneida Community Experiment," 377–78; Robert Allerton Parker, *A Yankee Saint: John Humphrey Noyes and the Oneida Community* (New York: G. P. Putnam's Sons, 1935), 253–61.

8. Klaw, *Without Sin*, 204.

9. "We should give up insisting" is quoted from Klaw, *Without Sin*, 201–2; "We had better set the world" is *Oneida Circular*, December 6, 1875; Fogarty, *Special Love / Special Sex*, 23–24.

10. John Humphrey Noyes, *Essay on Scientific Propagation* (Oneida, NY: Oneida Community, ca. 1872), as cited in Anthony Wonderley, ed., *John Humphrey Noyes on Sexual Relations in the Oneida Community: Four Essential Texts* (Hamilton College Library, Clinton, NY: Richard S. Couper Press, 2012), 140.

11. Noyes reprinted the article about the French cousins interbreeding to pro-
duce beautiful women in *Essay on Scientific Propagation* (Wonderley, *John Humphrey
Noyes*, 157–58). See articles in the *Circular* on March 27, 1869; September 13, 1869
(Jews); October 4, 1869; and February 28, 1870.

12. Wonderley, *John Humphrey Noyes*, 145; *Circular*, September 27 and September 13, 1869; Brian Connolly, *Domestic Intimacies: Incest and the Liberal Subject in
Nineteenth-Century America* (Philadelphia: University of Pennsylvania Press, 2004),
151–56. Noyes's 1870 article, "Scientific Propagation," was an early draft of the
monograph *Essay on Scientific Propagation* (Wonderley, *John Humphrey Noyes*, 128).

13. *Circular*, May 9, 1870.

14. Robert S. Fogarty, ed., *Desire and Duty at Oneida: Tirzah Miller's Intimate
Memoir* (Bloomington: University of Indiana Press, 2000), 72.

15. Maren Lockwood Carden, *Oneida: Utopian Community to Modern Corporation*
(1969; Syracuse, NY: Syracuse University Press, 1998), 63; Louis J. Kern, *An Ordered
Love: Sex Roles and Sexuality in Victorian Utopias: The Shakers, the Mormons, and the
Oneida Community* (Chapel Hill: University of North Carolina Press, 1981), 250; Fogarty, *Desire and Duty*, 20–22.

16. See, for example, Fogarty, *Desire and Duty*, 29–30.

17. Robertson, *Breakup*, 48–49.

18. Ibid., 32; "I attended several seances" is drawn from Jane K. Rich, ed., *A Lasting Spring: Jessie Catherine Kinsley, Daughter of the Oneida Community* (Syracuse, NY:
Syracuse University Press, 1983), 42.

19. Robertson, *Breakup*, 55.

20. Spencer C. Olin Jr., "The Oneida Community and the Instability of Charismatic Authority," *Journal of American History* 67, no. 2 (1980); Fogarty, *Special Love /
Special Sex*, 49; P. B. Noyes, *My Father's House*, 161.

21. Rich, *Lasting Spring*, 42.

22. Ibid.; Ira L. Mandelker, *Religion, Society, and Utopia in Nineteenth-Century
America* (Amherst: University of Massachusetts Press, 1984), 142, 158–59; Monique
Patenaude Roach, "The Loss of Religious Allegiance among the Youth of the Oneida
Community," *Historian* 63, no. 4 (2001): 787–807.

23. Robertson, *Breakup*, 91; see Anita Newcomb McGee, "An Experiment in
Human Stirpiculture," *American Anthropologist* 4 (October 1891): 323; Fogarty, *Special
Love / Special Sex*, 128, 184.

24. Wonderley, *John Humphrey Noyes*, 80–81.

25. Olin, "Oneida Community," 298; Klaw, *Without Sin*, 242. Ackley's comment
is in Stephen R. Leonard Jr., "Recollections," photocopy of unpublished manuscript
(Oneida Community Mansion House Archives, ca. 1951), 1. Fogarty, *Special Love /
Special Sex*, 133, and *Desire and Duty*, 163–64 ("Very much disaffected" and "Oh! Is
he a crazy enthusiast"); Ely Van der Warker, "A Gynecological Study of the Oneida
Community," *American Journal of Obstetrics and Diseases of Women and Children* 17,
no. 8 (1884): 789.

26. Fogarty, *Desire and Duty*, 154.

27. *Circular*, May 22, 1865.

28. Corinna Ackley Noyes, *The Days of My Youth* (1960; Hamilton College Library,
Clinton, NY: Richard W. Couper Press, 2011), 98, 120.

29. C. A. Noyes, *Days of My Youth*, 119.

30. Robertson, *Breakup*, 130, 170.

31. Edmund Wilson, *Upstate: Records and Recollections of Northern New York* (1971; Syracuse, NY: Syracuse University Press, 1990), 25.

32. Robertson, *Breakup*, 126.

33. Rich, *Lasting Spring*, 50.

34. Robertson, *Breakup*, 76–90; see Klaw, *Without Sin*, 243–44.

35. Helen Lefkowitz Horowitz, *Rereading Sex: Battles over Sexual Knowledge and Suppression in Nineteenth-Century America* (New York: Alfred A. Knopf, 2002), 335, 407–9, 413; Hal D. Sears, *The Sex Radicals: Free Love in High Victorian America* (Lawrence: Regents Press of Kansas, 1977), 166, 191–92; Robertson, *Breakup*, 76, 156.

36. Robertson, *Breakup*, 110; Fogarty, *Desire and Duty*, 173; P. B. Noyes, *My Father's House*, 158–59; Rich, *Lasting Spring*, 51.

37. Carden, *Oneida: Utopian Community*, 99–101; Van der Warker, "Gynecological Study," 795; Klaw, *Without Sin*, 241–42; Mary E. Odem, *Delinquent Daughters: Protecting and Policing Adolescent Female Sexuality in the United States, 1885–1920* (Chapel Hill: University of North Carolina Press, 1995), 13–14.

38. Carden, *Oneida: Utopian Community*, 99; Lawrence Foster, *Women, Family, and Utopia: Communal Experiments of the Shakers, the Oneida Community, and the Mormons* (Syracuse, NY: Syracuse University Press, 1991), 115–16; Klaw, *Without Sin*, 237; Olin, "Oneida Community," 298.

39. Robertson, *Breakup*, 272–75.

40. Fogarty, *Special Love / Special Sex*, 215.

41. Robertson, *Breakup*, 16; Lawrence Foster, ed., *Free Love in Utopia: John Humphrey Noyes and the Origin of the Oneida Community, Compiled by George Wallingford Noyes* (Urbana: University of Illinois Press, 2001), xxii–xxiii.

42. Klaw, *Without Sin*, 224.

43. Robertson, *Breakup*, 160; Fogarty, *Desire and Duty*, 178–79; Klaw, *Without Sin*, 253–54.

44. Carden, *Oneida: Utopian Community*, 119; Rich, *Lasting Spring*, 53, 60.

45. Robertson, *Breakup*, 297–98, 301–4; J. W. Towner, transcript of an untitled document dated August 17, 1875, Oneida Community Mansion House Archives.

46. *American Socialist*, June 26, 1879; C. A. Noyes, *Days of My Youth*, 65–66; P. B. Noyes, *My Father's House*, 71–72; *Pinafore* "wears well" quoted from Robertson, *Breakup*, 229.

47. Robertson, *Breakup*, 307–9.

48. Parker, *Yankee Saint*, 289–90; Robertson, *Breakup*, 309.

49. Holton V. Noyes, "A History of the Oneida Community, Limited," photocopied typescript (Oneida Community Mansion House Archives, ca. 1930), 12.

9. A Silverware Company

1. Pierrepont Burt Noyes, *My Father's House: An Oneida Boyhood* (New York: Farrar and Rinehart, 1937), 192–93, 260 ("the terror").

2. Ibid., 208–10.

3. Ibid., 213.

4. Constance Noyes Robertson, *Oneida Community: The Breakup, 1876–1881* (Syracuse, NY: Syracuse University Press, 1972), 224–25; Corinna Ackley Noyes, *The Days of My Youth* (1960; Hamilton College Library, Clinton, NY: Richard W. Couper Press, 2011), 155.

5. Grosvenor N. Allen, "The Background of Community Plate," *Oneida Community Journal* 8, no. 3 (September 1994): 2; "1877—the Iron Spoon, Wallingford," *Quadrangle* 6, no. 9 (September, 1913): 15–17; Walter D. Edmonds, *The First Hundred Years, 1848–1948: 1848—Oneida Community, 1880—Oneida Community, Limited, 1935—Oneida Ltd.* (Oneida, NY: Oneida Ltd., 1948), 24; Holton V. Noyes, "A History of the Oneida Community, Limited," photocopied typescript (Oneida Community Mansion House Archives, ca. 1930), 40, 58; Oneida Community, *Bulletin of the Oneida Community,* August 30, 1878 (Oneida: Office of the American Socialist), 5.

6. Robertson, *Breakup,* 282–83.

7. C. A. Noyes, *Days of My Youth,* 151–52; H. V. Noyes, "History," 44; P. B. Noyes, *My Father's House,* 215; Spencer C. Olin Jr., "Bible Communism and the Origins of Orange County, California," *California History* 58 (Fall 1979): 220–32.

8. P. B. Noyes, *My Father's House,* 215.

9. Pierrepont Burt Noyes, *A Goodly Heritage* (New York: Rinehart, 1958), 44.

10. H. V. Noyes, "History," 58, 63.

11. "1877—the Iron Spoon, Wallingford"; Stephen R. Leonard Jr., "Trap Book," photocopied manuscript in three parts (Oneida Community Mansion House Archives, ca. 1950), 2:52–53.

12. Carl Carmer, *Listen for a Lonesome Drum: A York State Chronicle* (1936; Syracuse, NY: Syracuse University Press, 1995), 197; "having been spiritually shepherded" quoted from P. B. Noyes, *Goodly Heritage,* 43; Stephen R. Leonard Jr., "Recollections," photocopy of unpublished manuscript (Oneida Community Mansion House Archives, ca. 1951), 99–100.

13. H. V. Noyes, "History," 64–65; P. B. Noyes, *Goodly Heritage,* 43 (Pitt who "had soft-pedaled his Spiritualistic leanings"), 44, 99–102.

14. H. V. Noyes, "History," 103, 109–10; P. B. Noyes, *Goodly Heritage,* 113, 122.

15. P. B. Noyes, *Goodly Heritage,* 69.

16. Ibid., 80–81; C. A. Noyes, *Days of My Youth,* 148.

17. P. B. Noyes, *Goodly Heritage,* 83–84.

18. H. V. Noyes, "History," 114–15.

19. P. B. Noyes, *Goodly Heritage,* 116.

20. Ibid., 95; P. Geoffrey Noyes, "The Oneida Community and the Oneida Community, Ltd.: The Offspring Makes a Success of Its Parent," paper delivered at the twenty-first annual Communal Studies Conference, October 6–9, 1994, Oneida, NY.

21. P. B. Noyes, *Goodly Heritage,* 43–44.

22. William Alfred Hinds, *American Communities and Co-operative Colonies,* 2nd rev., 3rd ed. (Chicago: Charles H. Kerr, 1908), 226.

23. Noyes, *Goodly Heritage,* 178–81; H. V. Noyes, "History," 226; Leonard, "Trap Book," 1:136–39.

24. H. G. Wells, *The Future in America: A Search after Realities* (New York: Harper & Brothers, 1906), 164–66.

25. Edith Kinsley, "Kenwood *Mores,* before and after the Break-up," *Oneida Community Journal* 16, no. 3 (September 2002): 6, 9.

26. P. B. Noyes, *Goodly Heritage,* 91.

27. Hinds, *American Communities,* 229–30.

28. Pierrepont Burt Noyes, "Basswood Philosophy: An Appreciation of the O. C. L., Part 5," *Quadrangle* 2, no. 3 (June 1909): 9.

29. P. B. Noyes, *Goodly Heritage*, 211.

30. "The Log Cabin," *Quadrangle* 2, no. 9 (December 1909): 1.

31. Prudence Skinner Wayland-Smith, "The Architecture of Theodore H. Skinner," *Oneida Community Journal* 4, no. 4 (December 1990): 1–6; Thomas A. Guiler, "Rebuilding Oneida: Ideology, Architecture, and Community Planning in the Oneida Community Limited, 1880–1935," *Communal Societies* 32, no. 1 (2012): 1–37.

32. Kinsley, "Kenwood *Mores*," 5–6.

33. Carlotta Cragin Kinsley, "Diary," photocopied typescript, dated June 12, 1923, to September 5, 1925 (Oneida Community Mansion House). The passages quoted are at October 12 and November 4, 1924.

34. Jane K. Rich, ed., *A Lasting Spring: Jessie Catherine Kinsley, Daughter of the Oneida Community* (Syracuse, NY: Syracuse University Press, 1983), 68, 159. Wayland-Smith, in contrast, interprets early twentieth-century Kenwood as an elitist and exclusionary place fearful of having its Oneida Community past publicized and secretly committed to inbreeding: see Ellen Wayland-Smith, *Oneida: From Free Love Utopia to the Well-Set Table—an American Story* (New York: Picador, 2016), 211–13, 220–21, 225–41.

35. P. B. Noyes, "Basswood Philosophy," 5:8; P. B. Noyes, *Goodly Heritage*, 69.

36. Dorothy Rainwater with Donna Folger, *American Silverplate*, rev. and expanded 3rd ed. (1968; Atglen, PA: Schiffer, 2000), 26.

37. P. B. Noyes, *Goodly Heritage*, 171–72; the letter of 1900 is cited from H. V. Noyes, "History," 159.

38. P. B. Noyes, *Goodly Heritage*, 171–72, 177.

39. Allen, "Background of Community Plate," 8; P. B. Noyes, *Goodly Heritage*, 186.

40. P. B. Noyes, *Goodly Heritage*, 177.

41. Ibid., 189.

42. Ibid., 187–92; "you can see for yourself" is at p. 200 of that work.

43. Allen, "Background of Community Plate," 5.

44. B. L. Dunn, *Dramatizing Community Silver into Prestige and Popularity* (Fulton, NY: Merrill, ca. 1914), 14.

45. Allen, "Background of Community Plate," 6.

46. Dunn, *Dramatizing Community Silver*, 12–13; P. B. Noyes, *Goodly Heritage*, 205–6; Allen, "Background of Community Plate," 6.

47. Edmonds, *First Hundred Years*, 39–41; P. B. Noyes, *Goodly Heritage*, 170–72, 183.

48. H. V. Noyes, "History," 289; Leonard, "Trap Book," 1:408; P. B. Noyes, *Goodly Heritage*, 206, 210.

49. Edmonds, *First Hundred Years*, 56.

50. *Sherrill, Smallest City in New York State, 1916–1966: 50th Anniversary Celebration* (Sherrill, NY: Anniversary Committee, 1966), 33; Constance Noyes Robertson, "The Story of Sherrill," ibid., 23–24.

51. P. B. Noyes, *Goodly Heritage*, 223.

10. Welfare Capitalism

1. Holton V. Noyes, "A History of the Oneida Community, Limited," photocopied typescript (Oneida Community Mansion House Archives, ca. 1930), 152–53.

2. Pierrepont Burt Noyes, *A Goodly Heritage* (New York: Rinehart, 1958), 152.

3. Ibid., 110–11, 126, 163; Pierrepont Burt Noyes, "P. B. N.," *Quadrangle* 6, no. 1 (January 1913): 9–11.

4. Edward K. Spann, *Brotherly Tomorrows: Movements for a Cooperative Society in America, 1820–1920* (New York: Columbia University Press, 1989), 164.

5. Edward Bellamy, *Looking Backward: 2000–1887* (Boston: Houghton Mifflin, 1889), 90.

6. Jessie Mayer, "Two Utopian Thinkers," *Oneida Community Journal* 17, no. 3 (September 2003): 4–8.

7. Gerald Zahavi, *Workers, Managers, and Welfare Capitalism: The Shoemakers and Tanners of Endicott Johnson, 1890–1950* (Urbana: University of Illinois Press, 1988), 23–28 ("the company pays" quoted from p. 21).

8. P. B. Noyes, *Goodly Heritage*, 112, 158.

9. H. V. Noyes, "History," 155.

10. Spencer Klaw regarded Hinds's book as "one of the best accounts ever written of the nineteenth-century's experiments, both religious and secular, in communal living": see Klaw, *Without Sin: The Life and Death of the Oneida Community* (New York: Allen Lane, Penguin, 1993), 237.

11. John H. Noyes in Constance Noyes Robertson, *Oneida Community: The Breakup, 1876–1881* (Syracuse, NY: Syracuse University Press, 1972), 105–6; H. V. Noyes, "History," 156.

12. *Daily Journal*, March 31, 1866.

13. H. V. Noyes, "History," 157.

14. Walter D. Edmonds, *The First Hundred Years, 1848–1948: 1848—Oneida Community, 1880—Oneida Community, Limited, 1935—Oneida Ltd.* (Oneida, NY: Oneida Ltd., 1948), 55; P. B. Noyes, *Goodly Heritage*, 224.

15. P. B. Noyes, *Goodly Heritage*, 228.

16. "When the Niagara Falls factory" is drawn from Edmonds, *First Hundred Years*, 55; H. V. Noyes, "History," 330.

17. P. B. Noyes, *Goodly Heritage*, 226; Edmonds, *First Hundred Years*, 53–54; H. V. Noyes, "History," 345.

18. Edmonds, *First Hundred Years*, 55, 73; Esther Lowenthal, "The Labor Policy of the Oneida Community Ltd.," *Journal of Political Economy* 35, no. 1 (1927): 122–23; P. B. Noyes, *Goodly Heritage*, 263.

19. P. B. Noyes, *Goodly Heritage*, 168–69; H. V. Noyes, "History," 338; Edmonds, *First Hundred Years*, 49; *Sherrill, Smallest City in New York State, 1916–1966: 50th Anniversary Celebration* (Sherrill, NY: Anniversary Committee, 1966), 42–43.

20. H. V. Noyes, "History," 333; Edmonds, *First Hundred Years*, 53. Pierrepont Noyes was one of the officials who went to Albany. When his daughter, Constance Robertson, authored a history of Sherrill on the occasion of its fiftieth anniversary, she briefly explained the city's birth in this fashion: The company delegation "waited on Governor Whitman to make the request: Sherrill wanted to be a city with a commission form of government. It had been understood that a population of ten thousand persons was necessary before a city charter could be obtained, but as no law to that effect could be found, the charter was granted." See Constance Noyes Robertson, "The Story of Sherrill," in *Sherrill, Smallest City in New York State, 1916–1966: 50th Anniversary Celebration* (Sherrill, NY: Anniversary Committee, 1966), 24.

21. H. V. Noyes, "History," 303, 221.

22. Stanley Buder, *Pullman: An Experiment in Industrial Order and Community Planning, 1880–1930* (New York: Oxford University Press, 1967), 36.

23. *Circular*, July 28, 1859; May 26 and October 27, 1873.

24. Charles Reade, *Put Yourself in His Place: A Novel* (1870; New York: Harper & Brothers, 1904), 5.

25. Buder, *Pullman*; Doris Kearns Goodwin, *The Bully Pulpit: Theodore Roosevelt, William Howard Taft, and the Golden Age of Journalism* (New York: Simon & Schuster, 2013), 185–86.

26. Edmonds, *First Hundred Years*, 8.

27. Ibid.

28. Lowenthal, "Labor Policy," 124–25.

29. Zahavi, *Workers, Managers, and Welfare Capitalism*, 2, 37–38.

30. Spann, *Brotherly Tomorrows*, 241; Stuart D. Brandes, *American Welfare Capitalism, 1880–1940* (Chicago: University of Chicago Press, 1976).

31. Keith L. Nelson, *Victors Divided: America and the Allies in Germany, 1918–1923* (Berkeley: University of California Press, 1975), 136–69; Pierrepont Burt Noyes, *While Europe Waits for Peace: Describing the Progress of Economic and Political Demoralization in Europe during the Year of American Hesitation* (New York: Macmillan, 1921).

32. H. V. Noyes, "History," 369–72.

33. Edmonds, *First Hundred Years*, 57–58.

34. Lowenthal, "Labor Policy," 117.

35. P. B. Noyes, *Goodly Heritage*, 262–63; Edmonds, *First Hundred Years*, 58; Lowenthal, "Labor Policy," 117; H. V. Noyes, "History," 337, 383.

36. "List of Articles Deposited in the Corner Stone Box of the New Administration Building," *Quadrangle* 1 (new series), no. 5 (October 1926): 28.

37. Edmonds, *First Hundred Years*, 59, 61, and 65.

38. Pierrepont Burt Noyes, "Summary of the President's Report to Stockholders of Oneida Community, Limited at the Annual Meeting, February 24, 1930," three-page printed document (Oneida Community Mansion House Archives).

39. Robertson, "Story of Sherrill," 26; Edmonds, *First Hundred Years*, 63.

40. Pierrepont Burt Noyes, Letter to the employees of the Oneida Community Ltd., April 8, 1933 (Oneida Community Mansion House Archives).

41. Carl Carmer, *Listen for a Lonesome Drum: A York State Chronicle* (1936; Syracuse, NY: Syracuse University Press, 1995), 198–99.

42. Pete Noyes quoted in Maren Lockwood Carden, *Oneida: Utopian Community to Modern Corporation* (1969; Syracuse, NY: Syracuse University Press, 1998), 173; Edmonds, *First Hundred Years*, 65–66.

43. Jane K. Rich, ed., *A Lasting Spring: Jessie Catherine Kinsley, Daughter of the Oneida Community* (Syracuse, NY: Syracuse University Press, 1983), 218.

44. Carmer, *Listen for a Lonesome Drum*, 177–79. Carmer was also struck by the fact that Kenwood social events involved participants of several generations: "Golf foursomes and tea parties are made up, without condescension on anybody's part, of people ranging in age from twelve to seventy" (p. 193).

45. Ibid., 179, 201–2.

46. Edmonds, *First Hundred Years*, 67–69. This passage is based on research conducted for *Wartime at Oneida, Ltd.*, a Mansion House exhibit I curated in November 2012. Most of the information derives from study of the *Community Commando*, Oneida Ltd.'s newsletter during World War II.

47. Personal conversations with Jim Colway (January 2012) and Paul Gebhardt (June–July 2014).

48. Edmonds, *First Hundred Years*, 69.

49. Ibid., 6–7, 73.

50. George Wallingford Noyes, ed., *The Religious Experience of John Humphrey Noyes, Founder of the Oneida Community* (New York: Macmillan, 1923); G. W. Noyes, ed., *John Humphrey Noyes: The Putney Community* (Oneida, NY: the author, 1931); Lawrence Foster, ed., *Free Love in Utopia: John Humphrey Noyes and the Origin of the Oneida Community, Compiled by George Wallingford Noyes* (Urbana: University of Illinois Press, 2001).

51. Foster, *Free Love*, x–xi; Klaw, *Without Sin*, 299.

52. William M. Kephart, *Extraordinary Groups: The Sociology of Unconventional Life-Styles*, 2nd ed. (1978; New York: St. Martin's, 1982), 127.

53. Carmer, *Listen for a Lonesome Drum*, 180. Noyes, for example, acknowledged that "the widest selections in cohabitation were encouraged and, in fact, insisted upon" in the Oneida Community; see Pierrepont Burt Noyes, *My Father's House: An Oneida Boyhood* (New York: Farrar and Rinehart, 1937), 8. Wayland-Smith's reconstruction of these events features a cynical Pierrepont Noyes, who, after censoring sex from his father's legacy, "proceeded to package up the rest into a socially acceptable mixture of masculine chivalry, Yankee business sense, and Christian charity (with some tantalizing ads of pretty flapper girls thrown in for good measure)" as a story to sell silverware. Wayland-Smith hypothesizes that the burning took place when top company officials learned that George Noyes was not only writing about complex marriage but was also in touch with outside researchers inquiring about sex in the Oneida Community. The records were destroyed to sanitize the past in the fear that Main Street America would buy less Oneida flatware if the sexual behavior of Oneida Community were better known. See Ellen Wayland-Smith, *Oneida: From Free Love Utopia to the Well-Set Table—an American Story* (New York: Picador, 2016), 225–41, 254–60 ("proceeded to package" on 225).

54. Robertson, "Story of Sherrill," 29.

55. Edmonds, *First Hundred Years*; Pierrepont Burt Noyes, letter included in the book *The Last Hundred Years*, distributed to employees, 1948 (Oneida Community Mansion House Archives).

56. Pierrepont Burt Noyes, text of remarks on July 31, 1948, Oneida Ltd. News Bureau Release (Oneida Community Mansion House Archives).

57. P. B. Noyes, *Goodly Heritage*, 274.

58. Lowenthal, "Labor Policy," 126.

59. *Sherrill, Smallest City*, 43; DuWayne E. Wilber, "A Brief History of the Vernon-Verona-Sherrill Central School System," photocopied typescript (Oneida Community Mansion House Archives, 1976).

60. Carden, *Oneida: Utopian Community*, 188.

61. Robertson, "Story of Sherrill," 31.

62. Oneida Ltd., "Oneida Ltd. Silversmiths Annual Report, Fiscal Year Ended January 31, 1958" (Oneida Community Mansion House Archives), 1–2.

63. Oneida Ltd., "Oneida Marks 100 Years of Leadership in the Tableware Field," *Oneida Silversmith* 4, no. 3 (March–April 1977): 3 (Oneida Community Mansion House Archives).

64. Carden, *Oneida: Utopian Community*, 184.

65. Ibid., 185–86.

66. Oneida Ltd., "Oneida Ltd. Silversmiths Annual Report, Fiscal Year Ended January 31, 1968" (Oneida Community Mansion House Archives), 4.

67. Pierrepont Trowbridge Noyes, "The Oneida Ltd. Creed," photocopied text dated January 1, 1967 (Oneida Community Mansion House Archives).

68. Carden, *Oneida: Utopian Community*, 180.

69. John P. L. Hatcher, Oneida (Community) Limited: *A Goodly Heritage Gone Wrong* (Bloomington, IN: iUniverse, 2016); Oneida Ltd., "Proxy Statement, 1977," 3; "Proxy Statement, 1982," 5; and "Proxy Statement, 1985," 5 (Oneida Community Mansion House Archives).

70. Oneida Ltd., "Proxy Statement, 1985," 6.

71. John Z. Noyes, "Newspeak," *Kenwood Association Newsletter*, no. 10 (April 1984): 2, which was published by the editor, J. Z. Noyes, out of his home in Greenbelt, MD (Oneida Community Mansion House Archives).

72. *Oneida Daily Dispatch*, May 27, 2004.

Conclusion

1. Holton V. Noyes, "A History of the Oneida Community, Limited," photocopied typescript (Oneida Community Mansion House Archives, ca. 1930), 186.

2. Maren Lockwood Carden, *Oneida: Utopian Community to Modern Corporation* (1969; Syracuse, NY: Syracuse University Press, 1998), 210.

3. Jane K. Rich, ed., *A Lasting Spring: Jessie Catherine Kinsley, Daughter of the Oneida Community* (Syracuse, NY: Syracuse University Press, 1983), 68; Constance Noyes Robertson, ed., *Oneida Community: An Autobiography, 1851–1876* (Syracuse, NY: Syracuse University Press, 1970), xii–xiii.

4. Spencer Klaw, *Without Sin: The Life and Death of the Oneida Community* (New York: Allen Lane, Penguin, 1993), 8 ("without"), 292 ("a thrilling voyage"), 294 (if one could put up).

5. Carden, *Oneida: Utopian Community*, xiv–xv, xxiv, 74, 106–7.

6. See, for example, Rosabeth Moss Kanter, *Commitment and Community: Communes and Utopias in Sociological Perspective* (Cambridge, MA: Harvard University Press, 1972), 226; Klaw, *Without Sin*, 291–92.

7. Robert S. Fogarty, "Religious Inventions in Nineteenth Century America," *OAH Magazine of History* 22, no. 1 (2008): 19–23.

8. A knowledgeable Christian scholar who has studied Noyes's religious doctrines concluded, "His analysis of Scripture is unsophisticated; his insistence on the occurrence of the Parousia [second coming of Christ] and the translation of the Primitive Church to Heaven at that time remains a stumbling block despite his efforts to prove the point. Theologically, many of his concepts are anthropomorphic and even offensive. If then, the value of Noyes's thinking stands or falls on the validity of his theology and Scriptural exegesis, one could not expect it to make any impact": see Richard DeMaria, *Communal Love at Oneida: A Perfectionist Vision of Authority, Property, and Sexual Order* (New York: Edwin Mellen, 1978), 221.

9. An obvious opportunity for presenting some kind of synthesis occurred in Noyes's 1870 book, which featured the Oneida Community as the most successful utopia among all the Owenite and Fourieristic experiments. Instead of offering an

interpretive summary, however, the chapter on Oneida comprises scarcely more than a list of chapter headings from *The Berean* (1847) to show "religious theory" and a list of section headings from *Bible Argument* (Oneida Community, 1849) to illustrate "social theory." See Noyes's *History of American Socialisms* (Philadelphia: J. B. Lippincott, 1870), 614–45.

10. Joanne E. Passet, *Sex Radicals and the Quest for Women's Equality* (Urbana: University of Illinois Press, 2003), 73; Dolores Hayden, *The Grand Domestic Revolution: A History of Feminist Designs for American Homes, Neighborhoods, and Cities* (Cambridge, MA: MIT Press, 1981).

11. Judith Wellman, *The Road to Seneca Falls: Elizabeth Cady Stanton and the First Woman's Rights Convention* (Urbana: University of Illinois Press, 2004), 198–200; Helen Lefkowitz Horowitz, *Rereading Sex: Battles over Sexual Knowledge and Suppression in Nineteenth-Century America* (New York: Alfred A. Knopf, 2002), 253; *Circular*, January 5, 1874.

12. Gage quoted in *Oneida Circular*, March 2, 1876; Passet, *Sex Radicals and the Quest*, 1–2, 14; David J. Pivar, *Purity Crusade: Sexual Morality and Social Control, 1868–1900* (Westport, CT: Greenwood, 1973), 43; Hal D. Sears, *The Sex Radicals: Free Love in High Victorian America* (Lawrence: Regents Press of Kansas, 1977), 8, 24. Acknowledging female sexuality was difficult because it challenged an entrenched image of woman as pure and passive, according to Mary E. Odem, *Delinquent Daughters: Protecting and Policing Adolescent Female Sexuality in the United States, 1885–1920* (Chapel Hill: University of North Carolina Press, 1995), 9, 43. Susan B. Anthony visited the Oneida Community but apparently expressed no opinion about it (*Daily Journal*, July 3, 1866).

13. *Oneida Circular*, December 27, 1875. For a sense of Woodhull as controversial see Mary Gabriel, *Notorious Victoria: The Life of Victoria Woodhull, Uncensored* (Chapel Hill, NC: Algonquin Books of Chapel Hill, 1998).

14. "Vile bodies" quoted from *Circular*, November 16, 1852.

15. Horowitz, *Rereading Sex*, 253, 256; Pivar, *Purity Crusade*, 43; Nancy F. Cott, *Public Vows: A History of Marriage and the Nation* (Cambridge, MA: Harvard University Press, 2000), 72.

16. Arthur Bestor, *Backwoods Utopias: The Sectarian Origins and the Owenite Phase of Communitarian Socialism in America, 1663–1829*, 2nd enl. ed. (1950; Philadelphia: University of Pennsylvania Press, 1970), 234, 265; Carl J. Guarneri, *The Utopian Alternative: Fourierism in Nineteenth-Century America* (Ithaca, NY: Cornell University Press, 1991), 174, 453 at note 1.

17. Horowitz, *Rereading Sex*, 405–15; Sears, *Sex Radicals*, 159–68, 191–92, 209–15; Taylor Stoehr, *Free Love in America: A Documentary History* (New York: AMS, 1979), 57, 60–61; Aldous Huxley, *Tomorrow and Tomorrow and Tomorrow, and Other Essays* (New York: Harper & Brothers, 1956), 148–50; Passet, *Sex Radicals and the Quest*, 148–50.

18. Peter von Ziegesar, "Reinventing Sex," *Lapham's Quarterly* 9, no. 4 (2016): 205; Kanter, *Commitment and Community*, 18; *Kaliflower*, about 20 digitized pages of the San Francisco communal publication e-mailed by Walter Parmenteau to Kelly Rose, August 5, 2013 (Oneida Community Mansion House Archives, ca. 1974); Jessica Bennett, "Polyamory: The Next Sexual Revolution?," *Newsweek*, July 28, 2009, as reprinted at http://www.newsweek.com/polyamory-next-sexual-revolution-82053.

19. Louis J. Kern, "Breaching the 'Wall of Partition between the Male and the Female': John Humphrey Noyes and Free Love," *Syracuse University Library Associates Courier* 28, no. 2 (1993): 115. See also Lawrence Foster, *Religion and Sexuality: The Shakers, the Mormons, and the Oneida Community* (1981; Urbana: University of Illinois Press, 1984), 121.

20. The importance and impact of utopias are notoriously difficult to measure. On the recurrent problem of significance see, for example, Yaacov Oved, "Communal Movements in the Twentieth Century," in *Utopia: The Search for the Ideal Society*, ed. Roland Schaer, Gregory Clacys, and Lyman Tower Sargent (New York: New York Public Library and Oxford University Press, 2000), 268–77.

21. Chris Jennings, *Paradise Now: The Story of American Utopianism* (New York: Random House, 2016), 7, 13, 19.

22. Kanter, *Commitment and Community*, 245–46.

23. Anthony Wonderley, ed., *John Humphrey Noyes on Sexual Relations in the Oneida Community: Four Essential Texts* (Hamilton College Library, Clinton, NY: Richard S. Couper Press, 2012), 89.

24. *Circular*, February 17, 1859.

25. Lawrence Foster, ed., *Free Love in Utopia: John Humphrey Noyes and the Origin of the Oneida Community, Compiled by George Wallingford Noyes* (Urbana: University of Illinois Press, 2001), 133 ("Improvement is the motive power here"); Francis Wayland-Smith, "What Held the O. C. Together," photocopy of eleven handwritten pages "given to Historical Committee by P. B. Noyes 5 Feb. 49" (Oneida Community Mansion House Archives, ca. 1910), 2 ("a brave and noble experiment"); Corinna Ackley Noyes, *The Days of My Youth* (1960; Hamilton College Library, Clinton, NY: Richard W. Couper Press, 2011), 29 ("a brave and noble experiment").

26. Huxley, *Tomorrow*, 29.

27. Klaw, *Without Sin*, 7.

28. William Hepworth Dixon, *New America*, 8th ed. (London: Hurst and Blackett, 1867), 2:229 and 246 ("made no rules").

29. Klaw, *Without Sin*, 292. Edmund Wilson's classic study of socialist engagement ranks the Oneida Community as the most successful of all communitarian ventures of the 1840s–1850s. See *To the Finland Station: A Study in the Writing and Acting of History* (1940; New York: Farrar, Straus and Giroux, 1972), 126.

30. Whitney R. Cross, *The Burned-Over District: The Social and Intellectual History of Enthusiastic Religion in Western New York, 1800–1850* (Ithaca, NY: Cornell University Press, 1950), 333, 335.

31. Pierrepont Burt Noyes, "P. B. N.," *Quadrangle* 6, no. 1 (January 1913): 10–11.

32. *American Socialist*, September 4, 1879.

33. Carden, *Oneida: Utopian Community*, xiv (what lies at the center); Rich, *Lasting Spring*, 67 ("a great example of unselfishness"); P. B. Noyes, "P. B. N.," 10 ("we are learning").

Bibliography

Certain references given in the text to serial publications of the Oneida Community and the Mansion House are stand-alone citations not repeated in this bibliography. The Oneida Community's periodical, a newspaper-like magazine usually published weekly, went through several changes of name: *Spiritual Magazine* (begun in Putney and published between 1848 and 1850 in Oneida), *Free Church Circular* (1850–1851), *Circular* (1851–1870), *Oneida Circular* (1871–1876), and *American Socialist* (1876–1879). A newsletter printed for internal consumption (*Daily Journal*, 1866–1868) was preceded by the "Community Journal" (1863–1864), which we have in typescript at the Mansion House. The *Quadrangle* was a journal published irregularly out of the Mansion House by Oneida Community descendants between 1908 and 1938. The *Oneida Community Journal* (1987–present) is the biannual periodical of the not-for-profit museum, the Oneida Community Mansion House.

The most popular book about the Oneida Community is that by journalist Spencer Klaw (*Without Sin*, 1993). The most substantial publications about the Community by Community descendants begin with those by George Wallingford Noyes (*The Religious Experience of John Humphrey Noyes*, 1923, and *John Humphrey Noyes: The Putney Community*, 1931). His account of the Oneida Community's first years was published by Lawrence Foster as *Free Love in Utopia* (2001). Pierrepont B. Noyes authored two memoirs, one concerning Community childhood (*My Father's House*, 1937), the other about company experiences (*A Goodly Heritage*, 1958). Corinna Ackley Noyes (wife of P. B. Noyes) composed another reminiscence of Oneida as *The Days of My Youth*, originally published in 1960. Constance Noyes Robertson (daughter of P. B. and C. A. Noyes) assembled an anthology of Community writings (*Oneida Community: An Autobiography*, 1970) and authored a study of the commune's final days (*Oneida Community: The Breakup*, 1972). Jessie Catherine Kinsley recalled youthful days in the Oneida Community as well as adult times in and around the Mansion House in the early twentieth century (*A Lasting Spring*, edited by Jane Rich, 1983). Ellen Wayland-Smith recently contributed *Oneida: From Free Love Utopia to the Well-Set Table—an American Story* (2016).

One scholarly work addresses the Oneida Community and its development into a company: Maren Lockwood Carden's *Oneida: Utopian Community to Modern Corporation*, originally published in 1969. Three books by academic authors examine the Oneida Community in conjunction with the Mormons and the Shakers: *Religion and Sexuality* (originally 1981) and *Women, Family, and Utopia* (1991), both by Lawrence Foster; and *An Ordered Love* (1981), by Louis J. Kern.

Achorn, Erik. "Mary Cragin: Perfectionist Saint." *New England Quarterly* 28, no. 4 (December 1955): 490–518.

Ackley, Joseph. "Joseph Ackley: An Autobiography." *Quadrangle* 1, no. 8 (November 1908): 10–11.

——. Letter to Corinna Ackley, November 26, 1892. Oneida Community Mansion House Archives, photocopy.

Allen, Gay Wilson. *Waldo Emerson*. New York: Penguin, 1982. First published in 1981.

Allen, Grosvenor N. "The Background of Community Plate." *Oneida Community Journal* 8, no. 3 (September 1994): 2–9.

Andrews, Edward Deming. *The People Called Shakers: A Search for the Perfect Society*. 1953. Reprint, New York: Dover, 1963.

Barkun, Michael. *Crucible of the Millennium: The Burned-Over District of New York in the 1840s*. Syracuse, NY: Syracuse University Press, 1986.

——. "'The Wind Sweeping over the Country': John Humphrey Noyes and the Rise of Millerism." In *The Disappointed: Millerism and Millenarianism in the Nineteenth Century*, edited by Ronald L. Numbers and Jonathan M. Butler, 153–72. Bloomington: Indiana University Press, 1987.

Barron, Alfred. *Foot Notes; or, Walking as a Fine Art*. Wallingford, CT: Wallingford Publishing Co., 1875.

Barron, Alfred, and George Noyes Miller, eds. *Home-Talks by John Humphrey Noyes, Vol. 1*. Oneida, NY: The Community, 1875.

Bates, Albert. "Architectural Design and 'Complex Marriage' at Oneida." *Communities* 95 (Summer 1997): 43–46, 95.

Beecher, Jonathan. *Charles Fourier: The Visionary and His World*. Berkeley: University of California Press, 1986.

Bellamy, Edward. *Looking Backward: 2000–1887*. Boston: Houghton Mifflin, 1889.

Bennett, Jessica. "Polyamory: The Next Sexual Revolution?" *Newsweek*, July 28, 2009. As reprinted at http://www.newsweek.com/polyamory-next-sexual-revolution-82053.

Bestor, Arthur. *Backwoods Utopias: The Sectarian Origins and the Owenite Phase of Communitarian Socialism in America, 1663–1829*. 2nd enl. ed. Philadelphia: University of Pennsylvania Press, 1970. First published in 1950.

Boswell, Charles. "Uncle Johnny's Woman Farm." *Men: True Adventures*, April 1959, 34–37, 50.

Brandes, Stuart D. *American Welfare Capitalism, 1880–1940*. Chicago: University of Chicago Press, 1976.

Brisbane, Albert. *Association; or, A Concise Exposition of the Practical Part of Fourier's Social Science*. New York: Greeley and McElrath, 1843.

Brown, Leanne E. "By Their Fruits Shall Ye Know Them: The History of Canning by the Oneida Community and Oneida Community, Ltd." MA thesis, State University of New York College at Oneonta and Cooperstown Graduate Program, 1998.

Buder, Stanley. *Pullman: An Experiment in Industrial Order and Community Planning, 1880–1930.* New York: Oxford University Press, 1967.

Carden, Maren Lockwood. *Oneida: Utopian Community to Modern Corporation.* Syracuse, NY: Syracuse University Press, 1998. First published in 1969.

Carmer, Carl. *Listen for a Lonesome Drum: A York State Chronicle.* Syracuse, NY: Syracuse University Press, 1995. First published in 1936.

Carver, Victoria, ed. *Oneida Community Cooking, or A Dinner without Meat, by Harriet A. Skinner, Oneida, N.Y., 1873.* 2013. http://tontine255.wordpress.com.

Connolly, Brian. *Domestic Intimacies: Incest and the Liberal Subject in Nineteenth-Century America.* Philadelphia: University of Pennsylvania Press, 2004.

Cott, Nancy F. *Public Vows: A History of Marriage and the Nation.* Cambridge, MA: Harvard University Press, 2000.

Cragin, George E. [attributed]. "First Canning in the Community." *Quadrangle* 6, no. 9 (September 1913): 3–6.

Cragin, George E. "The Hubbard Farm." *Quadrangle* 7, nos. 2–3 (February–March 1914): 9–11.

——. "Trap Making on Oneida Creek." *Quadrangle* 6, Part 1 (no. 4 [April 1913]: 1–2), Part 2 (no. 3 [May 1913]: 3–4), Part 3 (nos. 7–8 [June–July 1913]: 8–10), Part 4 (no. 8 [August 1913]: 1–2).

——. "Water Supply at Kenwood, 1848–1911." *Quadrangle* 6, no. 5 (May 1913): 9–12.

Cross, Whitney R. *The Burned-Over District: The Social and Intellectual History of Enthusiastic Religion in Western New York, 1800–1850.* Ithaca, NY: Cornell University Press, 1950.

Davies, John D. *Phrenology: Fad and Science—a 19th-Century Crusade.* New Haven, CT: Yale University Press, 1955.

DeMaria, Richard. *Communal Love at Oneida: A Perfectionist Vision of Authority, Property, and Sexual Order.* New York: Edwin Mellen, 1978.

Desroche, Henri. *The American Shakers: From Neo-Christianity to Presocialism.* Amherst: University of Massachusetts Press, 1971. First published in 1955.

Dixon, William Hepworth. *New America.* 8th ed. Vol. 2. London: Hurst and Blackett, 1867.

——. *Spiritual Wives.* 2nd ed. Philadelphia: J. B. Lippincott, 1868.

——. *Spiritual Wives.* 4th ed. Vol. 2. London: Hurst and Blackett, 1868.

Downing, A. J. *The Architecture of Country Houses.* 1850. Reprint, New York: Dover, 1969.

——. *A Treatise on the Theory and Practice of Landscape Gardening, Adapted to North America with a View to the Improvement of Country Residences.* 6th ed. New York: A. O. Moore, 1859. First published in 1841.

Dunn, B. L. *"Dramatizing" Community Silver into Prestige and Popularity.* Fulton, NY: Merrill, ca. 1914.

Eastman, Hubbard. *Noyesism Unveiled: A History of the Sect Self-Styled Perfectionists.* Brattleboro, VT: the author, 1849.

Edmonds, Walter D. *The First Hundred Years, 1848–1948: 1848—Oneida Community, 1880—Oneida Community, Limited, 1935—Oneida Ltd.* Oneida, NY: Oneida Ltd., 1948.

"1877—the Iron Spoon, Wallingford." *Quadrangle* 6, no. 9 (September 1913): 15–17.

Estlake, Allan [Abel Easton]. *The Oneida Community: A Record of an Attempt to Carry Out the Principles of Christian Unselfishness and Scientific Improvement.* London: George Redway, 1900.

Finney, Charles G. *Memoirs of Rev. Charles G. Finney, Written by Himself.* New York: Fleming H. Revell, 1908. First published in 1876.

"Fire at Brook Farm." *Harbinger* 2, no. 14 (1846): 220–22.

Fogarty, Robert S., ed. *Desire and Duty at Oneida: Tirzah Miller's Intimate Memoir.* Bloomington: University of Indiana Press, 2000.

——. "Oneida: A Utopian Search for Religious Security." *Labor History* 14, no. 2 (Spring 1973): 202–27.

——. "Religious Inventions in Nineteenth Century America." *OAH Magazine of History* 22, no. 1 (January 2008): 19–23.

——, ed. *Special Love / Special Sex: An Oneida Community Diary.* Syracuse, NY: Syracuse University Press, 1994.

Foster, Lawrence, ed. *Free Love in Utopia: John Humphrey Noyes and the Origin of the Oneida Community, Compiled by George Wallingford Noyes.* Urbana: University of Illinois Press, 2001.

——. *Religion and Sexuality: The Shakers, the Mormons, and the Oneida Community.* Urbana: University of Illinois Press, 1984. First published in 1981.

——. *Women, Family, and Utopia: Communal Experiments of the Shakers, the Oneida Community, and the Mormons.* Syracuse, NY: Syracuse University Press, 1991.

Funk and Wagnalls. *The Practical Standard Dictionary of the English Language.* New York: Funk and Wagnalls, 1927.

Gabriel, Mary. *Notorious Victoria: The Life of Victoria Woodhull, Uncensored.* Chapel Hill, NC: Algonquin Books of Chapel Hill, 1998.

Gerstell, Richard. *The Steel Trap in North America.* Harrisburg, PA: Stackpole Books, 1985.

Godwin, Joscelyn. *Upstate Cauldron: Eccentric Spiritual Movements in Early New York State.* Albany: SUNY Press, Excelsior Editions, 2015.

Goodwin, Doris Kearns. *The Bully Pulpit: Theodore Roosevelt, William Howard Taft, and the Golden Age of Journalism.* New York: Simon & Schuster, 2013.

Guarneri, Carl J. "Reconstructing the Antebellum Communitarian Movement: Oneida and Fourierism." *Journal of the Early Republic* 16, no. 3 (Autumn 1996): 463–88.

——. *The Utopian Alternative: Fourierism in Nineteenth-Century America.* Ithaca, NY: Cornell University Press, 1991.

Guiler, Thomas A. "Rebuilding Oneida: Ideology, Architecture, and Community Planning in the Oneida Community Limited, 1880–1935." *Communal Societies* 32, no. 1 (2012): 1–37.

H.A.N. [Harriet Noyes]. "History of the Printing Business of O. C." Ca. 1875. Photocopied typescript in the Oneida Community Mansion House Archives.

Hatcher, John P. L. *Oneida (Community) Ltd.: A Goodly Heritage Gone Wrong.* Bloomington, IN: iUniverse, 2016.

Hayden, Dolores. *The Grand Domestic Revolution: A History of Feminist Designs for American Homes, Neighborhoods, and Cities.* Cambridge, MA: MIT Press, 1981.

——. *Seven American Utopias: The Architecture of Communitarian Socialism, 1790–1975.* Cambridge, MA: MIT Press, 1976.

Herrick, James B. "In lumina tuo lumen videmus." *Quadrangle* 1, no. 2 (May 1908): 11.

Herrick, Tirzah C. "To the Editor of the Sunday World." *Quadrangle* 5, no. 11 (September–November 1912): 13–14.

H.H.S. [Harriet Skinner]. "A Community Transplanted, from Putney to Oneida, III." *American Socialist* 4, nos. 33–41 (1879; nine sequent issues, August 14–October 9).

Hinds, William Alfred. *American Communities and Co-operative Colonies.* 2nd rev. (3rd ed.). Chicago: Charles H. Kerr, 1908. First published in 1878.

Holloway, Mark. *Heavens on Earth: Utopian Communities in America, 1680–1880.* 2nd ed. 1951. Reprint, New York: Dover 1966.

Horowitz, Helen Lefkowitz. *Rereading Sex: Battles over Sexual Knowledge and Suppression in Nineteenth-Century America.* New York: Alfred A. Knopf, 2002.

Huxley, Aldous. *Tomorrow and Tomorrow and Tomorrow, and Other Essays.* New York: Harper & Brothers, 1956.

J. [James Herrick]. "Harriet Noyes Skinner." *Quadrangle* 1, no. 8 (December 1908): 10–12.

Jennings, Chris. *Paradise Now: The Story of American Utopianism.* New York: Random House, 2016.

Johnson, Paul E. *A Shopkeeper's Millennium: Society and Revivals in Rochester, New York, 1815–1837.* 2nd ed. New York: Hill & Wang, 2004. First published in 1978.

Judd, Wayne R. "William Miller: Disappointed Prophet." In *The Disappointed: Millerism and Millenarianism in the Nineteenth Century,* edited by Ronald L. Numbers and Jonathan M. Butler, 17–35. Bloomington: Indiana University Press, 1987.

Kaliflower. Digitized pages of the San Francisco communal publication, ca. 1974. E-mailed by Walter Parmenteau to Kelly Rose, August 5, 2013 (comprises about 20 pages with sections entitled "Oneida and Us," "Daily Meetings," "A Matter of Fate," "Criticism," "Perfecting Each Other," "Spudding Perfectionism," "Third Persons").

Kanter, Rosabeth Moss. *Commitment and Community: Communes and Utopias in Sociological Perspective.* Cambridge, MA: Harvard University Press, 1972.

Kephart, William M. *Extraordinary Groups: The Sociology of Unconventional Life-Styles.* 2nd ed. New York: St. Martin's, 1982. First published in 1978.

Kern, Louis J. "Breaching the 'Wall of Partition between the Male and the Female': John Humphrey Noyes and Free Love." *Syracuse University Library Associates Courier* 28, no. 2 (1993): 87–115.

——. *An Ordered Love: Sex Roles and Sexuality in Victorian Utopias; The Shakers, the Mormons, and the Oneida Community.* Chapel Hill: University of North Carolina Press, 1981.

Kinsley, Carlotta Cragin. "Diary." Photocopy of a 70-page typescript dated June 12, 1923, to September 5, 1925. Oneida Community Mansion House Archives.

Kinsley, Edith. "Kenwood *Mores,* before and after the Break-up." *Oneida Community Journal* 16, no. 3 (September 2002): 4–9.

Klaw, Spencer. *Without Sin: The Life and Death of the Oneida Community*. New York: Allen Lane, Penguin, 1993.

Klee-Hartzell, Marlyn. "'Mingling the Sexes': The Gendered Organization of Work in the Oneida Community." *Syracuse University Library Associates Courier* 28, no. 2 (1993): 61–85.

La Moy, William T. "Two Documents Detailing the Oneida Community's Practice of Complex Marriage." *New England Quarterly* 135, no. 1 (March 2012): 119–37.

Lankes, Frank J. *The Ebenezer Community of True Inspiration*. Gardenville, NY: the author, 1949.

Leonard, Stephen R., Jr. "Recollections." Unpublished manuscript, ca. 1951. Photocopy, Oneida Community Mansion House Archives.

———. "Trap Book." Unpublished manuscript in three parts, ca. 1950. Photocopy, Oneida Community Mansion House Archives.

"List of Articles Deposited in the Corner Stone Box of the New Administration Building." *Quadrangle* 1 (new series), no. 5 (October 1926): 28.

Lockwood, Maren. "The Experimental Utopia in America." *Daedalus* 94, no. 2 (Spring 1965): 401–18.

"The Log Cabin." *Quadrangle* 2, no. 9 (December 1909): 1–2.

Lowenthal, Esther. "The Labor Policy of the Oneida Community Ltd." *Journal of Political Economy* 35, no. 1 (1927): 114–26.

Major, Judith K. *To Live in the New World: A. J. Downing and American Landscape Gardening*. Cambridge, MA: MIT Press, 1997.

Mandelker, Ira L. *Religion, Society, and Utopia in Nineteenth-Century America*. Amherst: University of Massachusetts Press, 1984.

Mayer, Jessie. "Two Utopian Thinkers." *Oneida Community Journal* 17, no. 3 (September 2003): 4–8.

McGee, Anita Newcomb. "An Experiment in Human Stirpiculture." *American Anthropologist* 4 (October 1891): 319–25.

Meyer, William B. "The Perfectionists and the Weather: The Oneida Community's Quest for Meteorological Utopia, 1848–1879." *Environmental History* 7, no. 4 (2002): 589–610.

Miller, George N. *After the Sex Struck; or, Zugassent's Discovery*. Boston: Arena, 1895.

Murray, T. A. "1866: The Year of Croquet." *Oneida Community Journal* 28, no. 1 (March 2014): 12–14.

Nelson, Keith L. *Victors Divided: America and the Allies in Germany, 1918–1923*. Berkeley: University of California Press, 1975.

Nordhoff, Charles. *The Communistic Societies of the United States: Harmony, Oneida, the Shakers, and Others*. New York: Harper & Brothers, 1875.

Noyes, Corinna Ackley. *The Days of My Youth*. Hamilton College Library, Clinton, NY: Richard W. Couper Press, 2011. First published in 1960.

Noyes, George Wallingford, ed. *John Humphrey Noyes: The Putney Community*. Oneida, NY: the author, 1931.

———, ed. *The Religious Experience of John Humphrey Noyes, Founder of the Oneida Community*. New York: Macmillan, 1923.

———. "Sixty Years Ago." *Quadrangle* 1, no. 11 (February 1909): 5–6.

Noyes, Hilda Herrick, and George Wallingford Noyes. "The Oneida Community Experiment in Stirpiculture." *Eugenics, Genetics and the Family* 1 (1923): 374–85.

Noyes, Holton V. "A History of the Oneida Community, Limited." Unpublished typescript, ca. 1930. Oneida Community Mansion House Archives.

Noyes, John Humphrey. "Association." *Spiritual Magazine* (Putney, VT), vol. 1, no. 1 (March 15, 1846): 4–7.

———. *The Berean: A Manual for the Help of Those Who Seek the Faith of the Primitive Church.* Putney, VT: Office of the Spiritual Magazine, 1847.

———. *Confessions of John H. Noyes, Part 1: Confession of Religious Experience, including a History of Modern Perfectionism.* Oneida Reserve, NY: Leonard & Co., Printers, 1849.

———. *Dixon and His Copyists: A Criticism.* 2nd ed. Oneida, NY: Oneida Community, 1874.

———. *Essay on Scientific Propagation.* Oneida, NY: Oneida Community, ca. 1872.

———. *History of American Socialisms.* Philadelphia: J. B. Lippincott, 1870.

———. *Salvation from Sin: The End of Christian Faith.* Wallingford, CT: Oneida Community, 1866.

———. "Swedenborgiana—No. 13, Amphibious Morality." *Circular* 4, no. 17 (February 3, 1866): 369–71.

———. *The Way of Holiness: A Series of Papers Formerly Published in "The Perfectionist," at New Haven.* Putney, VT: John H. Noyes and Co., 1839.

Noyes, John Z. "Newspeak." *Kenwood Association Newsletter* (published by the editor, J. Z. Noyes, out of his home in Greenbelt, MD), no. 10 (April 1984): 1–2. Oneida Community Mansion House Archives.

Noyes, P. Geoffrey. "The Oneida Community and the Oneida Community, Ltd.: The Offspring Makes a Success of Its Parent." Paper delivered at the twenty-first annual Communal Studies Conference, October 6–9, 1994, Oneida, NY.

Noyes, Pierrepont Burt. "Basswood Philosophy: An Appreciation of the O. C. L., Parts 1–5." *Quadrangle* 1, no. 10 (January 1909): 11–12; 1, no. 12 (March 1909): 10–11; 2, no. 1 (April 1909): 9–11; 2, no. 2 (May 1909): 8–10; and 2, no. 3 (June 1909): 7–9.

———. *A Goodly Heritage.* New York: Rinehart, 1958.

———. Letter included in the book *The Last Hundred Years,* distributed to employees. 1948. Oneida Community Mansion House Archives.

———. Letter to the employees of the Oneida Community, Ltd., April 8, 1933. Oneida Community Mansion House Archives.

———. *My Father's House: An Oneida Boyhood.* New York: Farrar and Rinehart, 1937.

———. "P. B. N." *Quadrangle* 6, no. 1 (January 1913): 9–11.

———. "Summary of the President's Report to Stockholders of Oneida Community, Limited at the Annual Meeting, February 24 [1930]." Three-page printed document, Oneida Community Mansion House Archives.

———. Text of remarks on July 31, 1948. Oneida Ltd. News Bureau Release. Oneida Community Mansion House Archives.

———. *While Europe Waits for Peace: Describing the Progress of Economic and Political Demoralization in Europe during the Year of American Hesitation.* New York: Macmillan, 1921.

Noyes, Pierrepont Trowbridge. "The Oneida Ltd. Creed." Photocopy of a typed statement dated January 1, 1967. Oneida Community Mansion House Archives.

Odem, Mary E. *Delinquent Daughters: Protecting and Policing Adolescent Female Sexuality in the United States, 1885–1920.* Chapel Hill: University of North Carolina Press, 1995.

Olin, Spencer C., Jr. "Bible Communism and the Origins of Orange County, California." *California History* 58 (Fall 1979): 220–32.

——. "The Oneida Community and the Instability of Charismatic Authority." *Journal of American History* 67, no. 2 (September 1980): 285–300.

Oneida Association. Family Register, January 1, 1849–March 17, 1850. 23-page typescript. Oneida Community Mansion House Archives.

Oneida Community. *Bible Communism: A Compilation from the Annual Reports of the Oneida Association and Its Branches.* Brooklyn, NY: Office of the Circular, 1853.

——. *Bulletin of the Oneida Community.* August 30, 1878. Oneida, NY: Office of the American Socialist, 1878.

——. *First Annual Report of the Oneida Association: Exhibiting Its History, Principles, and Transactions to Jan. 1, 1849.* Oneida Reserve, NY: Oneida Association, 1849.

——. *Hand-Book of the Oneida Community.* Oneida, NY: Office of the Oneida Circular, 1875.

——. *Hand-Book of the Oneida Community: Containing a Brief Sketch of Its Present Condition, Internal Economy, and Leading Principles, No. 2.* Oneida, NY: Oneida Community, 1871.

——. *Hand-Book of the Oneida Community; with a Sketch of the Founder, and an Outline of Its Constitution.* Wallingford, CT: Office of the Circular, Wallingford Community, 1867.

——. *Mutual Criticism.* Introduction by Murray Levine and Barbara Benedict. Syracuse, NY: Syracuse University Press, 1975. First published in 1876.

——. *The Oneida Community: A Familiar Exposition of Its Ideas and Practical Life, in a Conversation with a Visitor.* Wallingford, CT: Office of the Circular, 1865.

——. *Second Annual Report of the Oneida Association: Exhibiting Its Progress to February 20, 1850.* Oneida Reserve, NY: Oneida Association, 1850.

——. *Third Annual Report of the Oneida Association: Exhibiting Its Progress to February 20, 1851.* Oneida Reserve, NY: Oneida Association, 1851.

"The Oneida Community." *Transactions of the New York State Agricultural Society, 1866,* vol. 26 (1867): 791–806.

Oneida Ltd. "Oneida Ltd. Silversmiths Annual Report, Fiscal Year Ended January 31." 1958. Oneida Community Mansion House Archives.

——. "Oneida Ltd. Silversmiths Annual Report, Fiscal Year Ended January 31." 1968. Oneida Community Mansion House Archives.

——. "Oneida Marks 100 Years of Leadership in the Tableware Field." *Oneida Silversmith* 4, no. 3 (March–April 1977): 3. Oneida Community Mansion House Archives.

——. Proxy Statement. 1977. Oneida Community Mansion House Archives.

——. Proxy Statement. 1982. Oneida Community Mansion House Archives.

——. Proxy Statement. 1985. Oneida Community Mansion House Archives.

Oved, Yaacov. "Communal Movements in the Twentieth Century." In *Utopia: The Search for Ideal Society,* edited by Roland Schaer, Gregory Clacys, and Lyman

Turner Sargent, 268–77. New York: New York Public Library and Oxford University Press, 2000.

Parker, Robert Allerton. *A Yankee Saint: John Humphrey Noyes and the Oneida Community.* New York: G. P. Putnam's Sons, 1935.

Passet, Joanne E. *Sex Radicals and the Quest for Women's Equality.* Urbana: University of Illinois Press, 2003.

Pellerin, Charles. *The Life of Charles Fourier.* Translated by Francis George Shaw. New York: William H. Graham, 1848.

Pivar, David J. *Purity Crusade: Sexual Morality and Social Control, 1868–1900.* Westport, CT: Greenwood, 1973.

Rainwater, Dorothy, with Donna Folger. *American Silverplate.* Rev. and enl. 3rd ed. Atglen, PA: Schiffer, 2000. First published in 1968.

Reade, Charles. *Put Yourself in His Place: A Novel.* New York: Harper & Brothers, 1904. First published in 1870.

Rich, Jane K., ed. *A Lasting Spring: Jessie Catherine Kinsley, Daughter of the Oneida Community.* Syracuse, NY: Syracuse University Press, 1983.

Roach, Monique Patenaude. "The Loss of Religious Allegiance among the Youth of the Oneida Community." *Historian* 63, no. 4 (2001): 787–807.

Robertson, Constance Noyes, ed. *Oneida Community: An Autobiography, 1851–1876.* Syracuse, NY: Syracuse University Press, 1970.

——. *Oneida Community Profiles.* Syracuse, NY: Syracuse University Press, 1977.

——. *Oneida Community: The Breakup, 1876–1881.* Syracuse, NY: Syracuse University Press, 1972.

——. "The Story of Sherrill." In *Sherrill, Smallest City in New York State, 1916–1966: 50th Anniversary Celebration,* 7–32. Sherrill, NY: Anniversary Committee, 1966.

Rowe, David L. *Thunder and Trumpets: Millerites and Dissenting Religion in Upstate New York, 1800–1850.* Chico, CA: Scholars Press, 1985.

Sears, Hal D. *The Sex Radicals: Free Love in High Victorian America.* Lawrence: Regents Press of Kansas, 1977.

Shambaugh, Bertha M. H. *Amana: The Community of True Inspiration.* Iowa City: State Historical Society of Iowa, 1908.

Sherrill, Smallest City in New York State, 1916–1966: 50th Anniversary Celebration. Sherrill, NY: Anniversary Committee, 1966.

Spann, Edward K. *Brotherly Tomorrows: Movements for a Cooperative Society in America, 1820–1920.* New York: Columbia University Press, 1989.

Stoehr, Taylor. *Free Love in America: A Documentary History.* New York: AMS, 1979.

Swedenborg, Emanuel. *A Compendium of the Theological and Spiritual Writings of Emanuel Swedenborg: Being a Systematic and Orderly Epitome of All His Religious Works. . . .* Boston: Crosby and Nichols and Otis Clapp, 1854.

Teeple, John B. *The Oneida Family: Genealogy of a 19th Century Perfectionist Commune.* Oneida, NY: Oneida Community Historical Committee, Mansion House, 1985.

Thomas, Robert David. *The Man Who Would Be Perfect: John Humphrey Noyes and the Utopian Impulse.* Philadelphia: University of Pennsylvania Press, 1977.

Towner, J. W. Untitled document outlining terms of membership in the Oneida Community, August 17, 1875. Typed transcript in the Oneida Community Mansion House Archives.

Van der Warker, Ely. "A Gynecological Study of the Oneida Community." *American Journal of Obstetrics and Diseases of Women and Children* 17, no. 8 (August 1884): 785–810.

Van Wormer, Heather M. "The Ties That Bind: Ideology, Material Culture, and the Utopian Ideal." *Historical Archaeology* 40, no. 1 (2006): 37–56.

Von Ziegesar, Peter. "Reinventing Sex." *Lapham's Quarterly* 9, no. 4 (Fall 2016): 200–206.

Wayland-Smith, Ellen. *Oneida: From Free Love Utopia to the Well-Set Table—an American Story*. New York: Picador, 2016.

Wayland-Smith, Francis. "What Held the O. C. Together." Ca. 1910. Photocopy of eleven handwritten pages "given to Historical Committee by P. B. Noyes 5 Feb. 49." Oneida Community Mansion House Archives.

Wayland-Smith, Prudence Skinner. "The Architecture of Theodore H. Skinner." *Oneida Community Journal* 4, no. 4 (December 1990): 1–6.

Wellman, Judith. *The Road to Seneca Falls: Elizabeth Cady Stanton and the First Woman's Rights Convention*. Urbana: University of Illinois Press, 2004.

Wells, H. G. *The Future in America: A Search after Realities*. New York: Harper & Brothers, 1906.

"When We Made Brick." *Quadrangle* 6, no. 12 (December 1913): 9–10.

White, Janet R. "Building Perfection: The Social and Physical Structures of the Oneida Community." MA thesis, Cornell University, 1994.

Wilber, DuWayne E. "A Brief History of the Vernon-Verona-Sherrill Central School District." Photocopy of 30-page typescript dated May 16, 1976. Oneida Community Mansion House Archives.

Wilson, Edmund. *To the Finland Station: A Study in the Writing and Acting of History*. New York: Farrar, Straus and Giroux, 1972. First published in 1940.

——. *Upstate: Records and Recollections of Northern New York*. Syracuse, NY: Syracuse University Press 1990. First published in 1971.

Wonderley, Anthony. "How Women Worked in the Oneida Community during the 1870s." *Communal Studies* 30, no. 2 (2010): 65–85.

——, ed. *John Humphrey Noyes on Sexual Relations in the Oneida Community: Four Essential Texts*. Hamilton College Library, Clinton, NY: Richard W. Couper Press, 2012.

——. "The Most Utopian Industry: Making Oneida's Animal Traps, 1852–1925." *New York History* 91, no. 3 (2010): 175–95.

——. "Oneida Community Buildings, Grounds, and Landscape, 1848–1880." Cultural landscape report prepared for the Oneida Community Mansion House, 2012.

——. *Oneida Iroquois Folklore, Myth, and History: New York Oral Narrative from the Notes of H. E. Allen and Others*. Syracuse, NY: Syracuse University Press, 2004.

——. "Watervliet Shakers through the Eyes of Oneida Perfectionists, 1863–1875." *American Communal Societies Quarterly* 3, no. 2 (2009): 51–64.

Worden, Harriet M. *Old Mansion House Memories, by One Brought Up in It*. Oneida, NY: Oneida Ltd., 1950.

Zahavi, Gerald. *Workers, Managers, and Welfare Capitalism: The Shoemakers and Tanners of Endicott Johnson, 1890–1950*. Urbana: University of Illinois Press, 1988.

INDEX

Page numbers in *italics* refer to figures.

Wells, H. G., 169
Wesley, John, 18, 37
Whitcomb, Jon, 196–97
Wilson, Edmund, 157, 254n29
women's rights movement, 34, 140, 208–9
    See also bloomer costume

Woodhull, Victoria, 209
Woolworth, William, 33, 78, 135
Worden, Harriet, 59, 83, 86, 105, 111
Worden, Marquis de Lafayette, 22
worker relations. *See* labor relations
Wright, Orrin, 166